The Cinema
of
FRANK CAPRA

The Cinema
of
FRANK CAPRA

An Approach to Film Comedy

Leland A. Poague

SOUTH BRUNSWICK AND NEW YORK:
A. S. BARNES AND COMPANY
LONDON: THE TANTIVY PRESS

© 1975 by A. S. Barnes and Company, Inc.

Portions of this work originally appeared as a dissertation,
The Cinema of Frank Capra, © 1973 by Leland A. Poague.

A. S. Barnes and Co., Inc.
Cranbury, New Jersey 08512

The Tantivy Press
108 New Bond Street
London W1Y OQX, England

Library of Congress Cataloging in Publication Data

Poague, Leland A   1948-
     The cinema of Frank Capra.

     Portions of this work originally appeared as the author's thesis, University of
Oregon.
     Filmography: p.
     Bibliography: p.
     Includes index.
     1. Capra, Frank, 1897-   2. Comedy films—History and criticism.   I. Title.
PN1998.A3C266   791.43'0233'0924   74-9295
ISBN 0-498-01506-8

PRINTED IN THE UNITED STATES OF AMERICA

dedicated,
with all my love,
to Susie

Contents

Preface

Readers will notice that the book is organized both by topic and chronology. The topic section, comprising the first six chapters, tends to be theoretical and academic, and intentionally so. It is my belief that much current film criticism suffers from a lack of scholarly honesty, a reluctance to face up to the aesthetic and psychological issues raised by the popular cinema. I have done my best, therefore, to face those isues, defining my approach, acknowledging my debts, and revealing, in the process, my shortcomings. The second section is altogether practical and historical in its orientation, focusing not on theory but on explication and interpretation, with the intention of making as much sense out of Capra's films as I possibly could. It is true, of course, that my practice is based on my theory, and that my theory is constantly modified by my practice, so that theory and practice are ultimately inseparable. Nevertheless, I believe that each chapter in this book is relatively self-sufficient, so that readers who find my theorizing at first rather too involved are urged to skip the initial chapters in favor of the more practical examples of my film criticism. Then, perhaps, the significance of my theory will be clear.

Acknowledgments

My heartfelt thanks are due to William Cadbury, for teaching me to *see*; to Irma Sherwood, Joseph Hynes, Tom Hyde, Bill Batty, Kitty Morgan, Bill Rothman, Dee Schofield, and William Cadbury, for reading and criticizing successive drafts of the manuscript; to Richard Heinzkill and Linda Batty for their help with research; to Patrick Sheehan and the Library of Congress Motion Picture Section, Charles Silver and The Museum of Modern Art/Film Study Center, the staff of the National Archives, David Shepard and The American Film Institute, Paul Scaramazza, Pierre Dunn and The University of Oregon Film Society, and Frank Capra, himself, for assisting me to see the films; to The University of Oregon English Department, Alan Jenson, and Lloyd Poague, for financial support; to Eric and Debbie Park, Dick and Midge Kean, and special thanks to Jon and Carol Sanford, for sheltering a wandering scholar; to Owen and Lynn Daly, for the loan of their typewriter; and to the many fine friends in Eugene, Oregon, whose *curteisye* knew no limits (God bless you everyone).

Illustrations appear through the courtesy and assistance of Kitty Morgan, Mark Ricci of The Memory Shop, Paula Klaw of *Movie Star News,* Cinemabilia, James Card and George Pratt of George Eastman House, Mary Corliss of The Museum of Modern Art/Film Stills Archive, the National Film Archive (London), Jack Kerness of Columbia Pictures, Ernest Kirkpatrick of National Telefilm Associates, and Ronald Perkins of United Artists. Thanks also to National Telefilm Associates for permission to quote dialogue from *It's a Wonderful Life,* and to Jerome Gottlieb of Screen Gems for permission to quote dialogue from Columbia Pictures.

Introduction

This essay builds upon two basic assumptions: (1) directors make movies, and (2) the movies they make are generally literary works. I do not mean to disparage cinema as an art form, nor to disregard the contributions of writers, photographers, and other cinematic craftsmen. But I believe I can demonstrate that at least in the case of Frank Capra both assumptions are warranted. Indeed, both assumptions are necessary to the proper understanding of Capra's films.

Capra's critics have generally attacked him for being too popular, too American, and too politically naive to warrant recognition as a major figure in cinema history. They most often describe him as a "populist" filmmaker: a man who makes movies for and about the "little people" of America, cataloguing their simple aspirations, painting with the heavy brush of caricature the fat-cat villains who oppose the common man's individualistic ethic, and finally demonstrating the wished for but seldom believed (at least by the critics) victory of this democratic ethic over the realpolitik of the Robber Barons.

This description is in itself a sort of caricature, exaggerating certain qualities of the Capra cinema, and ignoring other more important attributes. In the final analysis, then, it is a false description, false because it clearly and demonstrably misrepresents both the form and content of Capra's films.

Such critical misconceptions can be attributed to a lack of literary sophistication on the part of most early film critics, who saw themselves primarily as sociologists. Hollywood-the-dream-factory was their subject, and their first concern was to examine the mysterious relationship between mass appeal and

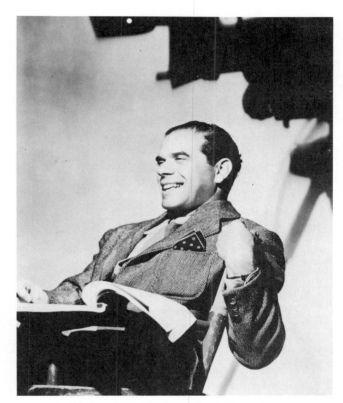

Frank Capra: the "populist" filmmaker.

mass production. Given their belief that films were data, not art, created by factories, not artists, it is not surprising that sociological critics found it difficult to appreciate the achievements of individual filmmakers. Even Capra, a man famous for his independence from studio interference, was generally treated more as a cultural weather vane than as a cinematic and literary author.

The "literariness" of the Capra cinema has thus gone generally unacknowledged and disregarded. And yet it is the literary qualities of Capra's films that define them as art. It is my assertion, then, that Capra and his films can best be understood in the context of literary history. This sort of analysis has seldom been attempted with cinema, but the study of aesthetic conventions and literary structures will provide, I believe, the sort of sophisticated criteria that will permit accurate descriptions and well-founded judgments of Capra's films.

However, critical sophistication can hardly exist in a critical vacuum, and therefore it is both necessary and useful, before we go on to discuss literary history, to consider the critical tradition of Capra scholarship: what do people, and particularly those people who function as accepted authorities, generally perceive as Capra's contribution to American and world cinema?

The Cinema
of
FRANK CAPRA

1

Capra and the Critics

There has been a remarkable consistency of critical evaluation among those few film scholars who have bothered to deal with Capra. Generally speaking, these scholars, with a few important exceptions, fall into two large groups.

The most important and influential of these groups derives its inspiration and authority from Richard Griffith. In his 1948 extension of *The Film Till Now,* Griffith describes the typical Capra film as a "fantasy of goodwill" in which "a messianic innocent, not unlike the classic simpletons of literature, pits himself against the forces of entrenched greed. His experience defeats him strategically, but his gallant integrity in the face of temptation calls forth the goodwill of the 'little people,' and through their combined protest, he triumphs."[1] Having thus described the Capra movie, Griffith goes on to question its social validity. "Nothing," he says, "could be further removed from the actual experience of American audiences than that triumph, and nothing could have suited them better. Such a blend of realistic problem and imaginary solution epitomised the dilemma of the middle-class mind in the New Deal period" (p. 452).

Capra thus becomes, for Griffith, a reprehensible spokesman for a reprehensible segment of American society. He sees Capra's "fantasy of goodwill" as being characteristic, despite its superficial kinship to New Deal optimism, of a group of essentially middle-class writers, Damon Runyon and Clarence Budington Kelland among them, who opposed the progressivism of Roosevelt with a resurrected sense of the good old days, an already bygone status quo when America was still "a great small town." It was in their eyes, Griffith continues, an "era of good feeling," a time when the classes were largely unconscious of class identities. "It was the individual who counted, who made his own way in the world and, feeling pity for those less strong and assertive than himself, helped his unfortunate fellows" (p. 450).

Capra's basic sympathy with this group of popular writers is evidenced, according to Griffith, by the frequency with which he went to them for story material. *Lady for a Day,* for example, purportedly Capra's first individually distinctive film, was based on Damon Runyon's short story "Madame La Gimp," and *Mr. Deeds Goes to Town* was adapted from Clarence Budington Kelland's *Saturday Evening Post* serial. In the latter film, Griffith goes on, this nostalgic feeling for the good old days "achieved the status of an idea," an idea "welcomed by huge sections of the American public." What need was there for the social reform of Roosevelt's New Deal if prosperity and peace could be assured simply by the "redemption of the individual?" (pp. 451-2).

Griffith implies in all this that Capra is naive at best, politically pernicious at worst, and intellectually bankrupt in any case. Capra's intellectual bankruptcy results, in turn, he contends, from the "popular" nature of the medium he works with. "It is clear," says Griffith, "that when the people em-

Capra's "fantasy of goodwill": George Bailey (James Stewart) meets his guardian angel (Henry Travers) in *It's a Wonderful Life.*

braced this new art they were bound to make it their own, and that therefore the most functional intellectual approach must be that of research into the economic, political, and cultural patterns which it was bound to reflect" (p. 421).

While I generally disagree with Griffith's basic premise here (for he fails to account for the fact that it is the people behind the camera who make the movies, not the people in the audience), at least Griffith takes Capra seriously. Capra's films are important (as sociological phenomenon), and therefore it is important to uncover and condemn Capra's political shortcomings (however mistaken Griffith's description of Capra's politics might be).

Perhaps it is the obvious seriousness of this sociological approach that makes it attractive. It does provide a respectable framework for critical discussion, and indeed many film scholars have adopted this framework without question. Thus we find critics as recent as Elliott Stein blasting Capra with the same sociological rhetoric originally employed by Griffith. "In retrospect," says Stein, "these 'fantasies of goodwill,' which at no point conflict with middle-class American status-quo values, appear as shrewdly commercial manipulative tracts. Their philistine-populist notions and greeting-card sentiments (a New Deal was hardly required—all social and political ills would melt away if one good John stuck to his guns) are not far removed from the simplism of such bottom-of-the-cracker-barrel movements as *Qualunquismo* in Italy and *Poujadisme* in France."[2]

The second group begins with Lewis Jacobs in *The Rise of the American Cinema* (1939). Critics of his persuasion tend to admit the naivete of Capra's vision, but they assign few negative associations to it. Indeed, Capra's naivete is the source of his charm, and his charm accounts for his popularity. As Jacobs puts it, Capra's films, "like O. Henry's stories, will be enjoyed as pastimes by millions, and as such are undeniably important."[3]

This position also has its recent adherents. In *Hollywood in the Forties* Charles Higham and Joel Greenberg describe *Meet John Doe* (1941) as "an impassioned plea for 'little people' and Democracy," which delivers "its naive utopian message with such fervour, such full-throated enthusiasm, and above all with such dazzling cinematic *panache* that, watching it, even the most cynical realist must succumb to its enchantment."[4]

As can be seen, this "enchanting pastime" view of Capra accords very nicely with the Griffith interpretation. In fact, both of these viewpoints share a common sociological bias: the films are important because they are popular, not popular because they are important. The essential difference between the two stances is that Griffith and his crew bear down very heavily on Capra's politics. But the political vision in Capra's films by itself can neither justify nor account for these ideologically motivated attacks. As I shall show, there is very little basis in fact for Griffith's political interpretations. To be accurate, Capra's films are only remotely concerned with politics. Given Griffith's sociological bias, the logical chain runs not from the films to the people (as it should were the films themselves at fault or in error), but rather from the people to the films. The American middle class is wrongheaded (*i.e.*, anti-New Deal), and accordingly the movies they most enjoy must be wrongheaded as well. Capra is thus guilty by association, too popular for his own critical good.

Jacobs and his followers, to the contrary, have no such ideological notions regarding the political validity of the middle-class ethic. Therefore they betray little concern with Capra's politics. They focus, rather, on the entertainment values of Capra's films. Thus Arthur Knight, for example, can discuss *Mr. Deeds Goes to Town* (1936) in the tradition of screwball comedies, "pictures that did anything and everything for a laugh."[5] The film is for Knight, as it was for Jacobs, a lightweight laugh getter, an amusing escapist tonic to cure for a brief moment the Depression blues.

These two superficially opposed (rejecting vs accepting) though essentially complementary viewpoints by and large dominate the critical debate: together they constitute the established wisdom regarding Capra's place in film history.[6] But recently a group of critics has begun to challenge this accepted evaluation. The most important of these revisionist critics are Penelope Houston, William Pechter, Andrew Bergman, and Stephen Handzo. Although each of them approaches Capra from a rather individualistic point of view, they all share a common belief that Capra's films are popular because they have something important and legitimate to say. Thus they reverse and refute the logic underlying the Griffith and Jacobs positions. The central critical premise is not, says Bergman, "that movie makers intuited the yearnings of a national unconscious, but rather that they felt the same tensions everyone else did and wanted to represent them in various ways."[7]

The first influential critic to challenge the Griffith-influenced opinion was Penelope Houston in her 1950 *Sight and Sound* article "Mr. Deeds and Willie Stark." Houston traces two cinematic responses to the social and political turmoil in the thirties and forties. One is the intellectual satire of such directors as Sturges (*The Great McGinty*), McCarey (*Duck Soup*), and Robert Rossen (*All the King's Men*), which exhibits beneath its hard and cynical surface an idealism that dares not expose itself to further disaster and disappointment. The other response is a "simple" one, reflecting the outlook of the average American. And its greatest exponent is Frank Capra. "He admires and believes in the little man," says Houston, and "he would like to believe that the meek will indeed inherit the earth; in a world dominated by power politics and big business he still finds refuge in idealism. The idealism, however, does not ignore the realities: Capra is always careful to build up a towering structure of dishonesty before he allows his hero to advance against it and knock it down, like the walls of Jericho, with his trumpet call."[8]

This perception of a realistic skepticism coexistent with Capra's fairy-tale optimism is an important insight, and it is the first step towards a thorough

Anything for a laugh: Gary Cooper and Douglass Dumbrille in *Mr. Deeds Goes to Town*.

The world of business and politics: Eugene Pallette, Claude Rains, and James Stewart in *Mr. Smith Goes to Washington*.

re-evaluation of Capra: he is not the naive simpleton that Griffith makes him out to be.

William Pechter takes much the same approach as Houston, pointing out a darker, less fantastically optimistic side to the Capra vision. In his chapter on Capra in *Twenty-Four/Times/A/Second*, Pechter quotes Griffith and offers the following analysis of the "fantasy of goodwill":

This ritual of innocence triumphant did little to ingratiate Capra to an intellectual audience to whom he represented only the triumph of the *Saturday Evening Post*. But though the apparent vein of cheery optimism which informs this ritual's re-enactment *is*, of course, precisely that quality which both endears Capra to his popular audience and alienates his intellectual one, yet, in seeing the films again, this quality seems strangely elusive, forever asserting itself on set occasions, but always dissipating itself finally in a kind of shrill excitement. There are even intimations of something like melancholy constantly lurking beneath the surface glare of happy affirmation.[9]

The majority of sociological critics, concerned for the most part with who wins or loses the social struggle, tend to take Capra's endings at their superficial face value, and they miss altogether the ironic undertones that critics like Houston, Pechter, and most recently Stephen Handzo have begun to perceive in their re-evaluation of Capra. "It is this formulized happy ending," Pechter continues, "which has always seemed the fatal weakness of Capra's films. . . . Yet this convention . . . seems, on closer look, to be curiously quarantined . . . and the observance of it has often been strangely perfunctory" (p. 127).[9]

Andrew Bergman in his very recent and very fine study, *We're In The Money: Depression America and Its Films*, takes yet another approach, one that attacks both the Griffith and the Jacobs interpretations. Capra is neither a political simpleton nor a mere entertainer. He is rather an artistic visionary. Bergman recognizes the artist's right to reflect upon the ideal as well as the real, and he considers Capra's success in the context of thirties screwball comedy, a genre Capra himself initiated with *It Happened One Night* (1934). The popularity of these films was not simply, according to Bergman, a function of their ability to evoke laughter. Rather, their success "had to do with the effort they made at reconciling the irreconcilable. They created an America of perfect unity: all classes as one, the rural-urban divide breached, love and decency and

Screwball comedy: a production still from *It Happened One Night,* featuring Clark Gable and Claudette Colbert.

neighborliness ascendant" (p. 133). In this context, then, Longfellow Deeds does not represent, as Griffith contends, a fantastic middle-class reaction against hard New Deal realities, but Deeds is rather a figure synonymous with Roosevelt himself, standing for the same kind of classless unity in optimism that swept Rooosevelt into office.

Bergman goes on to admit the fairy-tale nature of Capra's American myth, and he points out that even Capra himself had to abandon the notion of an all-encompassing social unity when it became clear that some villains (*e.g.,* Hitler) simply could not, even in the most fantastic dreams, be integrated into society. Unlike Griffith, however, Bergman sees nothing *a priori* reprehensible in Capra's myth-

making. It is enough for Bergman that Capra created films embodying his own visionary value system, and that people responded to that vision, seeing in it an image of their own legitimate egalitarian desires.

The last, the best, and the most troublesome of these revisionist critics is Stephen Handzo, whose article "Under Capracorn" appeared recently in *Film Comment.* There is a critical nonchalance to Handzo's eccentric approach that recalls Godard at his invigorating worst. Brilliant commentary and observation seem to appear out of nowhere, for there is no controlling idea to Handzo's essay.

If Handzo can be said to have a thesis at all, it is simply that Capra's films are worthy of the sort of

Backlit romanticism in Central Park: Gary Cooper and
Jean Arthur in *Mr. Deeds.*

lovingly precise and sensitive analyses that Handzo offers. And it is Handzo's facility for close analysis that makes him an important, indeed indispensable, critic. More than any other scholar, Handzo attends to the emotional realities of the Capra cinema.

A good example of Handzo's critical attention is his refutation of Raymond Durgnat, who follows Griffith in describing *Mr. Deeds* as "propaganda for a moderate, concerned, Republican point of view."[10] Handzo replies that such a political analysis "gives us no sense of what watching *Deeds* is actually like. Surely the face of Gary Cooper and *voice* of Jean Arthur are the film's real 'content'."[11] *Deeds* is, says Handzo, a film about love and feeling rather than politics, and as evidence he points out that "the nocturnal love scenes . . . played in the semidarkness of Joseph Walker's backlighting, are some of the loveliest romantic evocations this side of Borzage" (p. 9).

Similarly intelligent observations are to be found throughout the article, and accordingly we will frequently refer to Handzo, particularly since his place in the critical debate is a crucial one. Earlier critics, even those like Houston and Pechter who refute Griffith-inspired charges of naivete, are still arguing on Griffith's terms (*i.e.*, Capra is politically naive, or he is not politically naive). Handzo is the first critic to get to the heart of the matter, showing, however nonchalantly, that politics is not, as nearly everyone else has assumed, the central Capra issue. To the contrary, Capra's primary concern is with individuals, so that even in patently political situations (*e.g.*, *Deeds* and *Smith*) Capra tends to focus on the way individuals react to situations and each other rather than on the situation itself.

Handzo clearly points us in the right direction: Capra is primarily a poet of the personal and the moral, not the social and the political. Such an assertion, however, needs proof, and I intend in this essay to offer the evidence necessary to support such an evaluation. My general approach will be, as stated earlier, through the study of literary history, specifically the history of comedy and romance and the ways both forms traditionally deal with political and moral issues. Such a study will provide, I believe, a fresh perspective on Capra's films.

But we should be clear on one point: literary history is not simply the study of words. Words are obviously the medium of most literary works (and words are not unimportant in most films), but we are more concerned with principles of construction, the various ways in which artists put together their raw material. Generally speaking, the raw material of fictional literature is not words alone, but imagined experience, or, as Aristotle put it, imitated actions. Thus it is the ordering of imagined acts or events (and words can be considered imaginative events) that is "literary." Capra orders his imagined events in completely conventional, we might say classical, patterns. *It Happened One Night,* for example, reproduces with surprising exactitude the basic structure of *As You Like It.* Thus a study of conventional literary forms, comedy and romance in this instance, will clearly be useful for the study of Frank Capra. Indeed, given the oversights of earlier scholars, such a study becomes necessary, for it has been a drastic misunderstanding of literary structure (as I shall demonstrate) that has led most critics into error.

NOTES

1. Richard Griffith and Paul Rotha, *The Film Till Now* (1930; revised and enlarged 1949 and 1960, Middlesex: The Hamlyn Publishing Group), p. 452. Griffith's subsequent monograph, Frank Capra, New Index Series, no. 3 (London: The British Institute, 1951), is nothing more than the Capra section of *The Film Till Now,* and an extended filmography with occasional comment and excerpts from various newspaper and magazine reviews. The monograph is rare, and therefore I will continue to refer to *The Film Till Now* whenever possible.

2. Elliott Stein, "Capra Counts His Oscars," *Sight and Sound* 41, no. 3 (1972): 162.

3. Lewis Jacobs, *The Rise of the American Cinema* (1939; rpt. New York: Teachers' College Press, 1968), p. 479.

4. Charles Higham and Joel Greenberg, *Hollywood in the Forties* (New York: Paperback Library, 1970), p. 79.

5. Arthur Knight, *The Liveliest Art* (New York: New American Library, 1957), p. 241. "Screwball comedy," we should note, is less a generic than an historic term, applied rather loosely to such thirties and forties films as *It Happened One Night, The Thin Man,* and *The Awful Truth.* These films were generally "comedies," and we will define comedy presently, but "screwball" refers to a general quality of satire and self-deprecation.

6. Followers of Griffith include Jeffrey Richards, "Frank Capra and the Cinema of Populism," *Film Society Review* 7, no. 6 (1972): 38-46, no. 7-9 (1972): 61-71; Thomas Wiseman, *Cinema* (London: Cassell, 1964), pp. 72-73; and Manny Farber, *Negative Space* (New York: Praeger, 1971), p. 105. Critics of the Jacobs school include Harold J. Salemson, "Mr. Capra's Short Cuts to Utopia," *The Penguin Film Review,* no. 7 (London: Penguin Books, 1948), pp. 25-34; Bosley Crow-

ther, *The Great Films* (New York: G. P. Putnam's Sons, 1967), pp. 98-102; Martin Quigley, Jr., and Richard Gertner, *Films In America: 1929-1969* (New York: Golden Press, 1970); and David Zinman, *50 Classic Motion Pictures* (New York: Crown, 1970).

7. Andrew Bergman, *We're In The Money: Depression America and Its Films* (1971; rpt. New York: Harper & Row, 1972), p. xiv.

8. Penelope Houston, "Mr. Deeds and Willie Stark," *Sight and Sound* 19, no. 7 (1950): 277.

9. William S. Pechter, *Twenty-Four/Times/A/Second* (New York: Harper & Row, 1971), pp. 125-26. The chapter on Capra, "American Madness," appeared in *Kulchar,* no. 12 1963), pp. 64-72. See also Andrew Sarris, *The American Cinema* (New York: E. P. Dutton, 1968), pp. 87-88; James Price, "Capra and the American Dream," *The London Magazine* 3, no. 10 (1964): 85-93; and John Baxter, *Hollywood in the Thirties* (New York: Paperback Library, 1970), pp. 136-41.

10. Raymond Durgnat, *The Crazy Mirror: Hollywood Comedy and the American Image* (New York: Horizon Press, 1969), p. 125.

11. Stephen Handzo, "Under Capracorn," *Film Comment* 8, no. 4 (1972): 9.

2
Capra and the Comic Tradition

Most of Frank Capra's movies are comedies. Accordingly, we can better understand the films and their popularity by coming to terms with the comic conventions that Capra employed in creating them. In discussing Capra's place in the European comic tradition, however, we must consider the two major types of comedy he practiced: clown-oriented comedy of the Aristophanic and Chaplinesque sort, and plot-oriented comedy of the Shakespearean or Jonsonian sort. Both kinds of comedy are one in that they share a common history, a common form, common character types, and a common set of themes and concerns; but they differ in the way in which certain of these common elements are emphasized over others. Capra began his career with the first sort of comedy, working as a film editor, prop man, gag writer, and finally as a director, with a succession of silent comedians, including Mack Sennett and Harry Langdon. But once Capra left Langdon in 1927, he left clown comedy behind, and at the Columbia studios he turned his talents to more sophisticated problems and more complex plots, concerning himself less with the adventures of a single clown figure than with the complicated interaction of a variety of character types.

The most productive approach to the history of comedy has been the type of anthropological exploration pioneered by Francis Cornford in *The Origins of Attic Comedy* and expanded by Northrop Frye in *Anatomy of Criticism* and *A Natural Perspective*.[1] Cornford's early (1914) treatment of

Clown comedy: Harry Langdon as comic hero.

the comic form in light of ritual and myth was the first systematic attempt at understanding the total unity of comedy, the way various conventions of plot, character, and metaphor worked together as a whole. Cornford's primary contribution was to elucidate how comic conventions are not merely conventional mechanical devices whose primary function is to provide an excuse for witty dialogue and social satire. To the contrary, Cornford demonstrates that in the case of Aristophanes comic conventions provide both the structural bones and the emotional lifeblood of dramatic comedy.

Cornford's basic thesis is that the highly conventionalized form of Aristophanic comedy can only be explained by positing a preliterary ritual ancestor from which classical Greek comedy derived. Cornford compares the various elements in the Aristophanic plot to known religious and folk rituals in Greece and Europe (including England); and while he cannot supply all the missing links, he does pre-

sent a very convincing case for the proposition that the kernel event in European comedy is a fertility ritual (as Aristotle tells us in *The Poetics*) represented usually by a struggle deriving from the ritual combats of the Old and New Year, or by the marriage and feast deriving from the ritual weddings of Heaven and Earth, the New King and the Spring Queen, etc.

According to Cornford, the six formal elements of an Aristophanic play are as follows: (1) the prologue, (2) the *parados*, (3) the *agon*, (4) the *parabasis*, (5) the episodes of sacrifice and feasting, and (6) the *kômos* and marriage. The prologue serves to introduce the main character and explicate the problem he faces. The *parados* marks the

Buster and his bride in *Our Hospitality*.

entrance of the chorus (although it is usually not markedly discontinuous with the prologue). The *agon* is a formalized debate between the hero (the prot*agon*ist) and the villain (the ant*agon*ist). The *parabasis* is a choral interlude in which the leader of the chorus normally addresses (and abuses) the audience. After the *parabasis* we get scenes of sacrifice, feasting, and revelry leading finally to the marriage of the protagonist to his ritual reward, the bride.

Cornford asserts that "this canonical plot-formula preserves the stereotyped action of a ritual or folk drama, older than literary Comedy, and of a pattern well known to us from other sources" (p. 8). He then goes on to discuss the relationship of these conventionalized elements to well-known folk customs and rituals. Among these rites, we must pay particular attention to the types of fertility rituals underlying the three elements most relevant to our own discussion. These elements are the *agon*, the scenes of sacrifice and feasting, and the marriage and *kômos*.

Cornford classifies *agon*like fertility rites according to the manner in which the conflict between life and death, fertility and sterility, is symbolized. He lists four basic types of fertility rituals: the expulsion of Death/the bringing in of Life; the fight of Summer and Winter; the struggle of the Young and Old Kings; and the Death and Resurrection type.

The first ritual type, the expulsion of Death/the bringing in of Life, takes two complementary forms. The first involves the expulsion of a symbolic figure, in some cases dolls or animals, in other cases ritual actors, from the community. The expelled one is, in the Dionysian version, the *pharmakos* or scapegoat, the Christ-like one who takes the sins of the community upon his shoulders and carries them away. The second form reverses the movement, though it has the same ritual effect. Rather than casting Death out, Life is brought in. Harvest festivals and spring rites, like the English May Games, display this "bringing in of Life" pattern, aligning the community with the larger fertility of nature symbolized by the harvest and forest greenery.

The second type of *agon*like ritual, the fight of Summer and Winter, sees the principles of fertility and sterility personified by the appropriate natural season. There is thus a clear distinction between the opponents, and each is victorious and reigns in turn,

as Summer follows Winter and Winter follows Summer through the cycles of time. The third type, the struggle of the Young and Old Kings, while similar to the fight of Summer and Winter, recognizes the essential identity of the combatants: they are, "after all, only two successive representatives of the same principle" (Cornford, p. 57). It is frequently framed as an Oedipal conflict between father and son. Generally the victor gains not only the kingdom, but also the hand of a princess or queen, and the ritual concludes in their symbolic marriage.

The fourth type of *agon* ritual, the Death and Resurrection version, underlies not only the Aristophanic *agon,* but also the episodes of sacrifice and feasting as well. The hero, the spirit of life, is slain in the combat, and his triumph can only be brought about by his resurrection. The English St. George play demonstrates this pattern. St. George engages in combat with various opponents. As often as not St. George is slain, and he is resurrected by a Doctor who appears on the scene. One important variant of this resurrection pattern (and one that echoes the *pharmakos* motif discussed earlier) has the hero or hero-surrogate as the sacrificial victim. He is dismembered, cooked, and eaten in a sacramental feast. All the members of the community thus share the benign influence, and hence the god, as the focus of the newly rejuvenated community, is himself brought back to life. Many examples of such resurrected heroes are found in Greek mythology, but the most familiar example is, again, Christ, who is at once the scapegoat, the sacrificial victim, and the resurrected god. The Last Supper and Holy Communion are only slightly displaced versions of this sacrifice and feast motif.

The final Aristophanic plot element we shall consider, the ritual marriage, is the least problematic. It may be difficult to see at first what the ethical combat between Senator Paine and Jefferson Smith in *Mr. Smith Goes to Washington* (1939) has to do with fertility rites (although we can now see it as a conventional combat of the Young and Old Kings), but it is clear that the union of Peter and Ellie in *It Happened One Night* (1934) symbolizes a rejuvenated sense of human possibilities: the walls of Jericho fall and the lovers fulfill their roles as lovers. The ritual marriage, then, deriving from the marriage of Heaven and Earth, the victorious New King and the princess, etc, is the one plot element

A comic *agon*: Paulette Godard and Charlie Chaplin
battle the evil henchmen of *The Great Dictator*.

A comic couple: Longfellow Deeds (Gary Cooper) and
Babe Bennett (Jean Arthur).

to continue most clearly intact into the modern
European comic tradition.

Frye does for Shakespeare essentially the same
thing that Cornford did for Aristophanes: placing
the literary conventions of the playwright in the
context of the myths and rituals from which the
conventions derived. Frye briefly recounts the European history of the genre, through the New Comedy
of Plautus and Terence to Shakespeare, and then
offers the following description of the standard
comic formula:

The normal action is the effort of a young man to
get possession of a young woman who is kept from
him by various social barriers: her low birth, his
minority or shortage of funds, parental opposition, the
prior claims of a rival. These are eventually circum-

vented, and the comedy ends at a point when a new society is crystallized, usually by the marriage or betrothal of hero and heroine. The birth of the new society is symbolized by a closing festive scene featuring a wedding, a banquet, or a dance. This conclusion is normally accompanied by some change of heart on the part of those who have been obstructing the comic resolution.

(*A Natural Perspective*, p. 73)

And Frye then goes on to discuss this formulaic structure in terms of the three ritualistic components that we have already focused on in our discussion of Cornford, *i.e.*, the *agon*, the episodes of sacrifice and feasting, and the marriage and *kômos*. These elements are, according to Frye, "of particular importance for the comic structure" (*A Natural Perspective*, p. 73), in that they maintained their integrity as recognizable structural elements through Shakespeare's day, and, as I will soon demonstrate, even into our own period, where they regularly appear in romantic film comedy, specifically in the films of Frank Capra.

Of the three elements, the *agon* had by Shakespeare's time undergone the greatest modification or displacement. As we have seen in our examination of Cornford, the *agon* serves several functions, the most important normally being the rhetorical defeat of evil principles. But before evil can be defeated it must be recognized (*e.g.*, the scapegoat must be identified), and the corresponding movement in Elizabethan comedy usually involves the discovery of a general principle of social imbalance. Anti-comic sterility is not personified as a single figure, but becomes a shared social "humor," a type of bondage to destructive principles that can control the entire *dramatis personae* (*e.g.*, almost every character in *Love's Labour's Lost* gets so carried away by his "wit" that he cannot get carried away by love).

The episodes of sacrifice and feasting remained closer to their ritual origins in Shakespeare than they did in Aristophanes. In the plays of both writers, central characters undergo a kind of rejuvenation characteristic of death and resurrection rituals. In Aristophanes old men become young and sexually potent, but this renewal seems superficially incidental to the political satire. Shakespeare, however, is much more clearly concerned with personal rebirths, and the moral renewal of the leading char-

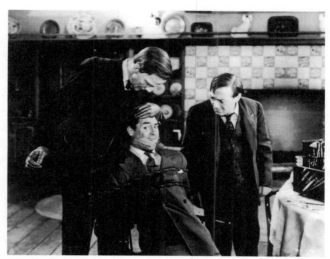

Comic bondage in *Arsenic and Old Lace*: Raymond Massey and Peter Lorre prepare Cary Grant for surgery.

acters becomes a central concern (*e.g.*, Benedick in *Much Ado About Nothing*, Bertram in *All's Well That Ends Well*). The sacrifice element that appeared in the original ritual as complete and actual loss of identity (*i.e.*, death) is seen in Shakespearean comedy as a confusion of identity: characters subject to social bondage become literally mad (*e.g.*, Malvolio, "sick of self-love"), and the central action of many Shakespearean plays has the leading character leaving society, abandoning a social role that is no longer tenable, and returning to a natural "green world," a place where viable social relationships, never far removed from necessary natural relationships, can be discovered and asserted. In keeping with the ritual concern with fertility, we frequently find that the confusion of identity becomes a confusion of sexual identity. Many major Shakespearean heroines (*e.g.*, Viola, Portia, Rosalind) masquerade as young men, and their disguise permits them to learn how they can best assert themselves as properly fertile young women.

The resurrection element, the literal rebirth of the slain god, becomes generally coincident with the final major structural element, the marriage and *kômos*. Almost all of Shakespeare's romantic comedies are concerned primarily with love, and the discovery of personal identity after a period of confusion usually takes the form of a properly motivated and aligned marriage. Personal identity thus

The confusion of sexual identity: Buster Keaton, second
from left, and friends.

becomes a matter of sexual identity, and the sexual
identity found in marriage is the comic assurance
of social renewal. The festive conclusions that we
see in Shakespeare are not, then, a matter of un-
motivated or unjustified frivolity. There is much
cause for rejoicing. The dangerous reign of illusion,
bondage, and sterility is ended, and the power of
love and fertility is reasserted.

We can see now that Cornford and Frye share a
common approach to comedy, an approach based
on a common belief in the utility and validity of
myth criticism, a mode of examination that undertakes the difficult but clearly rewarding task of comprehending literary works in the larger context of
human activity. As Ernst Cassirer and Suzanne
Langer, among others, have shown, literary works
share with myths and rituals a common adaptive
survival function. Human thought is defined by the
creation and utilization of symbolic forms. As
Langer puts it, "the symbol-making function is one
of man's primary activities . . . an act essential to
thought and prior to it' (*Philosophy in a New Key,*
p. 45). Symbols serve as our means of comprehending the vital aspects of human existence. But various
types of symbolic forms fulfill their adaptive functions in different manners, and it is important to be
aware of the differences between myth, ritual, and
literature.

Myths are, according to Frye, the stories that
accompany rituals, and thus the content of the
myth and the ritual (the wish for fertility in the
case of comedy) remains essentially the same. The

difference is one of intent and technique: the ritual attempts to effect by mimetic or sympathetic magic some change in the real universe, whereas the myth is *about* the changing universe, serving not so much to cause it as to interpret it.

Literature comes into being, then, when the distinction between ritual and myth collapses. Myth normally serves as a shared context of beliefs from which ritual acts take their meanings, but mythical beliefs are generally embodied in storylike narratives that tend to encompass and hence to destroy ritual, making the participants actors rather than celebrants, and moving from the realm of magic to the realm of dramatic fiction. The efficacy of ritual is more difficult to maintain than the efficacy of myth, and hence ritual, which must demonstrably affect reality in order to survive, tends to collapse into myth, which only requires a consistency of internal logic commensurate with the phenomena it seeks to explain.

Ritual and myth thus share the same content, tell the same story, and have the same outline of action; and when belief in ritual fails, once the collapse between ritual and myth takes place, we are dealing with literature, which is therefore *about* ritual and myth. Literature thus utilizes a structural form derived from ritual (as Cornford has shown) to reflect upon a content derived primarily from myth (as Frye asserts). Hence comedy is not a fertility ritual, but is *about* fertility rituals. Comedy derives its basic structure and concerns from ritualistic conventions, and while the surface issues of

Marriage as subject: the wedding ceremony in *Here Comes the Groom,* featuring Jane Wyman and Franchot Tone.

any given comic work may seem unrelated to the deep structural expectations characteristic of comedy (the issue of noise in Jonson's *Epicoene*, for example), the basic outline of comic action remains the same.[2] Comedy reflects upon the possibilities for life and fertility, and makes assertions as to how fertility should be promoted and life should be maintained. Any given set of surface issues can serve as metaphors for Life and Death, but the basic comic struggle between fertility and sterility remains constant.

The major types of comedy reflect upon this struggle in different fashions. Comedy generally celebrates "the sense of adequacy," according to Morse Peckham, and it does so by providing a set of elaborate conventional expectations and fulfilling them.[3] Similarly, the mythological content of comedy, deriving as it does from fertility rituals, celebrates an even more archaic and deep-seated form of adequacy, a sexual adequacy in tune with the entire reproductive cycle of nature. But once we accept this general description of comic conventions and themes, there is still no absolute necessity within the comic tradition that dictates what an artist can or must do with the comic form. We can see from simple observation that most of the works that we call comedies tend to assert without question the standard thematic implications inherited along with the ritual structure. The marriage at the end of a comedy, for example, usually implies social renewal and health as rewards for proper action, as it does for the most part in Shakespeare and Capra; but it may imply the exact opposite, the continuance of social corruption and disease, as it does in Ben Jonson's *The Alchemist*. An author (or auteur), then, may call the mythical content into question while still fulfilling the formal expectations of comedy. Thus Frye can answer the question "does anything that exhibits the structure of a comedy have to be taken as a comedy, regardless of its content or of our attitude to that content?" by saying "clearly yes" (*A Natural Perspective*, p. 46).

An artist is thus perfectly free, within his powers of reflection, to utilize whatever form he finds most appropriate to the statement he wishes to make. He may choose, for example, the comic form, as Shakespeare did in *Two Gentlemen of Verona*, to argue the basic insufficiency of abstract and outworn comic approaches to love in an experientially non-

Early Capra: Ralph Graves and Barbara Stanwyck in *Ladies of Leisure*.

comic universe. Nothing could or did prevent him. But the comic form in *Two Gentlemen* retains its integrity nevertheless, and if sterility is permitted to win in the play, the opposition of fertility and sterility is still very much the thematic issue. Comedy is thus a structure and a theme, not an answer. Comedy provides the symbolic form for thought, and the subject for thought, but it does not dictate the outcome of the artistic thought process.

With this proviso for artistic freedom in mind, however, we are free to examine the history of comedy to see how comic artists generally accomplish their comic purposes. Clown comedy, for example, focuses more on the central character of the fool or buffoon, while Shakespearean comedy centers primarily on contrasting sets of comic lovers. Important as clowns are in Shakespeare, they always play a subsidiary role. In Shakespearean comedy adequacy is defined by the rejuvenation of the whole social matrix, characters interacting, changing, and finally coming to a new and deeper sense of sexual and social selfhood. In clown comedy, on the other hand, comic adequacy is more often defined by the clown himself and is a function of his comic fortune. The great film comics (Chaplin, Keaton, Lloyd, and Langdon) are all clowns rich of character who move through the world, ignorant, innocent, or absentminded as the case may be, but who always manage to salvage their sense of selfhood out of the chaos of their environment.

Chaplin himself is clearly the most pathetic of the major comics, and his pathos can best be under-

Charlie meets the flower girl in *City Lights*.

stood as a matter of near-tragic inadequacy. One thinks particularly of the pathos in the closing moments of *City Lights* (1931) when Charlie's dreams of gentility and affection are completely dashed. The look on the flower girl's face tells Charlie that for all of his kindness and worth he is too scruffy a character to win her love. As James Agee observed, "it is enough to shrivel the heart to see, and it is the greatest piece of acting and the highest moment in movies."[4] But the inadequacy at the center of Chaplin's pathos is not altogether assignable to Charlie. One senses in his films that the world of Charlie the tramp and the world of society can never be reconciled. The typical plot movement in a Chaplin film sees Charlie walking into town along that ever-present dirt road. He interacts with society as he encounters it, seeking acceptance but seldom finding it, and thus he demonstrates society's inadequacy. Charlie is a spirit of life who is too alive. His comic intensity is too much for society to handle. Once rejected, Charlie gets right back on the road and heads out of town, stopping at the last moment to give that little hitch-kick that signifies that for all of the heartache Charlie has had to suffer, he is still at peace with himself.

The Tramp (1915) provides us with a classic example of this Chaplin type of clown comedy, and yet it also reveals a plot structure corresponding to the Aristophanic model. We first see Charlie walking along the road. As soon as he stops and sits down for lunch, however, he is attacked by hoboes, and the ensuing battle, which Charlie wins by virtue of his agility and good luck, is the comic *agon*. We then get scenes of sacrifice (Charlie is shot chasing the hoboes away from the farmer's house) and feasting (the farmer's daughter nurses him back to health), all revolving around the general issue of Charlie's identity: will he be a hobo (stealing the farmer's money) or a farmer (watering trees with a watering can)? The film then concludes with the final structural element, the comic wedding, as the farmgirl's sweetheart arrives. Charlie then understands that his dreams of marriage and life on the farm are dreams out of tune with the demands of reality, and he goes back to the road, leaving the farm and the farmer's daughter behind. The formal conventions of comedy are thus observed, and yet our feeling at the film's end is not one of complete rejoicing. Charlie has saved the farm from the threat of thieves, but Charlie is not allowed to share the happy results of his actions. The farm can never be his. He has insured the continuity of the farmer's family, but by so doing he condemns himself to further wandering. Charlie is thus a sacrificial victim, one who suffers rejection that life might go on.

There is thus a very tragic cast to *The Tramp*, a sense of loss and sorrow that is characteristic of Chaplin's greatest films. Nevertheless, Charlie can still manage to pick up his spirits and shuffle on to his next adventure with the hope that next time he will get the girl, as he does in *The Pawnshop* and *The Gold Rush* (1924). It is as if the entire Chaplin canon were one long comedy, a series of adventures in which Charlie wins as often as he loses, so that while individual films may reveal melancholic shading, like *City Lights* and *Limelight* (1952), there is still a Sophia Loren at the end of the rainbow to brighten up the darker moments along the way.[5]

Where Chaplin passes through society, Keaton, Lloyd, and Langdon always move towards integration with society. Lloyd is the eternal optimist who brashly pushes his way to success. Keaton is an intense stoic whose integrity and agility overcome obstacles standing between Buster and his rightful place as a valued member of the society. Lloyd and Keaton thus share this ability to take care of themselves. They make their own way in the world. In this ability they both differ from the last of the great clowns, helpless Harry Langdon, who always needs to be taken care of by someone more in tune with the demands of reality. Society (usually in the form of a maternal though occasionally shrewish female) makes room for Harry: he cannot make room for himself (see chapter 7 for a more detailed discussion of the Langdon films).[6]

It is clear then that the clown figure personifies the spirit of comedy. The clown *is* the comedy. Suzanne Langer describes hims as:

> the personified *élan vital;* his chance adventures and misadventures, without much plot, though often with bizarre complications, his absurd expectations and disappointments, in fact his whole improvised existence has the rhythm of primitive, savage, if not animalian life, coping with a world that is forever taking new uncalculated turns, frustrating, but exciting. He is neither a good man nor a bad one, but in his ruefulness and dismay he is funny, because his energy is

On the road again: Charlie Chaplin in *The Tramp*.

really unimpaired and each failure prepares the situation for a new fantastic move.[7]

Yet for all that people like Langer (and Fellini) can tell us about clowns, their historical derivation remains more vague than the derivation of comic plots. In *The Poetics* Aristotle tells us that comedy originated with "the leaders of the phallic songs" as they improvised and cavorted during the fertility rituals.[8] If this is indeed the case, we can see how character-oriented comedy of the clown type predates the more complex plot orientation of Shakespearen comedy. Even Aristophanic comedy, which serves as a plot prototype for Shakespearean comedy (in that the ritual form of Greek Old Comedy

The personified *élan vital*: Orson Welles as Falstaff (with Jeanne Moreau).

was transmitted through Roman New Comedy to Renaissance England), can be seen as a strongly character-oriented enterprise. Dicaeopolis, Strepsiades, Philocleon, Pisthetaerus; all are at the center of their respective plays (*i.e., The Acharnians, The Clouds, The Wasps,* and *The Birds*), and each is seen in conflict with his society. Much of this conflict, as would be the case in later film comedy, is carried out on a purely physical level: pratfalls and beatings abound. But for all of the slapstick and coarse humor to be found in Greek Old Comedy, it is still a relatively sophisticated form, and clowns are put to relatively sophisticated purposes.

But the fact remains that the clown as a folk-figure was not (and is not) the sole possession of the Greeks. European folklore abounds with clown types (see Langer). Wherever dramatic comedy develops, the clown figure is present. Even in sophisticated romantic comedy of the Shakespearean or Hollywood sort, the clown figure frequently retains many of his archaic functions (*e.g.,* poking fun at authority, mores, and social conventions), and in those works where the clown has dropped out as a recognizable character altogether, his functions are absorbed into the plot movement, so that the personal sequence of reversal and recovery that typifies the adventures of the clown becomes the social sequence of reversal and recovery symbolized by the course of comic love.

The themes of clown comedy can thus range from the castigation of social inadequacy, as in Chaplin and Aristophanes, to the celebration of social and personal renewal, as in Lloyd and Keaton. The line separating satiric abuse and comic acceptance is often a fine one, however, and sophisticated analysis is required if we are to properly comprehend the way approvable comic action is set over and against comically untenable behavior. It is impossible to have one without the other, for acceptance of an approvable stance of necessity requires a rejection of another less acceptable moral position; and similarly, the satiric abuse of immorality almost of necessity implies an understood moral standard. Nevertheless, almost all comedies tend to weigh one factor more than the other, so that while Ben Jonson and Shakespeare, for example, share the complex-plot orientation of Elizabethan comedy, they both display distinctively different tones of voice: Jonson attacks crimes and follies, while Shakespeare

reveals the infinite possibilities for human concern and loving interaction.

Two early, seldom seen, and, hence, seldom discussed Capra films provide us with an interesting set of contrasting comic structures, and serve to illustrate these two major strains of plot-oriented comedy.

The Younger Generation (1929) is similar in point and structure to Shakespeare's great play about money and money-making, *The Merchant of Venice.* Both works concern themselves with the kinds of risk necessary in personal relationships, and the fate of those who are unwilling to take such risks. Both Shylock and Maurice Fish (*né* Morris Goldfish) lose their families (if not their wealth) because they would not risk putting family first. But this unwillingness to take personal risk is, in both cases, placed in the context of mercantile capitalism, and Shylock, the usurer, and Maurice Fish, the art importer, reveal their basic human insufficiency through their addiction to the mercantile ideal.

Both works are thus about capitalism, but capitalism *per se* is not really called into question. Shakespeare's Antonio and Capra's Eddie Lesser are successful capitalists (in varying degrees), and they demonstrate that a people-oriented capitalism is possible. But the similarity between *Merchant* and *Younger Generation* is not simply a matter of surface issues. The point to make is that both works, for all of their surface concern with capitalism, display essentially the same type of comic pattern: the carrying out of Death.

The Younger Generation recounts the rise of the Goldfish family from Delancy Street to Fifth Avenue, and the varying relationships of the younger and older generations under the pressure of their rapid rise in social and economic status. Almost all of the central characters are thus involved in and affected by the capitalistic ethic. At the film's beginning, Papa Goldfish (Jean Hersholt) owns a push-cart full of tin goods that stands along with the other carts in the immigrants' street market. Much to the consternation of Mrs. Goldfish (Rosa Rosanova), however, Papa is seldom at his cart, for he is too busy telling jokes to his cronies to bother selling pots to potential customers. Young Morris, encouraged by a mother who thinks that "money talks," is a regular Ragged Dick (a Horatio Alger type), peddling papers and saving his pennies in a mantlepiece tin. The depth of Morris's commitment to the ideals of Horatio Alger is measured by his heroic act in the tenement fire (a fire started during a fight between Morris and his sister's boyfriend, Eddie Lesser). As the building burns down around him, Morris gathers up a large sheet full of goods and totes them out on his shoulder, boasting proudly to his mother of the possibility of a "fire sale." Even Eddie Lesser (Rex Lease), the comic hero of the piece, after a brief and half-hearted try at crime, becomes the proprietor of a music store, and a writer, himself, of best-selling pop songs.

So it is not just being a capitalist that is significant, but the kind of capitalist you are. The generation gap between the younger and elder Goldfish serves to symbolize the right-way/wrong-way opposition. Papa Goldfish, as we have already noted, is more than content to live on the East Side and ignore his pushcart for the sake of a good joke with old friends. On the other hand, Morris (Ricardo Cortez) obeys an almost obsessive urge to achieve economic and social success. He moves very quickly from fire sales to art importing, changing his name to "Fish" and his address to Fifth Avenue in the process. What he loses in the bargain is the warmth of human relationships (much is made of heat and cold in the film), so that he even resorts to denying his parents, calling them riff-raff servants lest they embarrass him before his rich friends.

The key incident in the personal degradation of

The Goldfish family in *The Younger Generation* (Ricardo Cortez, Rosa Rosanova, Lina Basquette, and Jean Hersholt).

Morris, however, is his treatment of his sister, Birdie (Lina Basquette). Once he has moved the family uptown, and assumed complete sovereignty, he insists that everything be subservient to his own social climbing, and Birdie's love affair with a "cheap songwriter" and an "East-Side bum" (*i.e.,* Eddie Lesser) is forbidden for bringing disgrace on the family. He is going to make "real people" out of them whether they like it or not. Morris thus stands square in the path of the comic movement, and the greater part of the film deals with the comic success of the lovers (despite nearly overwhelming difficulties) and the corresponding collapse of Morris's power. But it is Morris's misfortune, significantly, that seems to carry the emotional weight of the movie (just as Shylock often seems to overshadow the love affair of Portia and Bassanio in *The Merchant of Venice*). The film's final shot finds Morris before the hearth in the dungeonlike living room of his Italianate penthouse. He is alone, his father is dead, his mother gone to live with Birdie and Eddie, and he is cold, even before a roaring fire.

Morris's final gesture in this scene is significant. He puts his mother's fancy shawl around his shoulders in an attempt to ward off the moral chill. Much is made of the relationship between Morris and his mother. She favors him over his sister, sides with him in every argument, and most importantly, reinforces every one of his social moves. In a sense, he does everything for her, and her mercantile harping, while seeming jovial and innocent (should we say ignorant?), is certainly the cause of his obsession.

Morris realizes that something is wrong in this Oedipal relationship, that this kind of maternal domination should not be. He returns from dinner with the Kohns (rich jewel merchants), and hugs his mother in the parlor as he enters. In so doing, he looks over her shoulder at his father who stands in the opposite doorway with Mama's shawl around his shoulders (she had put it on him when he complained of being cold). A look of hurt and disgust passes over Morris's face, as if it were revolting that a man should wear a woman's shawl. But it is not just any woman's shawl, it is his mother's, and he is right to feel deeply disturbed at the image of a man (particularly his father) wrapped up in his mother's mercantile concerns. The shawl is elaborately and richly embroidered, and it is both the

The Younger Generation: Papa Goldfish (Jean Hersholt) bewails his fate, doomed to a joyless life on Fifth Avenue.

cause and the result of Morris's dedication to money and status. Under Morris's gaze, Papa too feels shame for wearing the garment, but it is not simply a matter of a man being ashamed to be seen in female garb, because it is what the shawl stands for that counts, and what it stands for is a dehumanizing dedication to things rather than people (when Mama puts the shawl on Papa she tells him how happy he should be to have such a nice house and such nice furniture).

When Morris puts the shawl on in the final scene, then, it is an admission of defeat, a gesture of accepting the personal failure that he brought upon himself. He knows that he is trapped beyond escape in the kind of obsessive capitalist quest that the shawl has come to represent. Morris literally takes the sins of the capitalist community upon his shoulders. He is, like Shylock, the scapegoat. He is not so much Death carried out as Death left to burn in its own cold sacrificial fires. Life has simply walked back to Delancy Street and left Morris to his penthouse prison.

Capra thus paints an ambivalent picture. We have seen enough of the real if stunted humanity in Morris to sympathize with him. We know that he is a logical product of his society. He is indeed the product of a specific Oedipal obsession to replace his father in his mother's affections, a task he accomplishes by giving her all the money she wants. But the point is not that he has an Oedipal problem so much as it is the way his society encourages him to deal with that problem, by making more money than his father. He thus represents what could happen to anyone (and almost does happen to Eddie Lesser) in a society where personal problems are most often solved by impersonal actions. Morris allows himself to become too much a capitalist and hence too little a human being.

The relationship between the comic deep structure and the economic surface issues is now clear. The personal risk that we talked about earlier is one that Morris could never take. He could not break away (as Birdie did) from the restricting and recurrent pattern of tooth-and-claw success, a success that, when thus pursued for its own sake, becomes the pattern of personal sterility. Morris could not risk breaking the only pattern of relationship that he knew to face the danger of being humanly free. The film shows us the comic joys of freedom (grandchildren, jokes, a song, and a glass of wine), but it also makes it clear how precious that freedom is, how little we need to change to become a person like Morris. Obsessive capitalism is thus an image for comic bondage, and it is this metaphor that unites the deep and the surface structures.

Structurally speaking, then, the film presents the struggle of wrong-way and right-way capitalism as personified by Morris and his father. The tenement fire at the film's beginning, and Morris's action in saving goods for a fire sale, serve to identify and define this wrong approach. The movement of the film is a movement from Delancy Street to Fifth Avenue and back to Delancy Street, from comic freedom to comic bondage and back again. The *kômos* of the film takes place at the deathbed of Papa Goldfish, when the entire family, including Morris, can laugh at Papa's immense joy at being a "grandpapa." It is a celebration of life in the presence of the dying grandfather, but even the dying can take joy in the presence of the living child. The comic movement proper thus ends with the departure of Mama Goldfish back to Delancy Street with Birdie, Eddie, and the baby, and the final scene is an ironic epilogue, calling to mind what has been lost, and what it means to be the man left out.

The Younger Generation, then, centers on the scapegoat figure, the one who represents the comic obstacle. This emphasis on the "blocking figure" is typical of satiric comedy, which is generally concerned with the attack and abuse of anticomic characters. *The Younger Generation* is unusual to the extent that it allows so much sympathy to anticomic figures (later Capra films would confront figures impossible to sympathize with), but it is a type of sympathy characteristic of great comic artists.

Platinum Blonde (1931) has exactly the same structure as *The Younger Generation*, from a two-room flat to an Italianate mansion and back again, but it reverses the comic emphasis. We no longer sympathize with the comic scoundrels, but are primarily concerned with those who manage to escape the bondage that the scoundrels represent.

Platinum Blonde takes place almost entirely indoors, and within four locations: the newspaper office where breezy, intelligent, ace reporter Stew Smith (Robert Williams) and his female "pal," Gallagher, work; the speakeasy bar where they relax after work; the Schuyler mansion where most of the film's actual "work" gets done; and Stew's two-room flat, which we hear about but never see until the last scene of the film. The personal dynamic of the film, Stew's initial infatuation and quickie marriage to Ann Schuyler (Jean Harlow) and his final return to Gallagher (Loretta Young), the "gal" he loved all along, is closely tied into this physical scheme. Indeed, there is one moment when the relatedness of people and place becomes almost a matter of physical identity. Ann charges upstairs to hurry Stew into his monkey-suit tuxedo. She is wearing a geometrically patterned black-and-white silk dress, and she is walking across a black and white geometrically patterned floor. Capra shoots it in long shot from above, looking down off a balcony, so that the pattern of Harlow's dress and white hair seems a part of the similarly patterned floor: she is obviously "in place."

Stew, on the other hand, is just as obviously out of place, a "bird in a gilded cage," as both his editor and Smyth, the butler, tell him. His problem is his inability to keep physical and emotional facts straight. Gallagher is an emotional "pal," but she is, as far as Stew is concerned, physically neuter, being, in her own words, "just one of the boys." Stew does not perceive her physical reality as a woman. Ann Schuyler, on the other hand, is physically a woman, an extremely entrancing and beautiful "thoroughbred" to Gallagher's "draft horse," but emotionally neuter. She is hard and cold (like the marble floor) and she sees Stew as pure physicality, "putty" (to use Stew's own term) to be molded into the little toy gentleman she wants (just as Morris attempts to make "real people" of his parents and sister in *Younger Generation*). Ann is apparently an experienced hand at this childish arts-and-crafts

Ann Schuyler (Jean Harlow), Stew Smith (Robert Williams, and Gallagher (Loretta Young) in *Platinum Blonde*.

Platinum Blonde: The "arts and crafts" approach to love.

approach to love, and we can speculate that the reason she picks Stew is his "consistency." He is not quite so easily molded as others she has known (witness his ability to refuse her first sexually loaded request not to print the story about her brother's love affair with the chorus girl).

Capra associates this unnatural and tidy split between physical and emotional reality with a kind of self-perpetuating, decadent, upper-class sterility personified in the Schuylers. This sterility is balanced against the natural union of emotional and physical facts that we see personified in Gallagher, who is less upset at the prospect of losing her face (as the Schuylers are) than with the fact that a lost face (or specifically an unattractive, lower-class nose) will result in her losing Stew.

The comic conflict, then, is between sterility (Ann) and fertility (Gallagher), and the battle ground is Stew Smith, the hero who undergoes a kind of death (marrying Ann) and resurrection (divorcing her). Here, too, place plays an important part. The "green world" motif that we discussed earlier in this chapter is central to the action and theme of *Platinum Blonde.* The film's two most important and revealing scenes take place in contrasting garden sets, and both sets, being outside, contrast with the film's usual indoor setups. Of course, both scenes do take place within the Schuyler garden, but the first, where Stew proposes to Ann, is set beside an elaborate fountain that glitters with an artificial light corresponding to the artificiality of Harlow herself. This correlation of light, water, and sex appears frequently in Capra, most memorably in *Ladies of Leisure* (1930) when Barbara Stanwyck strips for bed. Capra shoots the scene through rain-washed windows, picking up Stanwyck

A production still of the fountain scene.

against the light from a fireplace, and the effect is one of an overwhelming (yet natural) sensuality. But in *Platinum Blonde* the effect is ominously reversed: firelight is replaced by electricity, falling water is replaced by pumped water, and the things that should come naturally, including love, are forced and foreign. In any case, this first garden scene at the fountain contrasts with the second garden scene, also set within the larger boundaries of the Schuyler estate, but in relatively natural surroundings, real trees and real moonlight rather than artificial fixtures.

There is another Schuyler party going on, and Stew has fled the house to sit alone on a bench among the trees. Gallagher, substituting for the society editor, attends the party dressed in an extremely elegant yet naturally flowing white (as opposed to Harlow's normally black) gown. As soon as she arrives, she looks for Stew, and finds him in the garden. The scene is filmed in medium long shot, with Stew sitting on a bench in the foreground, and Gallagher walking down an incline behind him so that the moonlight catches in her hair and illuminates her dress. She is extremely beautiful. That fact finally dawns on Stew, and one of the first things he asks her is "Gallagher, what have you done to yourself?" What she has done is to dye her hair and wash her dress (or so she says, though her hair looks essentially the same as before), nothing abnormal or spectacular, and the change is not so much in

Gallagher's appearance (she has been pretty all along) but in Stew's perception of her: he finally sees her as a woman. The first battle of the war was won by the woman in tune with the artificiality of the setting; the final battle is engaged in and eventually won by a woman in tune with the naturalness of her surroundings. To be sure, we are talking about relative degrees of naturalness here. Nobody is running naked through the woods. But Gallagher is far more "natural," far more "human," than Ann. Gallagher is, in other words, "in place," and Stew's natural place is with her, not with Ann.

Our natural function as spectators in this comic scheme is to sympathize with the eminently sympathetic comic lovers, Stew and Gallagher. We feel no sense of loss (as we did with Morris in *Younger Generation*), but only one of elation and victory. Both *The Younger Generation* and *Platinum Blonde* are, then, about the risks necessary to insure such victory, like Gallagher's risk in continuing to love Stew despite his disregard for her, and the risk of moral disaster run by those like Stew and Morris who succumb to the sterile glamour of wealth.

Capra thus reveals quite early in his career a deep-seated distrust of wealth and the wealthy, and a healthy skepticism regarding the system that allows such people to prosper. Nevertheless, Capra refuses to completely condemn the capitalist system (Longfellow Deeds is but one of his right-way capitalist figures). This contradictory approach on Capra's part continued long after Capra himself had become a rich man. Even as late a film as *Here Comes the Groom* (1951) portrays the rich as humorously but somehow insufficiently human. It is better for Emmadel to remain a fisherman's daughter [and Cary Grant, we might note, is saved from the nuthouse in *Arsenic and Old Lace* (1944) because he is the son of a sea cook] than to be bred to a blue blood. But no matter how much Capra attacks wealth, he appreciates the freedom that money allows: freedom from hunger, care, and want (see chapter 14: *Pocketful of Miracles*). There is something of the immigrant's realistic intelligence in Capra's approach to economic fact and necessity. You have got to have money to survive, and those who have it are not going to give it to you.

Despite his satiric abuse of the upper classes, Capra is best described as an accepting and forgiving filmmaker. He generally chooses to empha-

The upper class in *Platinum Blonde*: Dexter Grayson (Reginald Owen), Mrs. Schuyler (Louise Closser Hale), and Ann (Jean Harlow).

size the victory of comic love rather than the defeat of anticomic sterility (a choice not reprehensible in itself). Even *The Younger Generation*, which focuses primarily on the fate of the comic obstacle, has a very strong comic love interest, so that satiric abuse is tempered with comic concern. Those critics who condemn Capra's "fantasy of goodwill" are clearly upset with this assertion of adequacy. They see Capra as being politically naive, inadequate as a filmmaker to the task of exploring the economic issues of the day, and they want him to be a political sophisticate (although he is probably more sophisticated than they give him credit for).

But love-centered comedy, which has its own deep-seated prepolitical validity, almost never deals in the kind of accurate socioeconomic analysis that sociologically oriented critics want. Comedy as a form does deal with economic issues, but it deals with such issues in moral terms. For example, the earliest extant European comedy, *The Acharnians* by Aristophanes, treats a complex political situation, the Peloponnesian War, in simplified moral terms. The war started, according to honest citizen Dicaeopolis, because three whores had been kidnapped. The war resulted, of course, less from a drunken kidnapping than from the expansionist schemes of Pericles and his faction, but the equation of the two, imperialism and sexual indulgence, implies a moral evaluation: both are a matter of exploitation. Even the plays of Ben Jonson and Bernard Shaw, both of whom were very much concerned with the effects of capitalism on English society, deal with social problems in individualistic and moral terms.[9] Capra utilizes a similar technique of caricature, simplification, and moral evaluation, and he makes no attempt at sophisticated economic analysis because he does not have to: it is not necessary given the form in which he chooses to work. To ask Capra to be a Hauptmann, a Gorki, a De Sica, or a Godard, is to demonstrate a perhaps commendable political stance, but an insufficient aesthetic awareness.

Comedy is of its very nature a highly conventional form, retaining a kind of primitive psychological force by maintaining a structure and a logic characteristic of the archaic rites and myths from which it derives. This type of mythical conventionality accounts in large part for the popularity of comedy, for the fulfillment of conventional expectations is one way of fostering the sense of adequacy that is comedy's thematic heart. But as Cornford has shown, the comic conventions are not artistic dead weight to be enlivened only by witty dialogue or unconventional turns of plot. Rather, the conventional comic elements of plot, character, and theme provide an aesthetic foundation, a deep, supporting structure that the comic artist can build upon, using whatever surface issues he pleases to embody deep-structure conflicts of life vs death, fertility vs sterility, and so forth. Thus the appeal of comedy is not simply a matter of illegitimate wish fulfillment. The rituals from which comedy derives may have been elaborately orchestrated social wishes for rain, human fertility, and the continued social health of the community; but no matter how fantastic the surface presentation of those wishes may have been (resurrected heroes and the like), the content of the wishes, the objects wished for, were far from improbable: rain will fall, babies will be born, and communities will cohere.

We can measure the real strength of these comic conventions by noting their persistency: the comic myth occurs with astonishing regularity from Aristophanes to Buster Keaton, and the surprising thing is not the near infinite number of variations on the comic formula, but the way in which all of these variations can be traced back to a small core of conventions. Thus to understand comedy at all is to understand how conventions serve as the comic language, providing the symbolic form for comic

thought. Comedy as a form of expression therefore cuts across boundaries between media. It is not a matter of print vs celluloid, literature vs cinema, stage vs screen, because comedy as a principle of design, as an aesthetic foundation, largely determines the final form of the finished aesthetic structure, regardless of which raw building materials are used. If we can employ linguistic terminology, we can say that the grammar of forms (comedy being one such form) is of such a nature that the kernel sentences (e.g., comedy) are subject to varying transformational rules according to the meduim in which they occur, so that while the deep structure of It Happened One Night, for example, is the same as the deep structure of As You Like It, the immediate surface, which is the medium in both cases, is obviously different, requiring different techniques, different sensitivies, and different capabilities. Shakespeare creates a Forest of Arden through poetry, and Capra creates his green world through photographic images. It would be folly to overlook such important differences, where those differences are in fact important, but it would be just as foolhardy to ignore the deep similarities that exist between novels, plays and films, for they are similarities that demand an inclusive rather than an exclusive aesthetic.

Capra's popularity can thus be seen as a function of the form he chose to work with and his skill at exploiting that form for his own comic purposes. Sociological critics like Richard Griffith clearly feel ill at ease with this sort of conventionality, preferring clear-cut and obvious social realism to the kind of subtle examination of personal reality that comedy at its best can achieve. For example, Griffith can thus condemn Ernst Lubitsch for attempting "nothing that was not well within the tried formulas" after 1931.[10] But by so doing, Griffith only reveals himself as incapable of understanding how the "tried formulas" can have meaning and importance sufficient enough to insure their persistent existence on the stages and screens of the world. Griffith implies in his criticism that artists simply should not be creating comedy in our anticomic epoch. We can more validly urge, however, that there has never been a greater need for the comic expression of belief in human fertility and adequacy than in an age of such overwhelming sterility, death, and despair. It is to this ability to be deeply comic that we

Celebrating fertility: Mary (Donna Reed) and George (James Stewart) fall in love in *It's a Wonderful Life*.

should attribute Capra's popularity. His success does not reside completely in his ability to make people forget their troubles, nor does it reside completely in his evocation of the American myth. Capra's popularity runs deeper than either of these explanations allows. It is not the topicality of Capra's films that insures their continued popularity. It is their comicness. Capra's movies plug into a deep-running stream of emotion and aspiration that Frye describes as the "comic mythos," of which the populist-agrarian myth is only one version. Capra celebrates the human virtues of fertility, maturity, integrity, and community, and he does so in a fully committed, deeply humanistic, and completely cinematic manner.

NOTES

1. Francis Cornford, *The Origins of Attic Comedy* (1914; rpt. Cambridge: Cambridge University Press, 1934;) Northrop Frye, *Anatomy of Criticism* (1957; rpt. New York: Atheneum, 1969) and *A Natural Perspective* (New York: Harcourt, Brace & World, 1965). I became acquainted with myth criticism through Ernst Cassirer, *The Myth of the State* (New Haven: Yale University Press, 1946) and Suzanne K. Langer, *Philosophy In A New Key* (New York: New American Library, 1942) and *Feeling and Form* (New York: Scribner's, 1953). For a good introduction to the philosophy and methodology of myth criticism see John B. Vickery, ed., *Myth and Literature: Contemporary Theory and Practice* (Lincoln: University of Nebraska Press, 1966) and Thomas A. Sebeok, ed., "Myth: A Symposium," *Journal of American Folklore* 68, no. 270 (1955). One of the best Shakespearean myth critics is C. L. Barber, *Shakespeare's Festive Comedy* (Princeton: Princeton University Press, 1959). Also see Charles W. Eckert, "The English Cine-Structuralists," *Film Comment* 9, no. 3 (1973): 46-51, for a discussion of the influence of Claude Lévi-Strauss and his structuralist approach to mythology on such critics as Peter Wollen, *Signs and Meaning in the Cinema* (Bloomington: Indiana University Press, 1969) and Jim Kitses, *Horizons West* (Bloomington: Indiana University Press, 1969). Kitses, we should note, owes more to Frye (he actually discusses *Anatomy of Criticism*) and Bazin than he does to Lévi-Strauss.

2. See Ian Donaldson, *The World-Upside Down: Comedy from Jonson to Fielding* (London: Oxford University Press, 1970) and A. N. Kaul, *The Action of English Comedy* (New Haven: Yale University Press, 1970).

3. Morse Peckham, *Man's Rage for Chaos* (New York: Schocken Books, 1967), p. 140.

4. James Agee, "Comedy's Greatest Era," *Life,* 4 Sept. 1949, p. 77.

5. See Theodore Huff, *Charlie Chaplin* (1951; rpt. New York: Pyramid, 1964); Walter Kerr, *Tragedy and Comedy* (New York: Simon and Schuster, 1967); Charles Chaplin, *My Autobiography* (1964; rpt. New York: Pocket Books, 1966); Northrop Frye, "The Great Charlie," *Canadian Forum,* Aug. 1941, pp. 148-150; André Bazin, *What Is Cinema?,* translated by Hugh Gray, 2 vols. (Berkeley: University of California Press, 1967 and 1971); and Robert Warshow, *The Immediate Experience* (Garden City: Doubleday & Company, 1962).

6. See J.-P. Lebel, *Buster Keaton,* translated by P. D. Stovin (South Brunswick and New York: A. S. Barnes and Company, Inc., 1967); David Robinson, *Buster Keaton* (Bloomington: Indiana University Press, 1969); and Donald W. McCaffrey, *Four Great Comedians* (South Brunswick and New York: A. S. Barnes and Company, Inc., 1968).

7. Langer, *Feeling and Form,* p. 342. See also John G. Neihardt, *Black Elk Speaks* (1931; rpt. New York: Pocket Books, 1972) and Paul Radin, *The Trickster* (New York: Philosophical Library, 1956) for discussions of the clown figure in American Indian society.

8. Aristole, *The Poetics,* in T. S. Dorsch, ed., *Classical Literary Criticism* (Baltimore: Penguin, 1971), p. 24.

9. See Brian Gibbons, *Jacobean City Comedy* (Cambridge: Harvard University Press, 1968).

10. Richard Griffith and Paul Rotha, *The Film Till Now* (1930; revised and enlarged 1949 and 1960, Middlesex: The Hamlyn Publishing Group), p. 479.

3

Capra's Comic Vision

In my last chapter I set forth an aesthetic for comedy, specified the model in terms of its structural elements, themes, and images, and applied that model in some detail to selected specific examples of Capra's work. The intention was to demonstrate how Capra's comic films could be reasonably understood in terms of an ongoing literary tradition. But while the tradition provides us with a set of terms particularly appropriate and enlightening for the study of Capra's comedies, the tradition in itself does not determine what Capra actually accomplished in his comic films. The comic tradition may supply a general form for artistic thought and a general subject for consideration, but only the artist himself can transform traditional possibilities into aesthetic realities. It is then the artistic works, the actual products of Capra's artistic endeavor, that we are concerned with here. How did Capra employ the comic form, and to what purpose? Is there a discernible pattern common to Capra's comedies, and how can we best describe it?

An analysis of three representative movies, drawn from different periods of Capra's career, should make it clear that there is indeed a recognizable pattern to Capra's comic films. Comparing the early *That Certain Thing* (1928) to a political period film like *You Can't Take It With You* (1938), and finally comparing both of these films to a later effort like *Here Comes the Groom* (1951) will reveal an amazing (and generally overlooked) consistency in

Charles, Jr. (Ralph Graves) and Molly "the gold digger" (Viola Dana) do the town in *That Certain Thing*.

both deep-structure comic form and surface-structure issues.

That Certain Thing was Capra's first film for Columbia Pictures and, in a way, the first film that he made for himself. While working with Harry Langdon, he was limited by the Langdon character that he, Arthur Ripley, and Harry Edwards cooked up on the Sennett lot (see chapter 7). His first feature without Langdon, *For the Love of Mike* (1927), was agreed upon script unseen, and Capra talks about it in his autobiography as a project he was little interested in. *That Certain Thing,* however, was evidently a story that Capra chose (or wrote?) on his own, and it stands as a surprisingly complete exposition of themes and characters that were to concern Capra throughout his career.[1]

That Certain Thing exhibits the classical New Comedy structure described by Frye in *A Natural Perspective.*[2] For reasons of class and wealth, the irate father forbids the marriage of his wastrel son and the son's beautiful but lower-class lover. A. B. Charles (Burr McIntosh), "the restaurant king," is convinced (rightly it turns out) that the girl, Molly (Viola Dana), is a "gold digger," only out after the Charles fortune. Molly comes from a working-class, immigrant neighborhood, and she is determined to escape her tenement. She naively talks about marrying her millionaire, but when the time comes, she genuinely falls in love with Junior (Ralph Graves). Thus at the very moment when the father's opposition crystalizes (he disinherits his son), the reason for the opposition evaporates. Molly is no longer the fortune-hunting gold digger, but a resourceful and independent young wife who puts her immigrant character to the task of making a working-class husband out of her upper-class lover.

The comic movement of the film has two parts then: the first involves the actual marriage and resulting disinheritance, and the second involves the financial resurgence of Molly and Charles, Jr., and the resulting reconciliation of father, son, and

Charles, Sr. (Burr McIntosh), disinherits his no-good son.

daughter-in-law. Money and *petit bourgeois* capitalism are thus as central to this film as they will be to later Capra movies. The father is the archetype of Capra's cigar-chomping, skinflint capitalist. Charles, Sr.'s notion of good restaurant management is to "slice the ham thin," and thus to take as many pennies per pound of ham as possible from the working-class men who frequent his string of restaurants. This self-centered form of capitalist enterprise is countered by the box lunch business established by Molly and Junior. On his first (and last) day on the construction job, Molly brings him a gargantuan lunch in an old shoebox. He cannot eat it all, and he gives a sandwich to a worker who has just left and is still hungry from eating lunch at one of Charles, Sr.'s restaurants. The worker comments on the quality of the sandwich, and Charles, Jr. gets the inspiration to go into the box lunch business in direct competition with his father.

The result is of course the comically predictable triumph of Molly and Junior over the old man. His restaurants begin to lose money, and he goes over to buy the "Molly's Box Lunch Company" from Molly, whom he does not know as his daughter-in-law. The thing to note, however, is the way in which Molly and Junior fight fire with fire and manage to quench much of the old man's capitalist flame in the process. The box lunch company has expanded as quickly as possible to meet demand, and hence they have plowed all of their capital back into the firm. They do not even have money enough to meet the payroll. Charles, Sr., comes in and is appropriately impressed by the hustle and bustle of the sandwich assembly line. Junior sees him coming and tells Molly to put on a big bluff that will convince the old man to buy them out at any price, no matter how high. Despite Molly's comic ineptitude, Junior manages to coach her via hand signals through the window in her office door, and she quickly ups the price from $5,000 to $100,000. In the meantime, Junior completes the deception by ringing cash registers helter-skelter and lugging in a large bag of washers as "the day's receipts." All the while Charles, Sr., becomes more and more convinced that he must buy them out or be ruined. He must uncover the mystery of the "sandwich with a secret." They finally accept the $100,000 offer, and the deception of the father is complete.

The closing of the deal is not the ending of the film, however. Junior comes in, and Charles, Sr., comments on the business sense of "Molly, the box lunch queen." He tells his son, "If you had only married a girl like her, I'd give another $100,000." Molly and Junior both hand him a pen to sign the check with, and Charles, Sr., true to his word, writes another check. At this point Molly takes the bag of washers, dumps the bogus coin on the desk, and deposits the checks daintily into the sack as if it were a purse. Charles, Sr., thus gets an appropriate comeuppance in terms he understands. He had been getting something for nothing by selling near-hamless ham sandwiches, and now he has bought $200,000 worth of nothing to learn his lesson. But of course he has not bought just nothing. He has paid the price for his greed, learned that the secret of the sandwich is "cut the ham thick," and the joviality with which he swallows his medicine reconciles him to his newly expanded family.

This concern with family values will be a constant one in Capra, and the greatest threat to the family ethic is the unrepentant capitalist whose sole concern is the further accumulation of wealth and power. The scope of this conflict is undeniably expanded in *You Can't Take It With You,* but the comic dynamic and the essential concerns remain the same despite the addition of more obvious political issues.

You Can't Take It With You has essentially the same character alignment as *That Certain Thing*: two families of different economic and class status are eventually united by a Romeo-and-Juliet-type love affair that cuts across class barriers. But the inner dynamics of this set of relationships are far more complex in the later film. The issue is not simply a matter of the rich father (Edward Arnold) disinheriting his son. Rather, it is the elder Kirby's attempts to make his son Tony (Jimmy Stewart) president of the world's largest munitions combine that represents the comic threat. But Kirby's scheme is not simply a threat to Tony's relaxed sense of self: the putting together of a financial empire in fact affects the fates of a multitude of people. Kirby's plan threatens to disrupt a large community of friends (those who live in or around the Vanderhoff place), further corrupt an already acquiescing government, as well as condemn a sizable portion of the human race to annihilation once the munitions works starts turning out the tools of destruction.

Charles, Sr., "swallows his medicine" and the family is reconciled.

The impetus behind Kirby's action, however, is not destruction *per se*. He comes from a long line of financiers, and he feels duty bound to make his son the wealthiest and most powerful financier in family history. It certainly says something about the state of society in general that the path to wealth and power lies along the road to the apocalypse, but it says something positive about Kirby that his basic motive is tied into a conception of family continuity, however perverse the manifestation of that continuity might be. Unlike the other capitalist power mongers played by Edward Arnold (*i.e.,* Jim Taylor in *Mr. Smith* and D. B. Norton in *Meet John Doe*), Anthony P. Kirby is clearly redeemable. We know that he once wrestled [something that re-

quires, according to Kolenkhov (Mischa Auer), a unity of mind and body], and he was once quite a harmonica player, both of which testify to a latent sense of humanity at work in Kirby's soul.

Set in direct conflict with Kirby's perverse sense of family is the Vanderhoff/Sycamore clan, a marvelous bunch of harmless eccentrics whose joyful mode of existence seems particularly in tune with their Walt Disney world (as Tony describes it). There is something of Langdon's childishness about them, and Providence favors them with an effortless existence. Their personalist ethic is in sharp philosophical contrast to the acquisition ethic of Kirby, but their personalism also poses a direct and immediate threat to Kirby's acquisitiveness. He

The Walt Disney world of the Vanderhoff clan in *You Can't Take It With You.*

wants to force his exfriend and competitor, Ramsey (H. B. Warner), out of business, and he plans to do it by purchasing all the property surrounding Ramsey's plant, hence preventing necessary expansion. The last parcel necessary for Kirby's plan is the old Vanderhoff place, which Grandpa Vanderhoff (Lionel Barrymore) refuses to sell. His reason for that refusal is again a personal one. His deceased wife still lives in the spirit and fragrance of the house, and to leave the house would be to leave her, something Grandpa cannot do.

Complicating and eventually resolving this economic conflict is the love affair of Tony Kirby and Alice Sycamore—granddaughter to old Vanderhoff (Jean Arthur). Alice is Tony's secretary, and Tony is

understandably more entranced by her charms than he is by his father's business schemes. Tony wants to marry Alice, but she rightly fears the opposition of the elder Kirbys. Tony is thus the central figure of the film. Kirby's financial plans revolve around Tony, as do the romantic hopes of the Vanderhoff clan (Grandpa thanks God for sending Tony to be Alice's husband). Tony is thus caught in the middle. He can either be another Kirby, which means he will lose Alice, or he can become a Vanderhoff, marrying Alice and carrying out his college dream of utilizing the energy in grass.

The subject of the film, then, is Tony's personal moral choice: what kind of person should he be, a Kirby or a Vanderhoff? But again, it is not quite that simple, because the difference between Kirby and Grandpa Vanderhoff is not that great. Vanderhoff was once a businessman, like Kirby plagued with gastric pains, until one day he just up and quit. Kirby thus represents what Grandpa would have become had he continued in business. Similarly, however, Vanderhoff represents what Kirby might become, someone free of the mental anguish symbolized by executive ulcers. We have, then, a continuum of characters, stretching from Kirby through Tony to Grandpa, and the movement of the film will be to push everyone towards the proper Vanderhoff end of the scale. Tony will marry Alice, the properly comic continuance of both families will be thus assured, and Kirby will give up his financial schemes, removing the threat not only to the neighborhood and the world but to himself.

Tony Kirby (James Stewart) woos Alice Sycamore (Jean Arthur).

Family harmony in *You Can't Take It With You,* with Lionel Barrymore and Edward Arnold.

The primary metaphor of the film is surely the family, but an important secondary symbol is music. Capra generally uses background music sparingly and unobtrusively, but many of his characters, particularly the sympathetic ones, are quite musically inclined, singing folk songs (Deeds with "Swanee River" or George Bailey with "Buffalo Gal") or playing folk instruments (harmonicas, guitars, sweet potatoes, etc). The Vanderhoff house, for example, is full of music and dancing, and *You Can't Take It With You* concludes in a *kômos*like celebration with Grandpa and Kirby dueting on harmonica while neighbors dance and Alice falls into Tony's loving arms. The harmonica that Alice gives Grandpa, and that Grandpa in turn gives to Kirby, thus serves to represent a childlike harmony of mind and body (recall the dancers in the park) that Kirby has lost in the quest for financial and political power. His taking up the harmonica again is thus beginning anew, returning to the integrity of childhood to celebrate the continuity of life. A grown man can wrestle, play the harmonica, and give up destructive schemes without destroying his real sense of personal dignity. Kirby rightly preceives that his financial schemes have destroyed the family tradition that he sought to maintain (in that Tony decides to leave the business) and that the only right road to family unity is the Vanderhoff path to eccentric personalism.

Like *The Younger Generation,* then, *You Can't Take It With You* tends to have a dual focus, paying nearly equal attention to the fate of the comic lovers and the fate of the comic obstacle. Both fates are intertwined, certainly, and they share a common motivation and conclusion. The film thus sets right-way personalism (Vanderhoff and the Sycamores) against wrong-way personalism (the Kirbys) and arrives at a comic conclusion that in fact rejuvenates both families. The Vanderhoff clan does not lose a daughter, but gains a son, a harmonica player, and a neighborhood as well. Likewise, the Kirbys do not lose a son but they gain themselves.

The deep-comic structure of *You Can't Take It With You* is thus of the ritual-combat type (as was the structure of *That Certain Thing*), with Tony aligning himself with the Vanderhoff clan in intial opposition to Kirby. There is also a secondary element of scapegoat ritual, with Kirby's competitor, Ramsey, dying of a business-induced (or Kirby-induced) heart attack. The sins of capitalism weigh Ramsey down unto death, and it is Ramsey's death that finally inspires Kirby's decision to quit business. The surface issues of economics and politics here serve, as they do repeatedly in Capra, as metaphors for comic bondage, for dedication to sterile principles. Capra's topicality is thus a matter of the metaphor he chooses to embody the death principle. This equation of capitalism with sterility reveals the same distrust of the American economic system that we have seen elsewhere in Capra, but again Capra stops short of total condemnation. Essie, Alice's sister, sells her homemade candies ("love dreams") and Paul Sycamore is in the fireworks business. This kind of small-change capitalism is acceptable because it does not demand the psychotic split between action and desire that characterizes the financial practices of Kirby or *The Younger Generation's* Morris Goldfish. Furthermore, this personalist capitalism endangers no one. Neighbors will not be forced from their homes by the various Sycamore enterprises. You can be a capitalist, but being too much of a capitalist, like Kirby, requires giving up "the perfume of life," something that Capra is loath to see people do.

Here Comes the Groom is a very relaxed film, devoid of the political overtones seen in *You Can't Take It With You.* As in many previous Capra films the issues in *Here Comes the Groom* revolve around questions of family and personal responsibility. Peter Garvey (Bing Crosby) is a reporter in Post-WW II Europe who helps run an orphanage. His concern for the children is moving and genuine, but it is clear that his continuing presence in Europe requires a corresponding absence from America and from an American girl, Emmadel Jones (Jane Wyman), who has been waiting faithfully for years to marry him. She has apparently threatened before in letters to go ahead and marry somebody else rather than wait for Pete and become an old maid in the process. But by the time of the film's beginning, she is so frustrated that she resorts to a talking letter (a record) to tell Pete that she is through. "I was born to be a mother," she protests, "not a poised pencil," and she informs him of her determination to marry the first "egghead" that catches her. She cannot "stare childless at the prospect of old age in a home for spinsters."

Peter is clearly convinced that she is right in her

You Can't Take It With You: Ramsey (H. B. Warner) confronts Kirby (Edward Arnold).

determination to have a family, so he packs up two orphans, Robert and Susie, and takes them (after much bother and delay) back to America as the first two installments of the Garvey family that he plans to raise with Emmadel. He is rightly convinced (as the film demonstrates) that she still loves him, despite her determination to eliminate him from her life.

But the bother and delay, and Peter's negligence in keeping Emmadel posted on his progress home, throw his plans out of joint. Emmadel has awaited one too many airplanes, and, figuring that Pete has stood her up once too often, she consents to marry her boss, Wilbur Stanley (Franchot Tone) of the Boston Stanleys. Peter's task, then, for the remain-

Here Comes the Groom, Bing Crosby, and his ready-made family of war orphans.

der of the film is to win Emmadel back, and in this he is amiably assisted by his rival, Wilbur, who knows of Emmie's past relationship with Pete and who wants her to make a free choice. Wilbur puts Peter and the kids in the guest house at the family mansion and gives them until the day of the wedding to talk Emmadel out of it.

So the moral question in *Here Comes the Groom* centers on Emmadel. She must choose between Peter Garvey and the easygoing exuberance of the life he leads, and Wilbur Stanley, whose grace and ordered elegance make the Stanley fortune all the more attractive. The relaxed nature of this conflict dictates the relaxed tone of the entire film. Crosby himself is relaxation personified, with his smooth voice and breezy gestures, and Wilbur is a quite splendid fellow as well, handsome and generous. Were it not for the fact that Emmadel really loves Pete and really belongs with him, we would not be

upset for a minute were she to marry Wilbur. But she would not just be marrying Wilbur. She would be marrying into the Stanley family, and there is a very unappealing, almost mummified stodginess about nearly all of Wilbur's relatives. We simply cannot imagine Emmadel becoming another old Stanley matron.

The insufficiency of the Stanley family is made clear when it is set against the Jones faimly, or at least the Jones family before Emmadel met Wilbur. Ma Jones (Connie Gilchrist) may once have been content to be the wife of a Gloucester fisherman, but the prospect of opulence is enough to make her quite happy with the proposed marriage. Pa Jones (James Barton), on the other hand, is convinced it is a mistake, and he wholeheartedly assists Pete to win Emmadel back. He does not want to spend the rest of his life in dry dock as a guest at the Stanley mansion. But what defines the spirit of the Jones

Pete (Bing Crosby) and Pa Jones (James Barton) discuss Emmadel's wedding plans.

family is a past of shared experiences. Pete is obviously the man for Emmadel, according to Pa, because Pete and Emmie grew up together. As Pa tells us, Pete taught her to "wrestle, and to box, and to bait a hook" during the summers they spent "scampering over the Gloucester rocks." Gloucester and the sea are thus important symbols for both Pa and Pete. They represent a world of childlike freedom and genuine experience. Pete had intended to take Emmadel to Pa's old Gloucester shack for their honeymoon (before he found out about Wilbur), and he repeatedly reminds Emmie of their Gloucester life together.

The Stanleys, by contrast, are, as a family, bound to sets of traditional relationships and actions that stifle rather than encourage freedom. Pa says that Wilbur is "not even a man—he's a tradition," and while he is wrong about Wilbur's manhood in partic-

ular (Wilbur is a champion athlete), Pa is correct about the Stanley clan in general. Indeed, even Wilbur is bound enough by tradition to insist on a formal wedding when Emmie, rightly sensing impending complications with Pete, begs him to elope and marry her before anything can go wrong. For once, Wilbur's Stanleyness comes through, and once is enough to insure that he will lose Emmadel.

But Wilbur is the least offensive of the Stanleys, and Wilbur's relatives are the proof that the rich Stanley pudding is rotten. The family has not produced a child in thirty years (according to Pa Jones), and it is clear that for all of Wilbur's good intentions, some members of the family, most notably Uncle Elihu (H. B. Warner), the horse breeder, see Emmadel as a "sharp, little filly" who will bring new vigor into the decaying Stanley bloodline. The family's primary method of expressing gratitude is

Wilbur Stanley (Franchot Tone) admires his "Cinderella" (Jane Wyman).

"the family wedding gift" of $500,000, with a "bonus besides for every colt." To be sure, Emmie would not mind bearing and raising children, but breeding is the only thing Stanley women are allowed to do, according to Aunt Amy (Adeline de Walt Reynolds). Emmadel is far too lively and intense a person to become a mere breeding mare, yet the Stanleys have two hundred years of sterile, male chauvinist tradition to weigh her down with. Thus, while marrying Wilbur is in itself perfectly acceptable, it is clear that marrying into the Stanley family carries a great deal of risk with it, a risk altogether unnecessary when the man she really loves offers such a completely healthy alternative to the oppressive atmosphere of the Stanley clan.

So the problem in the film is essentially one of knowledge and awareness. Pete becomes aware at the beginning of the film that he needs Emmadel, and that he has responsibilities towards her (the responsibility to give her children, for example). The greater part of the film involves Pete's attempts to make Emmadel aware that she needs Pete (at least more than she needs the Stanleys) and that she has a responsibility towards him, a responsibility to love the man who wants her and needs her the most.

The specific means that Pete uses to bring Emmadel to her comic senses are appropriate to the sexual and familial concerns of the film. He appeals to her maternal longings by means of the children. He has to be married within five days or the kids will be sent back to France. Emmadel is appropriately worried by this, but, unbeknownst to her, it becomes a nonproblem when Wilbur arranges to adopt the kids if Pete does not succeed. Pete's second tactic is to coach Wilbur's "kissing cousin," Winifred Stanley (Alexis Smith), in the fine art of seduction. She has been secretly in love with Wilbur for years, and as it turns out Wilbur has apparently been at least subconsciously interested in her, for, when she makes her concern evident, he rather welcomes her advances. Pete makes sure that Emmadel is aware of this budding relationship between Winifred and Wilbur. Emmie thus sees that Wilbur neither wants her nor needs her in the same way that Pete does.

Both of these schemes come to a head at the wedding scene [which recalls, as does much in the film, *It Happened One Night* (1934)]. Winifred (as maid of honor), Emmadel, and Wilbur are at the altar, but just as the ceremony is about to begin there is a commotion at the edge of the garden. An FBI agent is arresting Pete and the kids. Emmie still believes that Pete has to get married to keep the children (and Wilbur's decision not to tell her otherwise only indicates his growing regard for Winifred). Furthermore, Winifred is there to remind Emmie where Wilbur's interests have gone, and between these two apparent facts Emmie decides, with Wilbur's graceful assistance, to marry Pete at the last moment: And the FBI agent, it turns out, is a fake.

The film concludes, then, on the image of the entire Jones clan, newly enlarged by the addition of Pete and the children, singing "In the Cool, Cool, Cool of the Evening" as they ride down the road in Pa's old car. Emmie has forgiven Pete his deception (it only proves how much he loves her), and even Ma Jones seems happy with the eventual outcome. This musical *kômos* continues and concludes the musical metaphor that runs through the film. The Joneses are a singing family (the Stanleys never sing a note), and song as a metaphor for harmony ties in with the notion of the harmoniously fertile family that is the film's major image. There are six major production numbers throughout the course of the film, and each has to do with the relationships between people, defining and expressing their feelings for each other. "In the Cool, Cool, Cool" is apparently a song Pete and Emmie learned together in Gloucester, and, like the harmonica in *You Can't Take It With You*, the song carries associations of childhood and spontaneously meaningful emotions. At the film's ending, then, Pete and Emmie have come full circle. They are going back to Gloucester, singing the old Gloucester songs, but they are no longer children, however much they may retain the kind of emotional integrity typical of childhood. Pete and Emmie are parents now, and their task will not be simply to relive their old lives, but to help guide the living of new lives, teaching old songs to new singers, and thus continuing the viable tradition of life fully lived on the edges of experience.

The comic structure is thus essentially the same in *Here Comes the Groom* as it was in *That Certain Thing* and *You Can't Take It With You*. Each features a struggle between fertility and sterility, and the surface issues that metaphorically embody these basic principles are closely related across films, in that they all reflect Capra's basic value structure.

Emmie marries Pete and the kids in *Here Comes the Groom.*

Capra is concerned with moral questions having to do with class, economic status, life style as defined by class and economic status, past experience, personal value as defined by past experience, and above all with love and love's power to overcome barriers of history and position. *You Can't Take It with You* differs from the other two films only to the extent that the connection between big money and big government is made explicit, but this only represents a minor extension of Capra's general distrust of wealth and power, and it is in fact no exception to Capra's normal concerns, simply a slight refinement.

There is thus a strong consistency of form and theme to Capra's work, a consistency so strong that chronology seems much less important for Capra than for auteurs like Ford and Hawks. The only really concerted effort that Capra ever made across time seems to be the informal "populist trilogy" of *Mr. Deeds, Mr. Smith,* and *Meet John Doe,* which

Early Capra: Sam Hardy and Barbara Stanwyck in *The Miracle Woman.*

does demonstrate a recognizable shift in emphasis and form (see chapters 10-12). But this exception aside, the remainder of Capra's comedies are largely of a piece, exploring similar problems in similar manners. Capra is thus willing to test and re-examine his comic approach to life, but he seldom finds it lacking.

Nevertheless, for all of the similarity that Capra's consistency would seem to require, it also allows, by the very nature of its conventionality, a large measure of significance to otherwise slight changes and refinements. Understanding then that we are talking about relative degrees of importance, we can propose a rough but useful set of chronological categories for Capra's comedies based upon these slight but significant changes. Generally speaking, Capra's comic films fall into four major periods:

the city period, the country period, the political period, and the retrospection period.

The first two periods differ primarily in terms of setting (city vs country) and Capra's attitude towards the setting.[3] The city comedies take place in an urban milieu populated by reporters, immigrants, rich young men, rich young women, prostitutes, con men, financiers, etc. The tone is generally cynical, although romanticism always exists beneath the hard surface. The city-as-setting is clearly an appropriate context for the actions of these characters, but the city-as-symbol is still relatively neutral. The setting of the action counts, of course, but the sets that carry symbolic significance are usually various places within the city—uptown flats, Fifth Avenue penthouses, newspaper offices, public parks —but not the city as a whole. As always in Capra,

In the city: the newspaper office in *It Happened One Night*, featuring Clark Gable.

our primary concern is with characters, and the sets help to visualize the character dynamics. The Schuyler mansion in *Platinum Blonde* is important, for example, not because it is a mansion, but because the Schuylers live there.

The second period, which begins with *It Happened One Night* (1934), is characterized by the emergence of a positive alternative to the city milieu. Peter and Ellie flee the city at the film's end, and while negative associations are yet to be explicitly attached to the city, it is clearly a less preferable place for young lovers than roadside motels or moonlit hayfields. *Broadway Bill* (1934) repeats this "flight to freedom" motif, as Dan Brooks (Warner Baxter) gives up his job with the Higgins Cardboard Box Company and his marriage to Mar-

In the country: the barn in *Broadway Bill*, with Warner Baxter and Myrna Loy (both center).

The city-as-symbol in *Mr. Smith Goes to Washington*, featuring James Stewart.

garet Higgins to return to his life as an impoverished racehorse owner. *Mr. Deeds Goes to Town* (1936), the first film in this group to consciously set the city against the country, finds the city explicity deficient in the moral atmosphere necessary for life. Most of the people Deeds meets in the city are cynics of the worst sort (whereas most of the people we meet in *Platinum Blonde* are happy-go-lucky reporters). The city as a haven for cynics thus becomes a symbol for corruption and sterility, and Deeds is right to want to leave the city altogether. The final film of this group, *Lost Horizon* (1937), carries the city/country split to the greatest extremes (from London to Shangri-La). The Valley of the Blue Moon is Capra's attempt to actualize the imaginary paradise to which all men long to escape.

The third period, that of the political films, overlaps the second period, *Mr. Deeds* being at once the culmination of one tendency and the beginning of another. But for all of its topicality, *Mr. Deeds* generally avoids political issues, even though it is traditionaly considered the beginning of Capra's socially conscious cinema. *You Can't Take It With You* (1938) is actually the first film where the connection between big business, and big government is made explicit [*e.g.,* Kirby's Undershaftian (from Shaw's *Major Barbara*) confidence that the adminis-

Father (Samuel S. Hinds) and son (James Stewart) in
It's a Wonderful Life.

tration will not interfere with his munitions firm]. It is significant, however, that *You Can't Take It With You* also marks a return to the city. Anthony P. Kirby lives and operates there, but then so do the Sycamores and Grandpa Vanderhoff; so once again it is a question of character more than simply setting. A similar attitude is at work in *Mr. Smith* and *Meet John Doe*. Indeed, in *Mr. Smith Goes to Washington* (1939) the capital city is, in fact, a symbol for idealism rather than cynicism, and the corruption is clearly a function of the people who work there.

The retrospection period begins with *It's A Wonderful Life* (1946) and concludes with Capra's last feature film, *Pocketful of Miracles* (1961). Here Capra reconsiders the problems that are important to him, problems that he had dealt with in the past and felt compelled to treat again, but he always comes to the same comic conclusions. *It's A Wonderful Life* takes us back to the economic concerns of *Mr. Deeds,* and the country setting of *Broadway Bill,* but it utilizes a romance form (which we will discuss in the next chapter) to consider the issue of personal faith both in the universe and the utility of moral action. The remaining films in this group, *State of the Union* (1948), *Riding High* (1950), *Here Comes the Groom, A Hole in the Head* (1959), and *Pocketful of Miracles,* are characterized by a sense of the past. Two are out-and-out remakes of earlier films (*Riding High* is a remake of *Broadway Bill,* and *Pocketful* is a remake of *Lady for a Day*). *Here Comes the Groom* repeats the plot movement of *It Happened One Night* (the heroine leaves her upper-class fiancé at the altar to marry a reporter), and *A Hole in the Head,* with its eviction motif, recalls *You Can't Take It With You.* Tied in with this sense of the past is a feeling for age. For the first time with Capra, small children appear with regularity. Most of the adult characters are middle-aged (late 30s and 40s), most are maried (*e.g.,* Grant and Mary Matthews in *State of the Union,* George and Mary Bailey in *Wonderful Life*), and one is a widower with a young son (Tony Manetta in *A Hole in the Head*). Music tends to become more important in the films of this period: characters sing more than in earlier films (not surprisingly, when Crosby starred in two films, and Sinatra in another). There is also a quantitative decrease in dramatic tension. Capra seems more at ease with his subjects, and this is reflected in a more relaxed visual style (with the exception of *Wonderful Life*). We should also note that three of these films take place in the city, and Capra seems to feel little discomfort with this return to urban settings.

With these categories in mind, we can now understand one of the major critical problems. A quick glance at chapter 1 will show that most of the criticism on Capra focuses on the five political period films, as if they were the only movies that Capra ever made. Griffith's description of the Capra plot ("a messianic innocent . . . pits himself against the forces of entrenched greed") only fits the political films, if it fits any at all, and his monograph tends to see all the other films only in terms of what they foretell about these "real" Capra movies. But the fact of the matter is that Capra's primarily personal films (*e.g., It Happened One Night, A Hole in the Head*) are no less truly Capra than his political films. Indeed, Capra's political films, as we have seen and will see repeatedly, are no less personal than his love comedies. The comic value that we find in any of Capra's personal films is precisely the same value that we find in his political period films. Accordingly, we can offer the following description of the typical comic Capra plot, a description that applies with equal accuracy to all of Capra's comic movies.

Young lovers of integrity and feeling are faced with obstacles to their comic happiness. The obstacles can be internal, or external, or both, but they represent a combination of cynicism, self-indulgence, and acquistiveness characteristic of the extremely wealthy and powerful. In all cases the lovers manage to assert their emotional integrity, cement their relationship, and confront those in power with moral questions concerning the proper uses and abuses of wealth and influence. Moral victories are thus achieved, and in most cases social problems are resolved in the process. Sometimes this victory requires the help of Providence (*Mr. Smith Goes to Washington*) and sometimes even Providence cannot insure complete triumph (*Meet John Doe*), but in every instance proper personalism (*i.e.,* love) and individual moral responsibility provide comic rewards enough in themselves, whether or not the larger social questions are settled.

The value in all three of the comedies we have

Young lovers of integrity and feeling: Jeff Smith
(James Stewart) and Clarissa Saunders (Jean Arthur).

discussed in this chapter (and in all of Capra's comedies) resides in the personal comic triumph of the young lovers and of anyone else who is willing to join them in the assertion of proper values. Our function as spectators is simple and direct: we feel good about the good fortune of sympathetic characters, which means that we approve of the proper actions and the proper values that determine such good fortune. Of course, we can always reject Capra's moral viewpoint altogether, as some critics do, but for those of us who agree with Capra that personal integrity and community feelings are positive and praiseworthy, we are free to enjoy and appreciate without apology the work of a master filmmaker. Capra appeals to the best in us, and the strength of his moral commitment is the strength of the Capra cinema.

NOTES

1. Capra speaks in his autobiography as if he wrote the story for *That Certain Thing*. The filmography in the Griffith monograph credits the screenplay to Elmer Harris. The script for *You Can't Take It With You* was adapted by Robert Riskin from the Kaufman and Hart play. The screenplay for *Here Comes the Groom* was written by Virginia Van Upp, Liam O'Brien, and Myles Connolly from a story by O'Brien and Riskin.

2. Northrop Frye, *A Natural Perspective* (New York: Harcourt, Brace & World, 1965), p. 72.

3. This city/country opposition was suggested by Andrew Bergman in *We're In The Money* (1971; rpt. New York: Harper & Row, 1972), p. 136.

4

The Capra Romances

To this point we have been concerned almost exclusively with comedy, its derivation, its structure, and so forth. Yet interspersed throughout the Capra canon are several films that as a group can best be understood as romance, with "romance" to be understood as another generic form. The difference between comedy and romance is often a fine one, and many works are rightly understood to straddle the border line between the two. For Capra, however, the distinction between comedy and romance is important, and it is well worth our while to investigate the formal relationship between the two in some detail.

As Northrop Frye has often pointed out, "the mythical backbone of all literature is the cycle of nature, which rolls from birth to death and back again to rebirth."[1] Tragedy and irony focus on the first half of this natural cycle, and both are characterized by a sense of nature's inevitable logic: for every birth there is a death. Comedy and romance, on the other hand, are based on the second half of the mythic cycle, moving from "death to rebirth, decadence to renewal, winter to spring, darkness to a new dawn" (*A Natural Perspective,* p. 121). Comedy and romance are thus closely related. Not only do they share a common mythological ancestry, but they tend to display a similar pattern of action that emphasizes triumph and renewal.

Given this similarity of movement, then, the most easily perceived differences between the two forms are matters of character and setting. Romantic protagonists tend more towards the heroic than comic protagonists. The purest forms of romance exhibit characters "superior in degree to other men," heroes "whose actions are marvelous" but who are nevertheless identified as human beings.[2] Medieval romances in particular recount the adventures of such chivalric heroes, and works of this romantic sort generally function to provide "a self-portrayal of . . . knighthood with its mores and ideals."[3] Comedies, on the other hand, tend more towards the realistic in matters of characterization. As we shall see in our next chapter, comic heroes generally seem less archaic than their romantic counterparts. They are usually members of lower classes, and their dreams and desires are less idealistically oriented: they neither slay dragons nor worship virgins. To the contrary, comic protagonists generally circumvent barriers of class and station in the service of erotic rather than religious love.

This contrast between the mythic and realistic modes is repeated again in the matter of setting. The romantic universe is generally a fantastic one. As Erich Auerbach puts it, the romantic "landscape is the enchanted landscape of fairy tales; we are surrounded by mystery, by secret murmurings and whispers. All the numerous castles and palaces, the battles and adventures of courtly romances are . . . things of fairyland" (*Mimesis,* p. 130). Comedy too has its fairy-tale aspects, in terms both of character and setting. Shakespearean comedy in particular

Superior in degree to other men: Errol Flynn as *Captain Blood.*

projects a world of enchanted forests and magical beings. But Shakespeare was an exception even in his own time, and the Elizabethan norm was the sort of realistic and satiric type of comedy practiced by Jonson, Middleton, and Marston. Generally speaking, then, we can say that most comedies take place in rather realistic settings—the Roman crossroads, the Restoration drawing room, the modern city street—and Shakespeare's use of the fantastic serves more to foreshadow his own movement towards romance (*e.g., Tempest* and *Winter's Tale*) than a general tendency of comedy.

Romances, then, are mythic tales about godlike heroes. The stories themselves, which recount the adventures of these errant knights as they roam the romantic landscape, are thus a function of character: this sort of romantic hero performs and is defined by this sort of romantic exploit. A knight's place in the social order, what he *is* in relationship to the idealized society, is determined by the adventures he undertakes and his success at those adventures. As Auerbach puts it, "trial through adventure is the real meaning of the knight's idealized existence" (*Mimesis*, p. 135).

The plot of romance, the action of the hero, generally revolves around a heroic quest rather than a comic intrigue. But the romantic structure nevertheless displays a tripartite sequence similar and

A king and his court: General Yen (Nils Asther) and his staff in *The Bitter Tea of General Yen*.

parallel to the comic sequence previously discussed. Comic plots move from the *agon* through scenes of sacrifice and feasting to a *kômos* and marriage. The corresponding romantic movement involves an *agon* (the stage of the perilous journey), the *pathos* (the death-struggle), and the *anagnorisis* (the discovery or recognition of the hero). This romantic structure recalls the triumphal sequence we have seen in comedy, but as Frye points out, it "expresses more clearly [than comedy] the passage from struggle through a point of ritual death to a recognition scene" (*Anatomy of Criticism,* p. 187). In other words, romance is more clearly archaic and more clearly the descendent of idealized mythological desires than comedy, which generally strikes a less uneven balance between wish fulfillment and reality principles. Comedy normally guarantees life

in terms of the continuous community, a continuity insured by marriages and the promise of succeeding generations in time. Romance, to the contrary, generally lacks a strong sense of biological time, and continuity is a function of an eternal ideal, an almost platonic cultural conception of beauty and courtesy transcending time and space.

Dirigible (1931) is the most classical of Capra's romances, demonstrating both a recognizable romance form and Capra's own atypical approach to romantic idealism. The film can therefore provide us with a benchmark romance against which we can measure Capra's other romantic films.

Dirigible exhibits a typical romance structure: superheroes performing superdeeds in quest of a heroic holy grail. Dr. Rondelle is an aging explorer determined to reach the South Pole. Frisky Pierce

Planning the *Dirigible* expedition: Dr. Rondelle, Jack
Bradon (Jack Holt), and Frisky Pierce, (Ralph Graves).

(Ralph Graves) is an immature, glory-hounding
stunt pilot who ignores the physical and emotional
needs of his wife to cater to his adoring public.
Jack Bradon (Jack Holt) is the most realistic hero
of the three—concerned with glory, particularly as
that glory furthers the cause of the "lighter-than-air"
service—but intelligent enough to acknowledge failure and accept a desk job until a new dirigible can
be readied to replace the one destroyed on the first
ill-fated polar journey.

There are three major romantic episodes in
Dirigible (and such an episodic narrative is typical
of romance).[4] Each episode is a quest, the first two
in search of the South Pole, and the third in search
of the lost explorers from quest number two. Significantly, the first two quests fail, and it is only the
last one, where the prize is human life rather than

newspaper headlines, that succeeds. Such a multi-
quest structure is necessitated by the presence of
multiple heroes. But the tripartite structure is nevertheless a recognizable romance pattern. The first
quest, the abortive Bradon/Rondelle expedition, is
the *agon,* a preliminary adventure that defines the
nature of the romantic conflict. The second quest,
the Pierce/Rondelle polar assault, is the major
episode, the *pathos* where the major romantic issues
are resolved. Finally, the third quest, Bradon's
rescue of Pierce, functions as the recognition or
anagnorisis. But this recognition is not simply a
matter of the courtly society acknowledging a
knight's prowess. We have, rather, a range of inter-
related recognitions, and it is the entire package of
realizations that make up the film's point.

The movie is thus *about* romance: what does it

mean to be a romantic hero of this type as opposed to that type? This right-way/wrong-way opposition is personified in the characters of Jack Bradon and Frisky Pierce. Both are Navy fliers, Pierce in his pursuit planes, and Bradon in his cumbersome lighter-than-air dirigible. Their characters can almost be fully defined just in terms of the machines they fly. Pierce is a grandstanding individualist, and his various crazy stunts (flying through a hangar, looping-the-loop around the circumference of a blimp) serve to characterize his irresponsible romanticism. Bradon, on the other hand, is less an individualist than the commander of a team. He is aware from the beginning of his responsibility to the men under him. To be sure, blimps cannot loop-the-loop, but Bradon's dedication to lighter-than-air indicates no desire to go looping. He is as steadfast as the machine he commands, yet no less courageous than Frisky when the chips are down.

Just as the film provides us with right and wrong heroes, it also provides us with right and wrong grails, proper and improper goals of heroic action. The first is Helen Pierce (Fay Wray), Frisky's beautiful young wife. She is a very reluctant Penelope, not at all happy with her husband's romantic mania, who longs for a life of intimate domesticity (Frisky has been home a total of two months in two years of marriage). The other prize is glory in general, but it becomes specified as the glory to be gained upon reaching the South Pole. In an ironic

Cold death on the Antarctic ice: burying Rondelle.

fashion these two goals are brought together in the second quest.

Frisky, who had been prevented from participating in the first polar attempt at the request (unknown to him) of his wife, is determined to get to the pole, if only to show up Jack Bradon, who Frisky thinks ordered him off the expedition in order to get all the glory for himself. Helen begs him not to go, and before he leaves she gives him a letter to open when he arrives at the pole. It reads as follows: "Frisky, when you read this you will be all over the front page again, but maybe there will be room for this. I will be in Paris getting my divorce and begging Jack Bradon to marry me. I'm tired of being married to a headliner." Thus for Frisky to gain the pole is to lose a wife, and the thing to note is Frisky's complete obliviousness to the situation. He has no real conception of the way Helen feels. He makes promises he never intends to keep, and it does not strike him that Helen might one day get fed up with his antics. He is totally unaware of her as a human being towards whom he has important responsibilities.

Helen's choice of Bradon as a lover is thus appropriate, for he has that sense of human responsibility that Frisky lacks. But it is his sense of responsibility, even towards an irresponsible friend, that makes it impossible for Jack to marry Helen. Helen's choosing Jack means deserting Frisky, and when they learn that Frisky's plane has crashed at the pole, they both realize that they cannot go

Helen (Fay Wray) and Jack (Jack Holt) learn of the crash.

through with the marriage. It is no longer a matter of marriage to one another, but of mutual betrayal of Frisky, who needs them both.

Ironically again, however, it is Frisky's crash-landing at the South Pole that insures Helen's continued love. She naturally feels frantically concerned: she still loves him the same way she always loved him, faults and all. But once he has crash-landed and the plane has burned, the romanticism is burned out of him as well, and we now realize that he is truly worthy of Helen. His dreams of flaming glory come true, and he finds out that glory means broken bones, putrified flesh, and cold death on the Antarctic ice. Romanticism crashes into reality, and the false hero becomes a true hero, capable of admitting defeat, but not giving up. He is responsible for getting the other explorers to the pole, and he is determined to get them back. Two of them do not make it (one succumbs to injuries, the other commits suicide because of his injury), but Frisky and the fourth man are saved at the last minute by the appearance of Bradon in his new dirigible. As a matter of human responsibility, Bradon and his volunteer crew have braved the Antarctic storms to save their comrades, however foolish those comrades might have been in the first place.

The third quest, then, is successful, and it is successful in this case because it searches for the right prize, human beings. Proper values are thus asserted and rewarded. Frisky likewise asserts proper value, once his illusions are destroyed, and he thus becomes a realistic hero, like Jack Bradon. But even at the film's conclusion, there remains an important measure of difference between the two men.

As we had been led to expect, Frisky forgets to open the letter from Helen. By the time he does recall it, he is on the blimp flying home, but he is snow blind and has to have Jack read the letter to him. Jack of course decides not to read Helen's real message, and he makes one up himself: "Sweetheart, you've won the greatest triumph of your life. What can I say to make it any greater? Only this, that I love and adore you, and I hope and pray that you'll come home safe to your Helen." Given our new knowledge about the nature of heroism, we know that his "greatest triumph" is not reaching the South Pole, but rather his return from the bondage

of romanticism to the realistic freedom of an everyday marriage. Frisky thus rejects his overly romantic notions of glory in favor of the kind of comic family value, domestic rather than heroic, that is at the heart of Capra's personalist vision.

But realism for Frisky and realism for Jack are two different things. The Helen that Frisky gains is the Helen that Jack loses. The film's final shot sees Jack riding alone in a Fifth Avenue ticker tape parade. He is now the recognized but reluctant hero, and the grim look on his face reminds us of the pain that goes along with being a responsible being in a realistic universe.

Dirigible thus has two conclusions, and the ironic relationship between them is typical of Capra's romances. The major recognition in the film is a matter of responsibility. Each of the major characters comes to understand his own place in the community of duty and concern. The film's final moments focus on what this sense of duty and concern means, both to the characters and to Capra himself. For Jack Bradon it means self-sacrifice, giving up Helen. For Frisky and Helen it means self-fulfillment, loving each other without fear of Frisky's previous romantic foolishness. And for Capra it becomes another assertion that proper personalism is the right way towards integrity, if not happiness. The dual conclusion therefore recognizes both that integrity does not insure contentment, and that without integrity no measure of happiness is possible.

In terms of the film's structure, Capra sets the romantic conclusion, the public ticker tape parade, against a private and essentially comic conclusion, Helen and Frisky alone in their apartment. The presence of this final comic marriage (comic because it embodies Helen's initial desire for a normal sexual relationship) does not change the generic form of the film, for the overall shape is still clearly that of romance. But the intrusion of the comic element serves to undercut the sort of unquestioning hero worship that normally characterizes the genre.

We noted in our discussion of comedy the different purposes that a comic form can serve: it is even possible to have anticomic comedy. Similarly, it is possible to have antiromantic romance, using the romance form to call the romance content into question; and while Capra is generally content to play it straight with comic conventions and implications, his romances, and *Dirigible* in particular,

Dirigible: the hero returns.

tend to center on what we might term the "romantic fallacy." While Capra's comedies generally focus on supporting realistically plausible hopes and desires (*e.g.,* going back to Delancy Street, falling in love with the girl you have loved all along), his romances are concerned with debunking unrealistic and, hence, spiritually destructive dreams.

Dirigible is the clearest example of this opposition between our formal expectations (the knight as hero) and Capra's use of the genre. The protagonists are recognizable romantic types, literally members of the warrior class, but Capra puts them to an antiromantic purpose. In other Capra romances the protagonists are less clearly heroic, hence, the ease with which we can overlook important structural differences. Nevertheless, this particular Capra romance pattern, the dreamer disillusioned, can be

seen at work in a large minority of Capra's films, among which I would include not only *Dirigible,* but also *Long Pants* (1927), *Flight* (1929), *American Madness* (1932), *The Bitter Tea of General Yen* (1933), *Lost Horizon* (1937), *It's A Wonderful Life* (1946), and *State of the Union* (1948). Many of these films look very much like Capra comedies, *American Madness* and *Wonderful Life* in particular, in that their central characters are familiar Capra types, people right out of his memorable comic films. But Capra's point in the romances is this contrast between character types and generic structure. Comic heroes, says Capra, should not let themselves be trapped in such implausible and self-destructive romantic sequences. To do so is to betray the community in the service of false self-interest.

Another Jack Holt/Ralph Graves epic: *Flight*.

Capra has a strong tendency, then, to collapse romance into comedy. Such a collapse is possible because both forms follow a quite similar outline of action, and it is very easy to switch the emphasis at any given point from the romantic to the comic. The romantic *anagnorisis*, for example, which frequently involves the marriage of the hero to a virginal damsel (recently rescued by the knight), can easily become a comic *kômos*, for both structural elements celebrate the same triumph of Life over Death. The usual difference is, again, one of character and ethic: romance emphasizing the knight's chivalric deed over the fact of marriage, and comedy emphasizing the fact of mating rather than the fact of fighting. But despite the slippery nature of this romance/comedy distinction, it is a distinction with a meaningful difference; a difference that, put specifically in terms of Capra, can be readily perceived.

Capra's comic films generally place false notions, often overly romantic notions, in the path of the comic marriage, and they serve to obstruct the larger comic movement. The romantic films, on the other hand, almost always take place after the fact of marriage (*i.e., Long Pants, Dirigible, American Madness, It's A Wonderful Life, State of the Union*) so that the romantic threat is not simply a barrier to a comic conclusion, but a threat to already on-

going and established families; or, in the case of two of the three exceptions to this marriage rubric (*Flight, The Bitter Tea of General Yen*), it is a threat to already ongoing institutions (*i.e.,* The Marine Corps, Yen's government). The dragon of sterility looms larger in romance because it has more to destroy. It is an active agent of destruction rather than a passive agent of obstruction.

The validity of this generic approach is underlined by turning our attention to *Lost Horizon*, the one exception to this rule for romance. It is Capra's only real aesthetic failure, and it falls short of success because Capra failed to observe the minimal structural requirements for the romance form. Even Capra's own atypical sort of romance is based upon struggle and crisis, but *Lost Horizon* is much romantic ado about nothing, for it generally lacks any real dilemma whatsoever. Nothing is really threatened, and therefore nothing really happens.

The only substantive conflict in *Lost Horizon* is between the two Conway brothers: to leave or not to leave. To leave, as the young Conway insists upon doing, is to be an immature Frisky Pierce type of romantic, and, like Frisky, young George Conway (John Howard) has his romanticism, and his life, snuffed out when it comes up against the cold reality of ice, snow, age, and death. The philosophical (rather than adolescent) romanticism of Robert Conway (Ronald Colman), on the other hand, seems somehow vague, fuzzy, and unreal, like the light that illuminates Father Perrault (Sam Jaffee) as he passes the legacy of Shangri-La into Conway's keeping. Not to leave, then, means that Robert Conway has to let the abstract responsibility of Shangri-La outweigh his immediate responsibility to his younger brother; and Robert, like Jack Bradon in *Dirigible*, rightly gives the immediate personal situation precedence over the abstract ideals embodied in Shangri-La. He knows that George's attempt to flee the kingdom with the fairy princess is a lost cause (since she is really an old hag), but, like other inspired Capra fools, he goes along anyway. He does not doubt the truth of Shangri-La (as Hilton's Conway does) but he recognizes an overriding personal responsibility towards George.

So the problem of the film, then, is not simply its "sophomoric philosophy" (as Jacobs puts it), because its philosophy is perfectly consistent with its green world setting.[5] Shangri-La is a garden para-

Robert Conway (Ronald Colman) and Father Perrault (Sam Jaffe) in *Lost Horizon*.

dise where uncorrupted men live uncorrupted lives and "be kind" is philosophy enough. The real problem involves the dissociation between James Hilton's overt social criticism and Capra's customary concern for personal reality. The Hilton novel is a utopian satire that sets the purposeful serenity of Shangri-La against the apparently purposeless cruelty and horror of life in the civilized world. Hilton further underlines his condemnation of civilization by showing the most civilized of men, Hugh Conway, the man chosen to guide Shangri-La after Father Perrault's death, falling prey to doubt, turning his back on salvation, deserting the Valley of the Blue Moon, and therefore probably destroying Father Perrault's lamasery once and forever. As Hilton puts

it, Conway "was doomed, like millions, to flee from wisdom and be a hero."[6]

Capra apparently could not bring himself to condemn Conway in this manner. Capra admired Conway and Conway's ideals too much to make him the object of attack. Rather he shifts the focus of satire to the romantic younger Conway, who then assumes the "hero" role played by Hilton's Conway. As John Howard plays him, however, George Conway is not a very admirable character, and we are, accordingly, little concerned with his fate. He does not have the redeeming qualities of compassion and humor that make other romantic Capra heroes worth saving.

The film's "to leave or not to leave" question is

George Conway (John Howard) pleads his case for leaving Shangri-La.

thus robbed of its impact. The fate of Shangri-La does not depend upon George Conway's action. In Hilton, by contrast, the George figure, Mallinson, is not Conway's brother, only his friend. But Mallinson is no friend to Shangri-La, and he is determined, should he escape, to return and destroy the Valley of the Blue Moon. In Capra, to the contrary, George's escape attempt presents no real threat. He has no plans to destroy Shangri-La (although he would like to see it in ruins), and furthermore we are sure that Shangri-La will get along by itself until the elder Conway returns, as Chang assures us he will. All that rides on Robert Conway's decision is his own sense of personal integrity, and while that is important, particularly for Capra, it is out of tune with much of the film, which reproduces rather faithfully Hilton's basically satiric structure.

Lost Horizon thus seems like two different works: Hilton's utopian satire and Capra's romance of personal integrity. The dilemma is that the two seem insufficiently related. There is a relationship—the "brotherly love" that characterizes Shangri-La is the same sort of brotherly responsibility personified by Conway—but the relationship is a static one. Conway is a good man, Shangri-La is a good place, and neither is really called into significant question.

For most of the film, then, Conway is a hero without a dragon or a damsel, without a daring deed to do but sit tight and sip tea until the outside world destroys itself in an orgy of brutality. The static quality of this mission dictates the static quality of

most of the film, which contrasts so poorly with the spectacular montages of the wind-swept Himalayas. Neither Capra-as-director nor Conway-as-hero can attempt to debunk Shangri-La, for it is a dream they both obviously want to believe in, but neither can they generate much concern about it. It is not a sophomoric philosophy but a sit-tight philosophy, devoid of the kind of conflict that can maintain our complete engagement. Shangri-La is a Camelot already won, and the interesting thing would be to see it fall apart, which is clearly what Capra attempted in the conflict of the Conway brothers. But the kingdom is clearly in no danger, Conway refuses to fight his younger brother, and even the question of Conway's return is answered in advance. Thus Conway's crisis of integrity occupies only a brief section of the film. Most of what we see is a Hilton-inspired spring song in praise of Shangri-La and its fertile beauty; and while Capra's cinematic poetry is interesting, it is not interesting enough to require our deep concern and attention. Because we know that everything will work out, nothing really matters. As Conway himself puts it, we feel "far too peaceful to care about anything." *Lost Horizon* is thus less an antiromance along *Dirigible* lines than a nonromance, one that gets stranded in a placid Shangri-La of its own making.

Up to this point we have dealt with two romantic films that are atypical in some degree even for Capra. *Dirigible* involves heroes who are clearly heroes, flying knights of the sky. *Lost Horizon,* on the other hand, despite its general lack of conflict, still takes place in a fairy-tale setting that clearly marks it as having a potential for romance. But, as we have noted, most of Capra's romances involve more realistic, and indeed more comic, characters. Let us therefore conclude this discussion of the Capra romances by examining one of Capra's more representative romantic films.

American Madness (1932) is often discussed as Capra's first truly distinctive film, probably because it marked the first time he collaborated with Robert Riskin. But despite Riskin's collaboration, the film displays a romantic form typical of Capra. The characters are less clearly heroic than those in *Dirigible* and *Lost Horizon,* and the bank, for all of its castlelike potential, is clearly treated in a realistic fashion.

Like *Lost Horizon, American Madness* seems at

A spring song in praise of Shangri-La.

first viewing to be two different films, both with bank manager Dickson (Walter Huston) as the central character. The first "madness" concerns Dickson's banking practices: his board of directors wants him to keep more cash on hand and less cash on loan, particularly when the loans are to marginal *petit bourgeois* whose only collateral is their character. The second "madness" concerns Dickson's relationship to his wife. Mrs. Dickson (Kay Johnson) does not like playing second fiddle to Dickson's romantic notions about bank management (no more than Helen Pierce enjoys taking the back seat to her husband's stunt flying), particularly when Dickson repeatedly forgets their anniversary and the night on the town he had promised her. She retaliates by letting her husband's friend Cluett (Gavin Gordon)

take her to the theatre. Both films (or both "madnesses") come to a head as a result of a bank robbery that, in turn, triggers a bank run.

The run itself calls Dickson's personalist banking philosophy into question, and the investigation of the robbery, which implicates the guiltless Mrs. Dickson, calls into question the whole notion of individual honesty and faith that underlies Dickson's banking practises. Both issues are then a matter of personal faith, in one's wife or one's customers. And the muddle comes in Dickson's mistaken attempt to make the personal and the banking issues exactly equivalent. The film points out that you cannot trust your customers: ninety-five percent of them desert you in the pinch, and it is only by means of a Capra miracle that the bank does not

Cluett (Gavin Gordon) jokes with Mrs. Dickson (Kay Johnson) in *American Madness*.

collapse altogther. You can, on the other hand, trust your wife, and Dickson's mistake here is that he lets circumstantial evidence and his wife's understandable reluctance to admit immediately to going out with Cluett (who did indeed have a hand in the bank caper) convince him that she was totally faithless and untrustworthy. But one need not necessarily distrust his customers if he distrusts his wife, or vice versa, and it is Dickson's romantic extremism that sees trust as being a general either/or proposition that the film is concerned to discredit.

The film's strength, then, is its ability to give an accurate image for this kind of destructive moral confusion, this failure to understand the difference between mobs and individuals. Capra clearly distrusts mobs, and the spread of rumor and the assault on the bank by the depositors overshadow and give the lie to Dickson's naive faith in the common man.

Constance Cummings and Pat O'Brien plead with Dickson's depositors in the hope of stemming the *American Madness* bank run.

Even when some of customers respond to frantic pleas from Dickson's assistants and come to deposit money rather than withdraw it, Dickson admits that they stand only a ten to one chance of getting their money back. The little people are simply not big enough to keep the bank from closing down or to save Dickson. It is only when the members of the board of directors reluctantly agree to put their own fortunes behind the bank that disaster is averted. To be sure, the board members were shamed into assisting by the selfless action of the few faithful depositors, so that the customers are partly responsible for pulling things out of the fire, but the fact remains that the vast majority were a faceless crowd concerned only with their own shortsighted interest (precisely as the board members were at first).

Simple faith in the customer is thus portrayed as insufficiently realistic, so that Dickson, like Frisky Pierce in *Dirigible*, is a romantic who runs head on into reality, and becomes a better man for the collision. Of course, he may not change his banking style (the final sequence confirms this "back to normal" feeling), but Dickson is surely more aware of the risk he runs, and is less likely to confuse emotional and financial realities. As with other Capra heroes, it is not so much the ideals that must change (here Dickson's idealistic banking notions) as it is the character's unrealistic attitude towards those ideals. Evidence for this change in attitude is Dickson's renewed concern for his wife, and the last thing he does in the film is to ask his secretary to make reservations for himself and Mrs. Dickson on

Falling prey to cynicism: Dickson (Walter Huston) in *American Madness.*

an ocean liner. At least she will not be stood up again.

American Madness is thus similar to *Dirigible* both in theme and plot. As in *Dirigible*, we move through an *agon*, Dickson's initial conference with the board of directors, to a *pathos*, the bank run and Dickson's resulting suicide attempt, and finally to the *anagnorisis*, when Dickson's faith in his wife and some of his clients is restored. The first element, the confrontation with the board of directors, sets up the terms for the conflict. The directors argue for a no-risk policy of caution and distrust, while Dickson argues a neochivalric code of personal honor, judging people on their character, not their financial assets. But significantly, even as Dickson counsels risk, he reveals a respect for caution. He justifies a loan to a near-bankrupt business on the grounds that such adversity will only make a wiser businessman of the owner. Dickson thus provides the middle term for the film's romantic dialectic. Where the directors want no risk, and where Dickson-as-romantic prefers no caution, Dickson-as-comic hero, something he becomes through the course of the film, strikes a balance between the two, a crisis-born respect for the reality of a world where people are both trustworthy and untrustworthy at the same time.

Dickson thus becomes self-aware, a man capable of understanding that his initial trust in his depositors and most of his loan clients was unjustified: when called upon to support him they betray him. But by the same token he learns that his later distrust of his wife was similarly unjustified: she comes to his aid even after he has rejected her. The danger that Dickson falls prey to is a cynicism born of naivete. He believes that all people (except his board of directors) are trustworthy. His clients prove him wrong, and he naively assumes that all human trust is therefore pretense. Hence, he readily believes the charges against his wife and decides to kill himself. He lets his romantic expectations get the better of his common senses, and his faith turns to skepticism. But this sort of extremism is also a false alternative. There is no need to commit suicide. To do so is only to desert a community of duty and concern, a community made up of loyal bank employees and a few courageous depositors. Dickson's "to leave or not to leave" decision thus counts, where Conway's in *Lost Horizon* did not.

The bank will surely fail and people will surely suffer if Dickson takes his life. Dickson's wife then rightly points out that trust is viable given a realistic awareness of possible disappointments, and the film concludes with Dickson's providential recovery. He has recognized the realistic facts of his situation, and he is therefore better prepared to deal with future disasters.

We can see now that the three films here discussed demonstrate similar patterns of action and similar thematic implications. Taking these three as generally representing Capra's normal use of the romantic structure, we can say that the Capra romances serve as ironic leaven to Capra's comedies. His romances are antifantasies that recognize the disastrous possibilities inherent in any "fantasy of goodwill." The very existence of the romances in the Capra canon refutes the notion that he is somehow simply an overgrown child with a talent for improvisation. Capra recognizes that wishes can be destructive, and that wish fulfillment is not always

George Bailey (James Stewart) making overwishful travel plans in *It's a Wonderful Life*, with Thomas Mitchell.

appropriate to the demands of reality. Capra can thus be seen as the obverse of Howard Hawks. As Peter Wollen points out, Hawks uses his crazy comedies to comment upon and therefore balance the superhero stereotypes that populate his romances (and the western, we might add, is essentially a romantic genre).[7] Capra uses his romances in a similar fashion, for they likewise serve a qualifying function, commenting upon and therefore balancing the wishfulness that appears in his comedies.

NOTES

[1] Northrop Frye, *A Natural Perspective* (New York: Harcourt Brace & World, 1965), p. 119.

[2] Northrop Frye, *Anatomy of Criticism* (1957; rpt. New York Atheneum, 1969), p. 33.

[3] Erich Auerbach *Mimesis* (Princeton: Princeton University Press, 1953), p. 131.

[4] Frye, *Anatomy of Criticism,* p. 186.

[5] Lewis Jacobs, *The Rise of the American Cinema* (1939; rpt. New York: Teachers' College, 1968), p. 478.

[6] James Hilton, *Lost Horizon* (New York: William Morrow & Comp, 1933), p. 260.

[7] Peter Wollen, *Signs and Meaning in the Cinema* (Bloomington: Indiana University Press, 1969), p. 91.

5

The Capra Characters

The primary function of comic characters is to embody basic structural conflicts between life and death. Generally speaking, the historical tradition we have been discussing accomplishes this structural task by pitting comic lovers against sterile old authority figures. A secondary function has to do with verisimilitude. With the exception of the fantastical characters that we find in Shakespearean romantic comedy, comic characters generally appear and react as contemporaries of the audience. In the realistic comic tradition of Plautus, Jonson, and Wycherley, comic characters thus serve what we might term a "mirror function," reflecting, and permitting the artist to reflect upon, the mores and follies of the time.

Cinema has an advantage over theatre in this matter of verisimilitude: not only do characters appear to be real, but the world in which they move appears to be real as well. To be sure, we know that the reality of cinema is projectors, screens, and celluloid; but there is a metaphorical reality that resides in the accuracy with which an image represents its referent object. Documentary seeks to collapse the metaphor of cinema, asserting that what we see is not a symbol for a fact, but the fact itself. But the cinema of fiction attempts to present us with the essential form of reality, a symbolic sequence that allows us to think *about* reality. Comedy, we have noted, is a form that considers the possibilities for fertility and adequacy in the

world, and the closer the comic image is to the world it represents, the more ready we are to respect the validity of the comic conclusion.

And here we must clarify what we mean by the "comic world." Generally speaking, the comic world is a personal and moral universe, characterized by sequences of personal triumph and renewal. Thus it does not represent the entirety of the real world (*e.g.,* it does not represent tragic or ironic sequences of personal failure and death), and it certainly does not represent in any detail the political aspects of the real world that many critics think it should. But the question is not what it should represent, but how well it represents what it chooses to be concerned with. If we had, for example, two drawings of a cat, one a line drawing of the cat's entire silhouette, and another a detailed study of the cat's face, we would not apply the same standards of judgment to both images. The first pays attention to one aspect of the total reality of "cat," and the second pays attention to another aspect of that reality. To say that the first drawing is insufficient or untrue because it does not take into account both sides of the cat's face is to miss the point of both drawings. Similarity, if we were to condemn comedy for ignoring one aspect of reality, when it is in fact concerned with another aspect of the real world, we would be applying false criteria.[1]

The comic world is a world of personal interaction, and personal moral choices as revealed and

The "mirror function": contemporary costumes and props in *You Can't Take It With You,* featuring Jean Arthur (on stairway).

defined by that interaction. The "realness" that we find in Capra's films is a function of the personal reality of his characters. Within the given comic situation, Capra's feeling for the necessary dynamics of personal relationships is accurate and unfailing. He is fully aware of the various pitfalls that characters are liable to fall into, but he is similarly aware of the possibilities for personal fulfillment that await those who are willing to take necessary risks and assert proper values.

This sort of emotional and physical verisimilitude has always been at work in European comedy, and the comic films of Frank Capra present no real exception to this rule. His characters are, as critics delight in pointing out, genuine American types,

baseball players, reporters, industrialists, and so on. But they are also genuine comic types, and, for all of their contemporaneity, they are clearly descendants of the classic New Comedy characters.

The character nucleus of most comedy is the young couple, the lovers around whom the comic intrigue revolves. Such is the case in Capra, where at the heart of almost every film we find "young people in love." Generally, and within the context of each individual film, this involves the pairing of an innocent and a cynic. The best known examples of such pairings are in the "Mr." films, with the Cooper/Stewart characters being the naive idealistic romantics, and the Jean Arthur characters being the cynics, attuned to the demands of their self-

Young people in love: James Stewart and Jean Arthur
in *Mr. Smith Goes to Washington.*

seeking milieu; but it is a pattern that occurs repeatedly from *Long Pants* (1927) to *Pocketful of
Miracles* (1961).

There are two important things to note about
these central innocent/cynic pairings. The first is
that they always serve to mirror the larger conflicts
between the natural and the unnatural, the selfless
and the selfish, the personal and the impersonal,
the loving and the unloved, fertility and sterility.
And the second point to make is that these pairings
are not simply a matter of opposites but comple-
ments (as death is both the opposite and the complement of life). Innocents frequently become
cynics, and cynics just as frequently become or reveal themselves as innocents. A good example of
this tendency towards attitude reversal is the John
and Florence pair in *The Miracle Woman* (1931).

Innocence and experience: Sister Fallon (Barbara Stanwyck), Hornsby (Sam Hardy), and John (David Manners) in *The Miracle Woman.*

Florence Fallon (Barbara Stanwyck) is a minister's daughter [like Mary Brown (Gertrude Astor) in *The Strong Man* (1926)] whose Christian idealism collapses into cynicism when her father dies in her arms, the victim of a hypocritical and self-righteous congregation that fired him in favor of a younger pastor. With the help of another Capra con-man capitalist, Hornsby (Sam Hardy), she puts both her cynicism and Bible learning to work, becoming an evangelist and bilking her innocent followers. One person she reaches in an evangelical radio broadcast is John Carson (David Manners), a blind World War I aviator who is just on the verge of jumping out the window in desperation. Florence's speech condemning quitters and extolling the accomplishments of blind poets like John Milton is enough to change John's mind, and for the rest of the film John is an innocent in love with the woman who saved his life. Thus we have an almost schematic change of attitude and stance on the part of the leading characters, which allows each of them to experience both possible modes of existence. As we might expect, Capra sets things up so that the innocent position finally triumphs, but both John and Florence are self-aware romantics at the end of the film, people who know the kinds of mistakes that naive idealism is prey to, and presumably capable of avoiding the pitfalls of oversimplistic thinking.

It should be kept in mind that degrees of cynicism exist, and that cynicism can be accurately defined only within the context of each given film. An example of this relativity principle is the pairing in *Ladies of Leisure* (1930). Jerry Strong (Ralph Graves) is the son of a railroad millionaire. Jerry

Ladies of Leisure: Kay Arnold (Barbara Stanwyck), Jerry Strong (Ralph Graves), and Jerry's millionaire father.

is generally cynical about the life his father leads, and Jerry's own demeanor and deportment reveal a kind of lassitude in his own life, a spiritual exhaustion that permits him to float with the tide of high society. Kay Arnold (Barbara Stanwyck), on the other hand, is a "lady of leisure" who sells her services to the highest bidder. She too is dissatisfied with her life (we first see her leaving a party), but her general disposition is one of resignation to the bleak facts of her existence. She is the victim of a desperately circular logic: it is the kind of world where her kind of woman can get along only by prosituting herself.

On the surface, then, it looks as if we have a pair of skeptics rather than an innocent and a cynic. But within the generally cynical atmosphere of this city film, we find that Jerry is, by contrast with his peers, very much of a romantic. He is a playboy with a penthouse, certainly, but both the playboy and the penthouse are unusual. Jerry does not spend his days going from club rooms to race tracks and back. He rather occupies himself with painting, and his penthouse is his studio. Within the unnatural context of the city, his penthouse represents a natural oasis, bestrewed as it is with flowers and shrubbery. It is a "green world" where Jerry hopes to find something meaningful in his otherwise weary existence.

Kay fits into Jerry's romantic scheme because the beauty of her face seems, in his eyes, the very image of hope, and he wants to capture that image on canvas. Predictably, but only after much complication, Kay and Jerry fall in love. He convinces her

Jerry tells Kay to "look up" in *Ladies of Leisure*.

Alice Higgins (Myrna Loy) and Dan Brooks (Warner Baxter) in *Broadway Bill.*

to "look up" at the stars rather than down at the city streets, and his decision to marry her and take her to Arizona represents the kind of personal risk necessary for happiness in a world where happiness is a risky proposition (note that we have an early instance of the city/country split, although we never actually see Arizona).

If we now contrast the pairing in *Ladies of Leisure* to that in *Broadway Bill* (1934) we can get some idea of the range possible under this innocent/cynic rubric. Dan Brooks (Warner Baxter) begins *Broadway Bill* by fleeing from the oppressive influence of the Higgins clan ("it's not a family, it's a disease") to return to the race-track life that he really loves. He is fully aware of the risk he runs, and he runs it willingly and joyfully. His romanticism is not, then, a matter of real ignorance, as is often the Capra case, but a matter of confidence; confidence that Broadway Bill can win the big race if he only gets the chance. There are obstacles to overcome, surely, but they concern financial necessity: Dan has to get the money for the entry fee. Dan is aided in this struggle by his sister-in-law, Alice Higgins (Myrna Loy), who is, in the context of the film, the cynic. She is ceratinly no Kay Arnold, and her general cheerfulness seldom gives

The marriage critic applies for a marriage license: Cary Grant and Priscilla Lane *in Arsenic and Old Lace.*

way to outright gloom, but there is a sense of longing about her that is characteristic of Capra's romantic cynics (*e.g.,* Gable in *It Happened One Night*). Alice obviously loves Dan, believes in him, and wishes that they could be married. But she also loves her sister Margaret (Helen Vinson), and there is no way she can really express her love for Dan without breaking the bonds of sisterly responsibility. Alice is clearly right to respect Margaret's prior claim on Dan. But Margaret is a blue-blood sophisticate, unwilling and incapable of sharing Dan's vagabond existence, and Alice's rightness is rewarded when Margaret, true to her upper-class character, sues for divorce. Dan is then free to marry Alice, and he does so at first opportunity, arriving like a knight of old at the Higgins castle gate to spirit his princess away.

The comic pairing in *Broadway Bill* thus demonstrates a general confidence in the universe that seems lacking in the Jerry Strong/ Kay Arnold relationship in *Ladies of Leisure*. This faith in the universe is usually the key element in the innocent/ cynic dichotomy, innocents naively believing that things will work out all right, and cynics naively believing that nothing will work out correctly. In most cases, both stances are wrong. Naivete of both sorts gives way before the hard facts of existence, but one of those existential facts is that people can generally control their own lives, or at least their emotional lives, given a realistic awareness both of chances and responsibilities.

Awareness thus becomes a major theme in Capra's cinema. Unaware characters are made to face up to the realities of their existence, and the responsibilities that go along with that new knowledge. *Arsenic and Old Lace* (1944) in particular is concerned with uncovering the bodies in the cellar, and Mortimer Brewster (Cary Grant) rightly assumes the responsibility for getting his homicidal aunts into the asylum before they can serve any more of their murderous elderberry wine.

But the thing to note, in *Arsenic and Old Lace* as elsewhere, is how the original, cynical sin can be a function of the romantic imagination. Aunts Abby (Josephine Hull) and Martha (Jean Adair) see themselves as innocent, little old ladies putting dejected old men out of their misery. The Brewster sisters clearly see nothing wrong with murder. Perhaps they do not even see it as being murder. But

murder it is nevertheless, and murder is the ultimate, cynical act. The Karloff-like brother, Jonathan (Raymon Massey), makes clear the darker side of his aunt's actions, since they are not really different from Jonathan's own sadistic practices. Even Mortimer is tainted with the family curse, although at first it is difficult to see how he fits into this murder scheme. The fact is, though, that Mortimer's antimarriage tracts are, in the comic context of the film, just as murderous as Jonathan's scalpels. Marriage as a symbol for fertility is endangered by Mortimer's writings, although we should note that he has rightly disregarded his own advice by marrying the minister's daughter, Elaine Harper (Priscilla Lane).

The film is thus not against intellectuals *per se,* as Jeffrey Richards asserts, but the misuse of the intellect in the service of sterility.[2] Of course, Mortimer, it turns out, is not really a Brewster, but the notion of a family madness is a kind of Hitchcockian metaphor (and the film is surely an homage to Hitchcock) for a universal tendency towards brutality (recall the ball-game riots at the film's beginning). That Mortimer even considers annulling his marriage to Elaine is significant testimony to his new-found sense of responsibility, and the fact of his bastardy is reward for this new awareness. Mortimer can thus flee the city with Elaine, a man convinced of the sanity to be found in marriage, happy in the knowledge that he can properly handle his own tendencies towards cruelty without resorting to actual homicide as his foster aunts and foster brother do.[3]

Arsenic and Old Lace shows us, then, how closely romanticism and cynicism are related, and how this general innocent/cynic opposition can be seen working across the entire cast of a film. Generally speaking, this character continuum is at work in all of Capra's movies, and we can most profitably discuss the remaining Capra characters in terms of their position on this romanticism/cynicism scale.

At the cynical extreme of Capra's character scheme we find a group of wealthy and powerful capitalists, law-abiding or otherwise, as the case may be. They range from the outright gangster type, the vice-racketeer Steve Darcey (Sheldon Leonard) in *Pocketful of Miracles* (1961), to the relatively jovial and ultimately redeemable autocrats like Alexander Andrews (Walter Connolly) in *It Hap-*

Family madness: Raymond Massey, Cary Grant, Jean
Adair and Josephine Hull in *Arsenic and Old Lace*.

pened One Night (1934). In between we find people
like D. B. Norton and Jim Taylor (both played by
Edward Arnold) who function as power-hungry,
motiveless malignities. We know they want power,
but we do not know why they want it. In every case
these authority figures function as embodiments of
the comic obstacles, and they are the direct descendants of the Roman *senex iratus*. Again we have
degrees of villainy, and while it feels uncomfortable
to equate Jim McDivett in *The Strong Man* (1926)
or Mr. Potter (Lionel Barrymore) in *It's A Wonderful Life* (1946) with a Wilbur Stanley (Franchot
Tone) in *Here Comes the Groom* (1951) or a J. L.
Higgins (Walter Connolly) in *Broadway Bill*, the
fact remains that they all represent, each in his own
film, the same kind of capitalist self-centeredness.

All they generally think about is the continuing
acquisition of money, and as we have seen by now
this is completely antithetical to Capra's personalist
ethic.

Standing in frequent opposition to this paternal
sort of sterility is the maternal fertility represented
by the Ma Smith-type of woman. Sometimes these
women are actual mothers (*e.g.,* Ma Smith, Penny
Sycamore, Ma Mitchell, Mrs. Bailey, Sophie Manetta), and sometimes they are motherly house-
keepers [*e.g.,* Mrs. Higgins (Beryl Mercer) in *The
Miracle Woman* (1931), Mrs. Meredith (Emma
Dunn) in *Mr. Deeds* (1936)], but in all instances
they represent the cornerstone of familial virtue.
They are generally kind, concerned, generous, and
in short, motherly, with all of the positive connota-

The power-hungry capitalist: Edward Arnold as Jim Taylor in *Mr. Smith Goes To Washington*, featuring James Stewart.

tions that accompany that word. They are always too busy holding their family together to worry about themselves.

Of course, just as we get right-way (*i.e.*, small-time) and wrong-way (*i.e.*, big-time) capitalists, we get right-way and wrong-way mothers. A significant minority of these mother figures in Capra's films are more than happy to think only of themselves. Mama Goldfish (Rosa Rosanova) in *The Younger Generation* (1929) is the archetype of this kind of material-ist harpy, but there are others: Mrs. Strong in *Ladies of Leisure* (1930), Mrs. Schuyler (Louise Closser Hale) in *Platinum Blonde* (1931), Mrs. Jackson (Clara Blandick) in *The Bitter Tea of*

General Yen (1933), and Ma Jones (Connie Gil-christ) in *Here Comes the Groom*. These women are either rich, or they aspire to riches, and they are generally more than willing to sacrifice their chil-dren for the sake of material gain and social status.

Another important figure is the servant/clown. In Roman Comedy the clown figure was the crafty-servant character. He was generally intelligent and cynical, more than happy to assist his young master in outfoxing whoever needed outfoxing (normally the lad's father, but frequently a *miles gloriosus*), and content, within the social context of Roman society, to walk a fine line between anarchy and sub-missiveness. He delighted in outwitting any type of

Walter Brennan as Long John's potato-playing misan-thropic sidekick in *Meet John Doe,* featuring Gary Cooper.

authority, even if he eventually became subject once again to the very authority he subverted. He was a realist, knowledgeable in the ways of the world, and he guided his generally naive young master through the sexual adventures that constituted the comic movement.[4]

This clown figure appears in many Capra films as a realistic sidekick to the comic hero. Again, the best known examples of this figure are from the films of the trilogy. In *Mr. Deeds* we have Cornelius Cobb, (Lionel Stander), press agent for Longfellow, who helps guide Deeds through the cynical intricacies of the big city. Cobb is himself a cynic (recall the everyday manner in which he offers to pimp for Deeds), but he is intelligent, and, despite his cynicism, he is capable of coming to Longfellow's aid when the chips are down. Saunders (Jean Arthur) and Diz (Thomas Mitchell) share this function in *Mr. Smith Goes to Washington* (1939). Diz is the one at the press club who first disillusions Jeff, telling Jeff that he is only a do-nothing stooge. And Saunders is literally a crafty servant (or secretary) who masterminds Jeff's filibuster.

Perhaps the best example of this character type is The Colonel (Walter Brennan) in *Meet John Doe* (1941) [with Peter Falk's marvelous Joy Boy in *Pocketful of Miracles* (1961) being a close second]. As we shall see in chapter 12, it is The Colonel who constantly and correctly inveighs against the authority of the "heelots." The Colonel thus represents the voice of reality in a chorus of public relations illusions. He is almost a stylistic device, a human parenthesis.[5] Capra uses The Colonel as a sounding board, giving us brief cuts of The Colonel as he reacts to the various sentimental inanities that fly by (recall the scene in Mayor Lovett's office when the John Doe Club members tell Long John how wonderful he is). Like other such characters in Capra, The Colonel is the embodiment of a reality principle [just as D. B. Norton (Edward Arnold) in *Meet John Doe* is the embodiment of the death principle], and Capra uses him to demonstrate a realistic awareness of the limits of sentiment.

Another, and the most misunderstood, of Capra's stock characters is the populace that Capra is supposed to represent. Richard Corliss has described the "second law of Capracorn" as being that "the mob is (almost) always right," and people from

Richard Griffith forward have tended to accept this viewpoint with little question.[6] But the amazing thing to note is the total inaccuracy of this position. The mob is *always* wrong in Capra. No matter where it appears, the mob-as-mob is always to be mistrusted. From the gang in the Palace Bar in *The Strong Man* to the Jerry Marks (Keenan Wynn) entourage in *A Hole in the Head* (1959), we sense understanding but nevertheless complete disapproval on Capra's part.

The only instances in which the mob can be described as "right" are when the mob-as-mob is broken down into individuals. The farmers in *Mr. Deeds Goes to Town* are always farmers, men that Deeds can meet one-to-one across his desk. It is an individual farmer, we should remember, who awakens Deeds's conscience and consciousness about the unemployed. The same is the case in *It's A Wonderful Life,* where George Bailey (James Stewart) deals with his little mob by having them come one by one to the teller's window where he asks each of them individually how much they need. Even if we could say, in reference to these two films, that the mob was somehow morally correct, we would still be forced to describe the films as exceptions to the general rule. Mobs of one sort or another appear regularly in Capra: *The Strong Man, Long Pants, That Certain Thing, Flight, Ladies of Leisure, The Miracle Woman, American Madness, The Bitter Tea of General Yen, It Happened One Night, Lost Horizon, Mr. Smith Goes to Washington, Meet John Doe, Arsenic and Old Lace,* besides those already mentioned; and in each of these films the mob is portrayed as mindless, cynical, and potentially (or actually) vicious. Thus those few instances where Capra manages to align his sympathy with crowds of any sort are exceptional in the extreme.

The primary ambiguity in Capra's vision involves this distrust of mobs. Capra clearly wants to believe in "the people," but he conceives of those people as a loose collection of independent individuals. As soon as they start to herd together, however, as soon as they start to give over their individuality in favor of a mass identity, they become mobs, and mobs are, *a priori,* disastrous in Capra's imagination. They allow no room for Capra's kind of personalist ethic to operate. Individaul moral responsibility goes out the window and the impersonal momentum of the mob takes over. The line between neutral groups

The impersonal mob: *American Madness.*

and mobs is a fine one, surely, but it is a real one for Capra nevertheless, and it is defined by the kind of self-destructive action that mobs characteristically take (the mob in *Meet John Doe* for example).

The accuracy of Andrew Sarris's comment that Capra's films are somber Christian parables of "idealism betrayed and innocence humiliated" is a function of this populist ambiguity.[7] Capra wants to believe in a populist morality deriving its authority from the collective will of the people, but he is painfully aware of the way in which people tend to betray that moral trust, surrendering their moral prerogatives to the rich and influential, who then lead them down the path to lemminglike destruction. It is to Capra's credit that he never let this moral dilemma destroy his films. Where it does become an issue, in the films of the trilogy, he draws strength from the philosophical dialectic by making the personal dilemma the actual subject of the films. *Mr. Smith Goes to Washington,* for example, is a film about faith and freedom and lost causes, and it points out both how right it is to believe in the people, and the price one has to pay for maintaining that belief. *Meet John Doe* is likewise concerned with faith and responsibility, and it, too, demonstrates a realistic awareness of this mob/individual dichotomy. We can say then that Capra is a "populist" filmmaker, but he is deeply troubled by the manner in which the populace allows itself to be manipulated. He believes in the integrity of individuals, and hence in the ability of individuals to make reasoned and moral decisions, but he is also aware that personal integrity is difficult to maintain, particularly in a society that encourages the collapse of individual morality into the comfort of mob psychology. Capra can thus sympathize with

Mr. Smith: faith, freedom, and lost causes.

the members of mobs—they are frequently "little people" whose meager expectations have been cruelly disappointed by the machinations of wealthy and powerful crooks—but he disapproves of mob action nevertheless. People who join mobs are traitors unto themselves, and hence betrayal is another major Capra theme.

One final Capra character remains to be considered. We began by discussing the innocent/cynic pairings that we find at the center of every Capra comedy. We then went on to demonstrate the close relationship between innocent romanticism and experienced cynicism. The nature of this relationship is made even clearer when we consider the heroes that we find in the Capra romances, heroes that we can now understand as comic-Capra innocents carrying their naivete to the absurd extreme. Their

romanticism is so high flown that it requires a romance form to properly debunk it.

A good example of the self-destructive romantic hero is Panama Williams (Jack Holt) in *Flight* (1929). Panama is a Marine flight instructor in love with a young Navy nurse (Lila Lee). She in turn is in love with Panama's buddy, Lefty Phelps (Ralph Graves), whose claim to fame is that he ran the wrong way with a fumble in a bowl game (after Roy Riegles, a University of California lineman who ran a fumble the wrong way and won the 1929 Rose Bowl for Georgia Tech). The film is thus about the general problem of moving in the wrong direction, and Panama's wrong move is to desert his friend because he thinks his friend has stolen his girl. Of course, Panama's initial wrong move was to assume that Elinor was his girl in the first place, but

Flight: Lefty Phelps (Ralph Graves) and Panama Williams (Jack Holt) on the runway.

the film's moral dilemma arises after Panama has found out otherwise.

Panama, for all of his tough-guy appearance, had not been able to muster the courage necessary to propose to Elinor. With some difficulty he talks Lefty into doing the job for him, and Lefty predictably fails to get Elinor's consent. Elinor accompanies Lefty back to Panama's tent, and she tells Panama how it is between Lefty and herself. Panama's immediate reaction is to work Lefty over, but he is interrupted by the call to arms. Nicaraguan bandits are besieging a Marine outpost, and the flying corps must go to the rescue. In the battle Lefty's plane is shot down, and the moral issue comes to a head when Panama refuses to take part in the subsequent search mission.

Flight: Elinor (Lila Lee) with Lefty.

Elinor talks Panama back to his senses: *Flight*.

At this point Panama's romanticism has clearly given way to self-centered cynicism. He will not help save the guy who stole his girl; and why should he? But the answer is simple. Lefty did not steal Panama's girl, because she was never Panama's to begin with. Lefty proposed for Panama in good faith, and his deep friendship and concern for Panama is never in question. Panama ignores all this, and thus shirks his responsibility to a friend. But friendship is not the only possible motive that might encourage Panama to help in the search. Panama is a Marine, and Lefty is a Marine, and that alone should be reason enough for Panama to participate in the rescue mission. Panama thus disregards his military as well as his personal responsibility to Lefty.

In a very real sense, then, we can say that Panama has almost destroyed himself as a moral being. He makes the choice not to help in the rescue mission, and the film makes it clear that Panama is the only flier on the base capable of doing the job. Hence, Panama's decision not to search is tantamount to murder. To be sure, Elinor does talk him back to his senses, and Panama does eventually rescue Lefty, but the point to make in this discussion is that Panama's extreme romanticism made him all the more liable to become extremely cynical when his romantic expectations were disappointed.

Capra's romantic heroes thus tend to assert their own total personality without regard for others in precisely the same way that Capra's cynics do. Their motives arise from the depths of selfhood and demand satisfaction. We are no more sure why George Bailey in *It's A Wonderful Life* wants to go exploring than we are why Potter wants to own all of Bedford Falls. Both romantics and cynics are wrong in Capra, because they ignore the interpersonal responsibility that defines Capra's personalist morality. Total selfhood is thus as wrong as the total lack of selfhood characteristic of mobs, and what is needed is personal integrity within the context of personalist communities, families and neighborhoods, or even military units, as is the case in *Flight* and *Dirigible*.

The spectrum of Capra's characters can now be seen as a complete circle, ranging from the cynical to the romantic, and finally back to the cynical again as romantic expectations are frustrated. The unity of concern that auteur critics are so diligent in seeking is therefore, in Capra's case, reflected in character. Capra's characters embody his basic thematic polarities, *e.g.,* faith vs despair, life vs death; and each individual film works through this moral dialectic by means of characters drawn from different places on this character scale. No two films are precisely alike, because Capra continually juggles the balance of characters within his stock repertoire, utilizing different surface issues as those issues serve to concretize varying character conflicts. But no matter how different a film like *Flight* might seem from *Mr. Smith Goes to Washington,* we can now understand how closely they are related within the realm of Capra's imagination. Both are concerned with issues of faith and responsibility, however much they differ in terms of form. The Capra cinema is thus holistic and complex within its own limits, self-aware, cinematically intelligent, and totally committed.

NOTES

1. Cinema's unique relationship with reality has fascinated many critics, most importantly Siegfried Kracauer, *Theory of Film: The Redemption of Physical Reality* (London: Oxford University Press, 1960), and André Bazin, *What is Cinema?* translated by Hugh Gray, 2 vols. (Berkeley: University of California, 1967, 1971). I shall discuss Bazin further in the next chapter, but for a general overview of the Kracauer/Bazin position see V. F. Perkins, *Film as Film: Understanding and Judging Movies* (Middlesex: Penguin Book, 1972).
2. Jeffrey Richards, "Frank Capra and the Cinema of Populism," *Film Society Review* 7, no. 6 (1972): 46. The film is, says Richards, "a glorious joke at the expense of the intelligentsia, as personified by urbane and sophisticated drama critic, Mortimer Brewster (Cary Grant) who discovers that his entire family is insane and is himself reduced to the verge of insanity."
3. In *Magic and Myth of the Movies* (New York: Henry Holt and Company, 1947), pp. 121-131, Parker Tyler explores the sexual aspects and implications of this awareness motif.
4. See Erich W. Segal, *Roman Laughter: The Comedy of Plautus* (Cambridge: Harvard University Press, 1968).
5. Stephen Handzo calls this reactive character "a key to Capra's cinema" in his article "Under Capracorn," *Film Comment* 8, no. 4 (1972): 9.
6. Richard Corliss, "Capra & Riskin," *Film Comment* 8, no. 4 (1972); 19.
7. Andrew Sarris, *The American Cinema* (New York: E. P. Dutton & Company., 1968),p. 88.

6
The Capra Style

To discuss an artist's "style" is to discuss the history of his artistic choices: why did he shoot this scene? why did he shoot it this way? why did he cut it in this manner? and so on down to the smallest detail of the film. Of course, no artist has unlimited choice, particularly artists who make a living with their art, but seldom are they told precisely how to create what they create. And even when outside limitations are imposed, when producers or stars insist upon changes of one sort or the other, directors are still free to accommodate such changes after their own fashion, for almost every imposed limitation offers a new range of choices. For example, Capra did not want to cast Hope Lange for the Queenie role in *Pocketful of Miracles* (1961), but once she was imposed upon him, he was free, within the range of her acting abilities, to decide exactly how he was going to use her. He subsequently rewrote the part with her in mind, but he did so in a manner completely consistent with his own concerns. Instead of the cynic Capra originally intended, we get an ingenue, however she is a typical Capra ingenue nevertheless.[1]

But Capra was generally his own man, subject to little if any outside control. Indeed, he was a pioneer of the "one man, one film" principle (as he describes it in his autobiography), and he was perhaps freer for most of his film career than any other director in Hollywood. As long as he kept turning out hits, Harry Cohn of Columbia was generally

Frank Capra, holding Oscar, is congratulated by Harry Cohn.

happy to let Capra go his own way, undisturbed and unfettered. Capra thus had a range of choices unexcelled among his Hollywood contemporaries, and his individualistic cinema reveals the result of those choices.

According to this definition of style, then, everything in a film *is* style, since everything is the result of choice, whether it be totally conscious choice or not.[2] Everything that we can say about a film is thus a response to style. As we view a film, our ideas and emotions are effected by an unending flow of style from start to finish. Hence every word that I write about Capra is concerned completely with only one thing: the Capra style. His films are his style, and to talk about one is necessarily to talk about the other.

Of course, style is generally taken to refer to the visual components of a film, to the extent that they can be separated from plot, character, and so forth. But truly preceptive critics (I think specifically of Raymond Durgnat in *Films and Feelings* or Pauline Kael in *Going Steady*) understand that such separation means running a great risk, specifically that of falling into unending discussions of visual nuance at the expense of the dramatic heart of the film. Durgnat offers a constructive approach to the question of style that will help us to avoid such errors. He divides stylistic elements into three categories for the purpose of discussion: primary elements (what the camera sees), secondary elements (derived from the possibilities of photography), and tertiary elements (derived from the possibilities of editing).[3] For our purpose we can combine these last two categories into one larger set concerned with how we are shown what the camera has seen, but it is helpful to keep Durgnat's basic scheme in mind.

it is evident from the high degree of consistency of themes, characters, and concerns across the Capra canon that no matter where Capra went for story material, and no matter what he found there, he made it uniquely his own. The only possible exception might be *Arsenic and Old Lace* (1944), which Capra shot as an exercise in quickie filmmaking. But as we have seen in our last chapter, *Arsenic and Old Lace* continues Capra's comic exploration of the problems of personal integrity and responsibility. What throws most critics off is (1) the lack of a Deeds figure, and (2) the horror film, gothic visuals; but these differences, while certainly atypical, in no way make *Arsenic and Old Lace* the apocryphal outcast that many consider it to be.

More important than source study to the comprehension of Capra's success is an understanding of Capra's relationship with his script writers. Foremost among those writers was Robert Riskin, and the generally accepted notion is that Riskin provided Capra with the extra verbal snap that made their collaborative efforts the great hits that they

WHAT THE CAMERA SEES

(story and script, casting, makeup, costume, sets, props)

With a few exceptions [*For the Love of Mike* (1927), *Submarine* (1928), *Here Comes the Groom* (1951), and *A Hole in the Head* (1959)] Capra always chose his own stories. His background as a gag man for Hal Roach and Mack Sennett equipped him to develop vague story ideas into effective scenes, and these into effective films, even before the advent of sound and the corresponding ascendancy of detailed, written scripts. The coming of sound, however, found Capra already ensconced as the number one director at Columbia, free to choose his own projects from the script properties either already owned by the studio, or purchased at Capra's request.

It is not within the scope of this essay to begin a detailed source study, which would, given the high number of films that Capra based on literary ancestry, be a large enough undertaking in itself. But

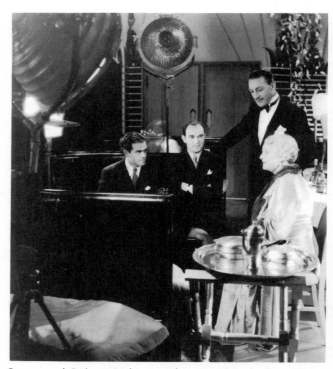

Capra and Robert Riskin on the set of *Lady For a Day*, featuring May Robson.

were. Capra clearly credits Riskin with primary responsibility for the naturalistic wit that characterized their pictures. Capra describes their working relationship in *The Name Above the Title:* "We worked together on scripts, sparking and building on each other's ideas. We were both creators and audiences. In general, I stayed ahead of him, thinking up the next batch of scenes, which, when agreed upon, he would put into dialogue-script form. And never was there a better 'ear' for the spoken word than Riskin's" (p. 148).

There is no reason to quarrel then with the judgment that Riskin was greatly responsible for the overall quality of the Capra/Riskin films, at least to the extent that Riskin's dialogue contributed to that quality. But given what we know about the character of the collaboration, it is doubtful that Riskin's contributions were decisive in shaping the Capra vision. Some critics have tried to collate all the various factors, thus to assign certain thematic or stylistic elements to Riskin, but such attempts have so far failed.

Stephen Handzo not only credits Riskin with his "ear for dialogue," but asserts that Riskin was likewise responsible for both an improvement in story construction and the "subject of the little people who march to their own drum and become prey for the cynical."[4] Richard Corliss has similarly attempted to show that Riskin was responsible for the "obligatory confession scene" that Sarris assigned to Capra. He points out that Riskin's plots "before, during, and after his association with Capra" demonstrated this confession motif.[5] But all of these assertions simply ignore the facts of the situation.

Handzo seems never to have seen Capra's Langdon films, where the "subject of the little people who march to their own drum and become prey for the cynical" is first introduced. Futhermore, Handzo does not account for the fact that Capra's films were getting increasingly better even before Riskin arrived, and continued to get better after Riskin left. Indeed, most of Capra's best films were done with other collaborators (of the nine films I devote individual chapters to, only three are Riskin's work). Corliss likewise ignores the fact that Capra's first confession scene appeared in *That Certain Thing* (1928), three years before Riskin showed up on the Columbia lot. If anything, we can better conclude that Riskin probably learned more from

Capra than Capra did from Riskin, and that the Capraesque nature of Riskin's non-Capra scripts— e.g., *The Whole Town's Talking* (director, John Ford, 1935), *When You're In Love* (director, Riskin, 1937), *Magic Town* (director, William Wellman, 1947)—bespeaks Riskin's basic affinity for Capra's kind of cinema.

The crucial factor in Capra's success was not the entrance of Riskin alone, but the overall improvement in the Columbia writing staff between 1930 and 1931. Harry Cohn understood that talking pictures demanded literate scripts, so he imported young writers (novelists, short-story writers, journalists, playwrights) from New York, and had them try their hand at screenwriting. Both the Bob Thomas biography of Cohn (*King Cohn*) and Capra's autobiography are full of anecdotes concerning the fates of these neophyte screenwriters. Most of them got sacked quickly. Cohn kept only the best.[6]

Among those that Cohn did keep on the Columbia payroll, four are of particular importance to Capra: Riskin, Jo Swerling, Sidney Buchman, and Edward Paramore. Riskin was the primary writer for eight films (*American Madness, Lady for a Day, It Happened One Night, Broadway Bill, Mr. Deeds Goes to Town, Lost Horizon, You Can't Take It With You,* and *Meet John Doe*) and he had a minor hand in five others (*The Miracle Woman, Platinum Blonde, Riding High, Here Comes the Groom,* and *Pocketful of Miracles*). Swerling had a major hand in four films (*Dirigible, Ladies of Leisure, Rain or Shine,* and *The Miracle Woman*) and a minor hand in four others (*Platinum Blonde, Forbidden, The Bitter Tea of General Yen,* and *It's A Wonderful Life*). Buchman and Paramore each did but one film with Capra, but those are two of Capra's best. Paramore adapted the Grace Zaring Stone novel *The Bitter Tea of General Yen,* and came up with a script that appealed to the darker side of Capra's imagination. Buchman scripted *Mr. Smith Goes to Washington,* and the film was clearly the best of Capra's populist epics.[7]

It is evident then that Capra did not depend solely on Riskin to make or break his career. If anything, Riskin was too much of an alter ego for Capra, and while this rapport resulted in the lazy masterpieces of the mid-thirties, it is clear that their artistic inbreeding could only be sustained for so long. For all of its considerable virtues, *Meet John Doe* is the

Capra's first confession scene: *That Certain Thing*, featuring Viola Dana and Ralph Graves.

least satisfactory of Capra's major films, and we can speculate that some of the problems with the film resulted from the lack of constructive feedback in the early stages. Riskin and Capra finally had to ask for outside assistance, calling in Myles Connolly, Capra's close friend and occasional collaborator (*It Happened One Night, State of the Union, Here Comes the Groom*), and "Doctor" Jules Furthman to take a look at their sick script; but nothing could be done to supply a completely satisfactory conclusion to *Meet John Doe* (see chapter 12). The Capra/Riskin team had run out of steam. Perhaps they had said all that they could say together. In any case, Capra's subsequent films clearly benefited from changes in collaborators. Riskin still earned story credit on occasion (*Here Comes the Groom*), and two of Capra's final films were remakes of earlier Capra/Riskin efforts, but Riskin ceased to play an active part in the making of Capra's retrospection-period films.

Given Capra's improvisational shooting methods, his own considerable writing abilities, and his habit of working closely with his scriptwriters in the early phases of preparation, it is fair to say that Capra personally molded and shaped every shooting script to reflect his own concerns.[8] Capra realized that he did not have the kind of writing talent capable of formulating an entire script unaided, but he was

The discarded ending of *Mr. Smith Goes to Washington*: Jeff (James Stewart), Saunders (Jean Arthur), and Paine (Claude Rains) ride in triumph through the streets.

genius enough both to get the best possible writers and to get them to write precisely what he wanted.

But even once a script was completed, Capra felt free to cut and rearrange it both as the shooting proceeded and in the cutting room. In *Mr. Smith Goes to Washington,* for example, Capra excised large sections of the Buchman script, including an anticlimactic ending with Jeff riding in triumph through the street of his hometown. Similar cuts, aimed primarily at eliminating verbal redundancy, are to be found by checking the script of *It Happened One Night.*[9] There can be little doubt that Capra made similar economies in most of his films.

Generally speaking, then, the overall consistency of Capra's output, despite the changing lineup of his collaborators, leads us to the firm conclusion that Capra was indeed the auteur of his films. He made the movies that he wanted to make, coherent reflections of his own artistic vision, and he made them the successful films they are by surrounding himself with highly talented contributors.

Another important factor in Capra's success has to do with the high caliber of acting in his films. We noted that the "realness" we find in Capra's films is a function of the personal reality of the characters. Capra's primary means of achieving this sense of personal reality was intelligent if intuitive casting. "To me," Capra says in his autobiography, "films were novels filled with living people. I cast actors that I believed could *be* those living people. Gary Cooper *was* Longfellow Deeds; he *was* Long John Doe. Jimmy Stewart *was* Jefferson Smith and George Bailey" (p. 389).

Capra of course was fortunate to find actors capable of this kind of comic realism. But Hollywood in its heyday had a surfeit of fine performers. It is certainly impossible today to imagine *Mr. Smith* with anyone but James Stewart in the lead role, and it is similarly impossible today to conceive of *It Happened One Night* featuring anyone but Gable and Colbert. But this unity of actor and character was something Capra consciously strived for. There is no reason then to believe that Capra could not have succeeded without Stewart or any other specific actor or actress. Capra could convince even bit players that they were "real flesh and blood human beings living a story" (Capra, p. 247), and his ability to invest a given role with an emotional import sufficient to inspire even neophyte actors

allowed him to achieve even greater force and impact when he had top-notch performers to work with.

Of course, we do not want to discount the iconographic value of Capra's leading players. By the time Jimmy Stewart, for example, came to play George Bailey in *It's A Wonderful Life* (1946), he had become a symbol for Capra's brand of good neighborliness. George Bailey is a Tony Kirby in *You Can't Take It With You* (1938) or a Jeff Smith in *Mr. Smith Goes to Washington* (1939) who has matured and assumed adult responsibilities. The continuity of this idealistic character type is underlined by the visual presence of Stewart playing all three roles. But we should remember that Capra was the one who discovered that persona in the first place. *Mr. Smith* was Stewart's first truly major role, and it gained him his first Oscar nomination.[10] Capra sensed affinities between the parts he had to cast and the actors he finally decided to use, and in large measure he encouraged actors to play themselves. Once he had cast the parts for a film he gave his actors great freedom to develop that sense of selfhood that would make them truly convincing. Some actors tended to stick close to the role as written, while others (I think specifically of Gable in *It Happened One Night*) would end up paraphrasing nearly the entire script. Thus we can see many of Capra's actors functioning as secondary auteurs, and Capra encouraged this kind of creativity. He knew that his films could only benefit from this kind of emotional involvement on the part of his actors, because emotional realism was his comic bread and butter.

Generally speaking, Capra's use of makeup and costume was consistent with his overall urge towards visual realism. He wanted his characters to be realistic in their appearance as well in their emotions. This usually meant no makeup at all (except for normal makeup on women, lipstick, etc), and where makeup was employed, it was used in the interest of naturalistic illusion.

An exemplary instance of this naturalizing makeup technique occurred during the filming of *The Bitter Tea of General Yen* (1933). Capra searched long and hard for a Chinese actor to play the role of the General, but he could not find one tall enough to convey the impression of overpowering authority. He finally settled on a Swedish actor, Nils Asther, whose tall good looks were accompanied by a hesitant and slightly British accent, perfect for the part of the cultured if ruthless Mandarin. The problem then was to transform Asther's Nordic features into convincingly Oriental ones.

Capra solved this problem in an unusual fashion. He studied Chinese features, and decided that the standard method of transforming Caucasian eyes into Oriental eyes, by stretching and taping the outer ends of the eyes back towards the ears, was worthless, "fooling nobody" (Capra, p. 141). Capra concluded, rather, that the major difference between Chinese and Caucasian eyes was not the slant alone, but the shape of the eyelid and the length of the eyelashes as well. Accordingly, Capra had Asther's upper eyelids covered with false skins, smooth and round rather than creased, and his eyelashes clipped to one third of their natural length. The effect was perfect. Asther's eyes had a natural yet decidedly Oriental appearance. Similar techniques were used

Naturalizing makeup technique: Nils Asther as a Chinese warlord in *The Bitter Tea of General Yen*, also featuring Barbara Stanwyck.

to transform Sam Jaffe into a two-hundred-year-old monk in *Lost Horizon* (1937), and in both cases the concern was for near-perfect physical verisimilitude.

Capra's use of costume parallels his use of makeup. He wanted to convey a sense of the contemporary (all but two of his films were contemporary to their own era), and the general policy at Columbia was that actors would wear their own clothes where contemporary apparel was in order (Thomas, p. 110).[6] Capra seemed content with this costume policy, as it served to reinforce naturalistic characterization. Even in his postwar films, when he worked with such costume designers as Edith Head, Capra maintained the same approach fairly consistently. But the thing to note is how Capra still managed to utilize clothing and costume as a sort of subliminal symbol system, despite the everyday nature of the costumes involved.

The earliest example of this occurs in the appropriately titled *Long Pants* (1927), where Harry's change from knickers to trousers symbolizes a change from the childish to the adolescent. This changing-clothes motif appears with great frequency in Capra, and a recurrent scene sees the comic hero changing out of his ill-fitting, upper-class monkey suit and back into his working-class threads. The best example of this is in *Platinum Blonde* (1931), when Stew Smith strips off his smoking jacket and puts on his old clothes. He is altogether fed up with life at the Schuyler mansion, and while his wife, mother-in-law, and Gallagher look on, he runs around the bedroom, gathering up his belongings in a battered, old satchel, and telling the Schuylers just what they can do with their upstairs bedrooms, their smoking jackets, and their oppressive stuffiness.

This correspondence of clothing, class, and character is often at work in Capra's films. All three of the populist heroes undergo similar costume changes, and Longfellow Deeds looks just as inappropriate in his smoking jacket as Jefferson Smith does in his diplomatic collar. Occasionally this class conflict is worked out as the opposition of character and costume rather than by having one character changing clothes. Peter Warne (Clark Gable) and his comfortably sloppy reporter's gear are thus set against King Westley (Jameson Thomas) and his streamlined, black business suit in *It Happened One Night* (1934). We find a similar setup in *Here Comes the*

Stew packs his clothes: Loretta Young, Robert Williams, and Jean Harlow in *Platinum Blonde*.

Groom (1951), where Peter Garvey (Bing Crosby) and Wilbur Stanley (Franchont Tone) are contrasts in appearance as well as in class status.

This clothing symbology is by no means limited to male characters. Women change clothes more often in Capra than men, and the relative variety of female apparel allows an even greater range of contrasts.

A good example of this kind of clothing symbolism occurs in *Ladies of Leisure* (1930). Jerry Strong (Ralph Graves), a playboy and a painter, is engaged to Clair Collins, a girl of his own class, but through the course of the film he falls in love with his current model, Kay Arnold (Barbara Stanwyck). After the initial portrait sitting, Kay and Jerry go into the front room just as Standish (Jerry's cognac-sot buddy) and Clair come in. After a few preliminaries, Clair orders Kay to come over so she

can get a good look at Jerry's "fascinating model." The contrast between the two women is complex and striking. Clair wears an elegant white dress, simple of cut and flowing, but there is a very uptight feeling to it. There is a scarf knotted almost hangman fashion at her neck, and she wears a very close-fitting cap, stretched tight across her forehead, revealing only a few wisps of hair. Kay, by contrast, wears a flouncy, black, print dress with stars all over it (recall how stars function as symbols for hope and freedom in the film). The dress is clearly much less expensive than Clair's, and it is flowingly open at the front, revealing a similarly sensual white blouse. Kay wears no headgear at all, and her hair is as free flowing and sensual as her attire.

This contrast in clothing between Kay and Clair thus reveals much more than just different class status. Clair clearly represents a sterile and restric-

Clothing symbolism in *Ladies of Leisure* (Barbara Stanwyck, far left, and Ralph Graves, center right).

tive sexuality, whereas Kay represents a kind of
sensual freedom that Jerry obviously aspires to. The
women thus embody the comic conflict of freedom
and bondage, and Jerry's choice between the two
will be a moral act of great significance. Costume
is used to symbolize the basic issue between fertility
and sterility that simple class conflicts do not necessarily reflect. Costume thus serves to elucidate and
clarify the film's underlying comic concerns.

In should be kept in mind, however, that the
context is as important here as it was in the discussion of character types. While it may be generally
true that upper-class people and their upper-class
attire spell trouble in Capra, it is not always the
case that expensive clothes are, *a priori*, suspect. A
comparison between the Stanwyck characters in
Meet John Doe (1941) and *The Bitter Tea of Gen-*

eral Yen will clarify how this relativity principle
works in the matter of costume (recall that Stanwyck played Kay Arnold in *Ladies of Leisure*).

One of Ann Mitchell's problems in *Meet John
Doe* is that she is almost childishly enamored of
D. B. Norton's fortune and estate. From Ann's point
of view, Norton (Edward Arnold) represents the
kind of financial stability she has always longed
for. Thus she can work for him without any major
qualms. Norton's primary method of rewarding and
reinforcing Ann's loyalty is by showering her with
luxurious presents: jewelry and expensive clothes.
Ann is clearly wrong to let herself be bound to
Norton this way, and the practical effect of her
error is that she inadvertently gives John (Gary
Cooper) proof of her unwitting political collaboration. Long John confronts Norton and Ann with

Evidence of collaboration: Ann Mitchell's (Barbara Stanwyck) costume in *Meet John Doe, featuring* Gary Cooper.

the speech nominating Norton for President, and he accepts at face value the physical evidence of Ann's betrayal. He sees her jewels, her evening gown, and he concludes (rightly, from his point of view) that Ann has sold out. Of course, she had not sold her soul, because she really had not known what was going on, but John was clearly right to assign oppressive associations to Ann's luxurious clothing. His only mistake is to assume that Ann is one of the oppressors rather than one of the oppressed.

In any case, no matter if John is correct in his immediate evaluation of Ann's character, it is clear that rich apparel and jewels carry their normal suspect connotations in *Meet John Doe.* This situation is reversed in *The Bitter Tea of General Yen.* The Stanwyck character in *Meet John Doe* changes from street clothes to luxurious attire, and that is clearly a wrong move in that film. The Stanwyck character in *Bitter Tea,* on the other hand, makes the same move, from street clothes to bejeweled gowns, but in the context of the film it is clearly the right action to take. Rather than an expression of collaboration, changing clothes becomes an expression of love and devoted concern (see chapter 8).

Another example of this relativity notion can be

seen in *Pocketful of Miracles* (1961). Along with *Lost Horizon*, where the timelessness of Shangri-La makes "contemporary" a meaningless term, *Pocketful of Miracles* is the only Capra film to really approach the status of a period piece. In remaking his own *Lady for a Day* (1933), Capra wisely decided to retain the Prohibition-era setting, realizing that updating the story would deprive it of its charm. Accordingly, the costumes are truly "costumes," intended to validate a sense of the past rather than a sense of the present. Nevertheless, despite its period status, the film does set up the normal Capra opposition between riches—Steve Darcey (Sheldon Leonard)—and middle-class sufficiency—Queenie (Hope Lange). But our concern here is with clothing imagery, and the major action of the film involves changing Apple Annie's image by changing her clothes, as well as her address and hairdo.

The nature of Annie's change is from rags to apparent riches, and the direction of that movement is generally seen as misguided in Capra. The odd thing about *Pocketful*, then, is that while the film generally disapproves of wealth, it clearly understands and accepts the rightness of Annie's transformation. She changes from tattered beggar's rags to exquisitely royal gowns, from apples to pearls, and yet we feel a sense of absolute propriety in Annie's changed appearance and demeanor. We certainly know that Annie (Bette Davis) will soon be back on the street, but we also feel in our heart of hearts that Annie deserves every moment of comfort, every passing minute of fairy-tale happiness. Annie's clothes are thus a means to an end, ensuring her daughter's happy future, and a symbol of Annie's motherly virtue: she is a queenly woman, and we cannot begrudge her one moment of queenly beauty and glory. It is not a matter of Annie betraying her own nature, but of the world momentarily recognizing her true royalty.

Capra's use of sets evidences once more his concern for cinematic realism. This again reflects Capra's early background at Columbia, where money for expressionistic experiments was in short supply (Thomas, p. 72).[6] Most of Capra's early films were shot either on strictly functional studio sets, which were constructed to represent the real world of tenements, newspaper offices, mansions, and so on; or they were shot outdoors on location. To be sure, Capra actually tells us very little about the art direction in his films. He does talk about the sets for *Mr. Smith* in his autobiography, and there he goes into great detail to catalogue the efforts necessary to create an exact duplicate of the U.S. Senate. But as often as not we are left guessing, for it is frequently difficult to determine if particular scenes were shot in the studio, or in actual hotels, city rooms, etc. And yet the very fact of our guesswork is testimony to the resourcefulness of Capra's set construction. We can thus generally assume, I think, that Capra took great care with all of his studio sets to insure the highest degree of verisimilitude.

One of the ways Capra achieved this sense of physical reality in his sets was by filling them with real objects. Even if the walls of any given set were only painted flats, it was easy to reinforce the realistic illusion by cluttering up the rooms with mirrors, chairs, desks, and other such small pieces of reality, along with the characters themselves. Again, as with clothing, Capra used these props to fulfill a double function. They were at once a device to insure realistic accuracy, and at the same time they are symbols, usually relating to the kind of person who normally occupied the set. It is impossible to catalogue all of the brilliant touches that Capra achieved by turning inconspicuous physical objects into cinematic symbols, but we can discuss a few representative examples.

One object that appears in almost every Capra film is a photograph, usually a portrait of a loved one. Harry (Langdon) has his snapshot of his beloved Mary Brown (Gertrude Astor) in *The Strong Man* (1926), and Apple Annie has a portrait of her "darling Louise" (Ann-Margaret) in *Pocketful of Miracles*. There is hardly a film in the Capra canon that does not have a photograph serving a similar function. In some cases the pictures are of political idols (Lincoln, Washington), but more often they are parents, children, or lovers. Most of these pictures are framed, and they either hang on the wall or stand upon a desk or dressing table. They serve to personalize the room or set, and one of the most striking aspects of Capra's work is this ability to create a unity of place and person.

But photographs are not Capra's only means of achieving this unity. Photographs usually carry positive connotations, and those who are concerned enough to keep reminders of their loved ones or their ideals are usually good people to start with (*e.g.,* Helen Pierce in *Dirigible*) or they are clearly redeemable (Tony Manetta in *A Hole in the Head*). And yet not all of Capra's characters are to be admired or approved, and just as Capra has icons of goodness, he has symbols of evil.

The most prominent of these demonic symbols are statues or busts of Napoleon. There is a statue in the Schuyler mansion in *Platinum Blonde*, a statue on D. B. Norton's desk in *Meet John Doe*, and busts of Napoleon are found in both of Potter's offices in *It's A Wonderful Life*. Another demonic symbol is the cigar. A few of Capra's cigar smokers are eventually reformed, but most cigar smokers are literally fat capitalists, and their cigars are ostentatious symbols of their power, neophallic expressions of their ability to burn the lower classes:

indeed, Jerry Marks drops cigar ash down the cleavage of his concubine in *A Hole in the Head*.

There are three major exceptions to Capra's normal use of realistic sets: *The Bitter Tea of General Yen, Lost Horizon,* and *Arsenic and Old Lace. Bitter Tea's* expressionistic surface, though, is more the result of lighting than it is of set construction, for the *Bitter Tea* sets are in fact as realistic as the sets elsewhere in Capra. The exception they represent has to do with the style of architecture reproduced. The Chinese summer palace cooked up by the Columbia Art Department does appear foreign and unreal, unlike Columbia's usual everyday setup, and Joseph Walker accentuates this strangeness by the use of deep-focus, low-angle photography, extensive back lighting, and darkly atmospheric shadows.

General Yen's summer palace (From left: Richard Loo, Walter Connolly, Barbara Stanwyck, and Nils Asther).

Lost Horizon: fantasy made concrete (Ronald Colman and Jane Wyatt in foreground).

One suspects that Capra's artistic (though not financial) success with *Bitter Tea* encouraged him to attempt *Lost Horizon*. Both films take place in the strife-swept Orient, and both offered an opportunity for a certain atypical grandeur of design, in terms of both subject and sets. But the sets in *Lost Horizon* do not carry this grandeur off. As Richard Griffith puts it, "the specific Utopia which appears is (as often happens when fantasy is visualized) cold, unconvincing, and strangely uninviting."[11] The problem with the *Lost Horizon* sets is not simply that they differ from Capra's earlier realistic sets, but that they do not differ enough. Shangri-La looks too real, too much like a junior college library, and therefore the "to leave or not to leave" question becomes even less significant. Were it not for the dangers and discomforts of the immediately surrounding territory, one could easily imagine departing for Paris in the spring with little if no regret.[12]

Arsenic and Old Lace, on the other hand, succeeds where *Lost Horizon* fails: the expressionistic set, with its leaf-stewed graveyard, its angular overhanging oak tree, and its Lang-like *Metropolis* skyline serves as an effectively fantastic background for the macabre goings-on. The set in effect provides the negative image of Capra's normal green world. In *It Happened One Night* we met with love newborn among the haystacks, while in *Arsenic and Old Lace* we encountered corpses newly-buried in the expressionistic cemetary. Capra apparently designed the *Arsenic and Old Lace* set himself, and his plans were realized by the Warner Brothers Art Department (Capra, p. 310). Capra clearly knew what he was doing in set design, and we can only speculate that he had a major hand in the art work on most of his films, just as he did with *Arsenic and Old Lace.*

VISUAL PRESENTATION

(editing, camera movement, deep focus,
lighting, color, Panavision)

The primary concern of Capra's cinema (the Capra "what" *i.e.,* what the camera sees) is people and their relationships to each other. The primary vehicle of human relationships is language, and Capra rightly pays attention to the way relationships are revealed and played out in conversation. Capra

does not seem stagey in this emphasis on words (despite the fact that a full quarter of his films are based on stage plays). Indeed, conversation is as much an action to be followed with the camera eye as is the purely physical action of Mr. Deeds sliding down the banister or Mr. Smith climbing the steps of the Lincoln Memorial. The majority of significant scenes in Capra (all are, of course, important, but some are more significant than others) are conversations or confrontations, and the camera's job is to pick up and expand the structure of nuance and implication that always accompanies such human interaction.

It is this overriding concern for the nuance of relationships that dictates Capra's visual style. It is a style, as William Pechter points out, based primarily on editing, the successive and economical use of various camera angles and depths of focus calculated to reveal and highlight the emotional undercurrents of conversation.[13] Capra always shot his films with the cutting room in mind, and he personally supervised the editing of all of his movies.[14]

Since Capra demonstrated his ease with dialogue sequences early, the examination of a scene from *Platinum Blonde* may serve as a representative example of Capra's treatment of conversation. We have already discussed *Platinum Blonde,* and we have seen how Stew Smith (Robert Williams) falls for the psysical attractions of Ann Schuyler (Jean Harlow) only to discover that she lacks the emotional integrity of Gallagher (Loretta Young), his one real "pal" on the newspaper staff. The scene considered takes place after Stew's first confrontation with Ann. Stew and Gallagher are at the local speakeasy and he tells her about Ann Schuyler's beauty. The scene begins with a full shot of the cafe, with Stew and Gallagher sitting at a circular table. Stew shows Gallagher the story he wrote up on the Schuyler scandal. The cuts and conversation then proceed as follows (as transcribed directly from the film):

Shots	*Dialogue*
medium closeup shot across table, STEW screen left, GALLAGHER screen right	GALLAGHER: You're certainly going to be poison to that junior leaguer from now on. STEW: Gosh, I hope not. I gotta call on her this morning.

shot past STEW's shoulder to close-up on GALLAGHER as she leans toward him; STEW in profile and GALLAGHER in full front

GALLAGHER: You What? (she sits up straight).

STEW: Sure. I must drop in and see the wench. Her wounds need soothing.

GALLAGHER: For heaven's sake Stew, are you completely bats. What for? // I thought that story was cold. You can't go back there.

STEW: Sure the story's cold, but I'm not. I'm sizzling, look (puts finger to mouth and then to the back of his other hand) pzzz.

GALLAGHER: Oh. . . . came the dawn, came the dawn (she leans away from him into a tight medium closeup: no change in camera setup).

STEW: And with it came love. Oh Gallagher, you've got to meet her, she's it . . .

GALLAGHER: . . . and that . . .

STEW: . . . and those and them . . .

GALLAGHER: Well, I've seen her pictures and I don't think she's so hot.

medium closeup across the table

STEW: Ah, // you don't appreciate her. Pictures don't do

shot past STEW's shoulder to tight medium closeup on GALLAGHER

her justice. Oh Gallagher, she's queenly, she is queenly (GALLAGHER looks at newspaper, then off into distance, obviously disturbed) and I know queens, and Oh has she got herself a nose, and I know noses too. That little schnozzle of hers is the berries I tell you. And is it cute, when she throws that schnozzle to the high heavens (he lifts his nose towards the ceiling).

GALLAGHER: // Of course I haven't got a nose.

STEM: Sure, sure, you got a nose, Gallagher, you got a nose, but that's different. Women are different, Gallagher, you know, like brewery horses and thoroughbreds.

GALLAGHER: Oh now Stew, I wouldn't be too hard on her. I wouldn't call her a brewery horse.

STEW: Gallagher, she's the real McCoy.

GALLAGHER: And the rest of us are truck horses?

STEW: There you go, talking like a woman.

GALLAGHER: Well . . .

STEW: Well, you're my pal aren't you (she bites her lip) and don't go turn female on me. // Pay that check, will you Gallagher. I'll give it back to you some time, maybe. I go, I go with Conrad in quest of my youth. Fry those tomatoes, will you Gallagher. //

full shot of room from STEW's side of table as he gets up and walks out in background closeup on GALLAGHER as she takes a mirror out of her purse and pushes her nose; almost on the verge of tears; fade out (time 2 minutes)

Platinum Blonde: The "arts and crafts" approach to love.

We can describe the typical features of this sequence as follows. At the beginning of the scene we get a full shot orienting us to the setting and the placement of the characters within the set. The camera is at eye level, and it generally tends to move in toward the characters, for it is the characters that Capra is concerned with. Most of the shots are medium closeups (from the thighs up: MC) and tight medium closeups (from the chest up: TMC). This middle range is where Capra feels most comfortable, and also, according to Bazin, where the viewer feels comfortable, "the natural point of balance of his mental adjustment."[15] Closeups (shoulders up: CU) and tight closeups (full face: TCU) are used primarily as a matter of emphasis. The cutting is aimed primarily at significant reaction, but Capra goes to neither extreme of cutting on conversation or cutting against conversation. It is not a matter of cutting from one person to another, because both are almost always in the picture. The logic of the cutting is such that the camera emphasizes the person speaking where what he has to say and the way he says it count more than the reaction of the person he says it to, and it emphasizes the person reacting where the reaction counts more.

This scene from *Platinum Blonde* is a good example of Capra's cutting logic. Most of the scene is shot past Stew, so that he is in three-quarter profile, to a full-front medium closeup on Gallagher. She is the one who is learning about Stew's infatuation with Ann Schuyler (we already know), and she is the one who is most affected by the news. When we do switch our viewpoint from one side of the table to the other, it is to emphasize Stew's rapturous description of Ann Scuhyler as a queenly thoroughbred with a schnozzle. Gallagher is still in the picture, and still reacting, but the foolishness of Stew is underlined by shooting him from the front while he lifts his nose to the "high heavens." We quickly cut back, however, to a shot emphasizing Gallagher, and her pain at discovering that she is just a "pal" to Stew. She never has to say that she is sexually interested in Stew, because it is clear just from her reaction when she finds out that Stew is not interested in her. The final closeup on her makes this absolutely apparent ("if only my nose were the real McCoy").

We cannot really say that this sequence of cuts

itself "means" anything. The cuts themselves show us something that means, and the something they show us is actors interacting. Generally speaking, Capra's visual style is transparent. As Capra puts it in his autobiography, "the audience must never become aware that there is a camera within a thousand miles of the scene" (p. 249). We seldom sense the camera because it never gets in our way: it always shows us what we want to see, and what we see is what counts. There are, however, moments in several films in which a cut can be said to "mean" something, by showing us something that is dictated not necessarily by the logic of conversation but rather by the overall logic of the film. To stay with *Platinum Blonde,* for example, we can examine the scene in which Stew first meets the Schuyler family in his role as a newspaper reporter investigating the scandal involving Ann's brother.

Stew walks in and introduces himself: "My name is Smith, Stewart Smith, no relation to John, Joe, Trade, or Mark. Of course, you can't have everything." Right after he says "you can't have everything," however, Capra cuts to medium closeup of Harlow smiling at Stew, and the effect is an Eisensteinian clash of sound and image, synthesizing a new meaning. The "everything" that Stew cannot have is Ann Schuyler, and we now know, if he does not, that he had best stay away from her altogether. Similar scenes are to be found in *Mr. Smith* and *Pocketful of Miracles.*

I noted that the conversation scene from *Platinum Blonde* serves to demonstrate Capra's usual editing style. Generally speaking, all of his conversation scenes are presented in a similar fashion, and, unless I note otherwise, the reader can assume that conversations quoted in this essay are similarly cut. But it is not true that Capra always shot his dialogue scenes in this manner. He is frequently willing to let the camera sit tight and film a lengthy conversation in one or two long medium closeup takes. But he generally does this as it corresponds to the emotional tempo of the movie.

In *Lost Horizon,* for example, there is a long conversation scene between Edward Everett Horton and Thomas Mitchell that is shot with only one or two cuts, and it serves as a relief from the frantic cutting of the previous scene in which the plane is loaded and takes off amid milling crowds and a hail of bullets from rebel rifles. There is a similar scene

Platinum Blonde: Stew meets the Schuyler family for the first time (From left: Robert Williams, Jean Harlow, Louise Closser Hale, Reginald Owen, and Donald Dillaway).

in *Mr. Smith Goes to Washington.* The montage of Jeff's tour of Freedom's shrines is cut in with the frantic attempts of McGann, Saunders, and Paine to locate the boy wonder. When Jeff finally shows up at his office he explains to Diz and Saunders how he just naturally climbed on the sightseeing bus, and this is shot in one long medium closeup take of the three of them standing together. Note that in both instances the easing up of editing corresponds to an ease in tension on the part of the characters and presumably on the part of the audience.

Of course, tension is as integral a part of a film structure as anything else. Capra's mastery of ten-sion and pace is certainly the most readily acknowl-edged of all of his many talents. He never wastes an inch of film upon anything that does not con-tribute directly to the emotional flow of the movie, and since the emotional tension in his films is gener-ally high, we expect, and do in fact observe, an editing style that underlines the urgency of his stories.

Generally speaking, we can say that the frequency of cutting in Capra demonstrates an intensity of in-terest corresponding to the emotional magnitude of a given scene in its given context. In other words, as suspense increases, so does the frequency of cut-

Three shot in *Mr. Smith* (Jean Arthur, James Stewart, and Thomas Mitchell).

ting. But we must remember how suspense works in Capra. We are concerned with characters and the fates that befall them. We identify with their fortunes, and the more important the characters are to us, the more concerned we are regarding their success or failure. Hence cutting tends to increase during moments of emotional and moral significance, when our own interest and moral curiosity reach a peak.

Capra is always intensely interested in the fortunes of his characters, and therefore he tends to cut more frequently than most of his Hollywood contemporaries. Indeed, the only person to my knowledge who seems to approach Capra in editing style is the existential Howard Hawks. But the thing to keep in mind is the importance of context to the analysis of style. We get a similar frequency of cut-

ting in the wedding scene in *It Happened One Night* (1934) and in the final confrontation scene in *Mr. Smith Goes to Washington* (1939). But the frequency in neither determines how we feel, desperate or otherwise. Cutting may determine the magnitude of our emotion, but the content of that emotion is determined by what is actually happening to characters we identify with. Hence we feel a sense of freedom and release when Ellie charges across the lawn with her train and veil trailing behind her, and we feel a sense of ominous foreboding in *Mr. Smith,* where our sense of desperation is more a matter of the emotional content than the cutting of the scene. Both scenes share the same magnitude of emotion, but the emotion (and hence the meaning) is different in both cases.

So far we have considered editing in conversation,

and the overall frequency of cuts. One final editing concern remains to be dealt with before we move on to matters of camera movement and depth of focus.

A characteristic feature of Capra's editing style is his use of what we might term "time-lapse montage." In almost every film Capra employs montages of newspaper headlines and other immediately significant symbols as devices to bridge time and to convey important plot information. Capra can thus dramatize the undramatic, and do so without destroying the emotional pace of his films.

In *Meet John Doe* (1941), for example, Capra encapsulates the time-consuming proliferation of the John Doe clubs into a few moments of highly effective montage, combining newspaper headlines, shots of Long John and Ann in trains and airplanes, John Doe posters, maps and pins signifying John Doe chapters, John speaking, John Doe buttons, farmers, miners, and so on; all calculated to render an accurate image of the wildfire spread of the John Doe movement. Through the course of this sequence we are shown the impact of the movement not only on the John Does of the country, but upon the politicians as well. Capra shows us the headquarters of both major political parties, where party functionaries recount their failure at lining the John Does up behind their own political banners. We can say then that this particular montage sequence fulfills three functions: compression of time, an explication of information, and a tertiary function of reinforcing the realistic immediacy of the film. Newspaper headlines in particular provide a sense of up-to-the-minute topicality, and the shots of the real farmers and miners serve to underline further the realistic context of the film (although we should not forget how complicated this notion of realism is).

Another characteristic use of montage, one which accords naturally with the comic struggle between fertility and sterility, involves parallel editing, cutting from the forces of good to the forces of evil as a means of highlighting the moral battle. This is the central technique of the *Why We Fight* (1942-45) films, and Capra uses it for great effect in nearly all of his movies.[16] Because he is usually so casual about this alternation of attention, it does not strike us with the immediate effect of Griffith's parallel montage in *Intolerance* (1916), but there are moments when Capra utilizes classical Griffith-type con-

structions to make his point. One thinks immediately of the sequence in *Mr. Smith Goes to Washington* where Capra cuts between the big-time Taylor newspaper presses and the *Boys' Stuff* news operation, or between Jeff's struggle in the Senate, and the Boy Rangers' struggle against the Taylor thugs in the streets of Jeff's home town.

A final montage technique should be mentioned before moving on (although it is clearly impossible to catalogue every stylistic nicety that Capra ever demonstrated). On several important occasions Capra uses what we might term "semisubjective montage." The best example of this again comes from *Mr. Smith,* and it involves Jeff's tour of Washington, D.C. The framework of the sequence is a sightseeing expedition, and the camera objectively watches Jeff watching the sights. But the real impact of the scene is a matter of its subjective moments, when the camera eye is clearly Jeff's eye, and we all gaze in admiration and awe at the symbols of freedom and democracy. For the moment of the montage we all become Jeff Smith, and the tempo of the editing matches Jeff's exhilaration at beholding the monumental symbols of his ideals. Of course, Capra does not always use objective montage in this manner. We should recall the scenes in *Meat John Doe* where John imagines himself beset by the terrifyingly immense faces of the people accusing him of fakery and fraud. The technique is not strictly subjective, but we experience much the same effect. The personal identification of character and audience that we generally assume as a matter of course is made explicit through this use of these subjective sequences.

To this point, we have established that Capra's style is generally based on editing. Within this overal stylistic context, however, Capra does utilize other cinematic techniques. Capra clearly knows how to employ moving camera, for example, and if he uses it sparingly, he nevertheless uses it effectively, particularly as it contrasts to his normal mode of presentation.

The most striking camera movement in Capra's repertoire is the subjective track shot. This usually occurs in moments of emotional intensity, when a character's attention is drawn to some object symbolic of his plight or situation. The best example of this can be found in *Dirigible* (1931), when Frisky Pierce and Hansen discover that they have been walking in circles in their attempt to reach their base camp after the plane crash. They have just avoided one disaster, cutting themselves loose from their sled only moments before it plunges down a crevasse, and as Hansen looks up in relief he sees a crosslike ice ax sticking up out of the snow in the distance. The camera swiftly tracks in to reveal the frozen corpse of Dr. Rondelle, encased in a transparent grave of ice. They had buried him days earlier, and now they are back where they started from. This zoomlike effect carries tremendous emotional impact, at once overpowering and arresting. We know what it feels like to have one fact at the center of our universe, particularly when that fact spells death. Of course, Capra does use this kind of shot in less gloomy circumstances [recall the scene in *Flight* (1929) when an airsick Lefty Phelps spies a bucket to heave in], but it is certainly a spectacular shot no matter where it occurs. Indeed, perhaps Capra felt it was too spectacular, for he hardly uses it at all in his later films. Once he mastered the technical aspects of cinema, Capra became more interested in the story value of his movies, and such self-conscious visuals became fewer and farther between.

A far more normal use of moving camera is Capra's devotion to unobtrusive and functional pan shots, used to follow characters in action without breaking up the world they are acting in any more than is necessary. Examples of this abound in Capra (*e.g.,* the scene in *Platinum Blonde* when Stew collects his belongings and leaves the Schuyler mansion, or the scene in *It Happened One Night* when Ellie searches the bus depot after missing the bus) and we need not discuss it in any great detail.

A final use of moving camera involves tracking with conversation. Capra's characters talk a great deal, but they do not always do it sitting down or standing in one place. Accordingly, Capra is ready to keep up with his characters, following them, staying beside them, or even on occasion ahead of them, in order to pick up their conversation. One thinks readily of the scene on the road in *It Happened One Night* just before the hitch-hiking routine, when Capra follows Peter and Ellie with the camera, keeping them in full shot and in microphone range. Capra reverses his point of view in a similar situation in *Mr. Deeds Goes to Town* (1936), tracking backward to keep Cooper and Jean Arthur in

medium closeup as they walk towards the camera. Generally speaking, Capra evidences a respect for the integrity of human action, and when that action involves movement across space, he will keep his camera focused on the action as long as necessary.

This respect for the physical world is further evidenced by Capra's use of deep focus. Of course, here again we must keep in mind that the center of the physical Capra universe is characters, but Capra is not the least bit hesitant to describe their relationships to each other via deep focus where deep focus is appropriate.

The most characteristic deep focus setup is a linear organization with the axis of interest running diagonally from foreground to background. A good example occurs in *It's A Wonderful Life* (1946), when George Bailey (James Stewart) leaves the reception for his newly returned and newly married younger brother to have a smoke out on the front porch of the family house.

Here again, context is the crucial factor that allows significance to the camera setup. George's younger brother, Harry Bailey (Todd Karns), was supposed to come home from college and take over the family business so George could have his chance to leave Bedford Falls and get an education. Harry came home as planned, but he brought a new bride with him, and with the new bride came a very good job opportunity. George rightly decides that he cannot hold Harry back from pursuing his big chance, but he feels a great deal of resentment nevertheless.

In the shot in question, George comes into the close foreground, leaving the porch and walking towards the front gate and the camera. Over George's right shoulder we can see Harry and his wife in the doorway. At this moment a train whistle sounds off in the distance and the entire thematic and visual gestalt of the film comes together. George's romantic dreams of travel and adventure are frustrated by the kind of familial responsibility imaged in the marriage of Harry and Ruth (Virginia Patton). George clearly wants to turn his back on his home and his hometown, thus ignoring what the film defines as his real duty, but George rightly remains in Bedford Hills, however begrudgingly, and this refusal to shirk responsibility is similarly reflected in this shot. He would not be agitated and upset had he made the wrong decision. This one deep-focus shot thus sets forth all of the basic issues of the film's moral conflict.

Generally speaking, Capra's normal use of deep focus follows a similar pattern (indeed, this same porch setup is frequently repeated). He tends to stay as close to his characters as possible (George was in a closeup in this last scene), and he usually avoids really long shots, as they tend to dehumanize his characters. The only time Capra normally makes extensive use of radical, deep-focus setups is when photographing a mob, where dehumanization is the very fact he wishes to convey.

Capra's normal use of lighting also reflects his concern with reality. He wants to make things look real, and accordingly he has his cameraman light his sets in a functional realistic fashion. This normal lighting setup remains a constant across Capra's canon, despite changes of photographers (he worked with some fifteen different photographers over the course of his career). But once again the aspect of Capra's visual style that we remember is not the norm, which is generally straightforward and sunny, but the exception, and the exceptional expressionistic setups in Capra's films should be attributed to Columbia's ace photographer, Joseph Walker.

Walker came to Columbia in 1928, and he is usually credited with the luminous surface generally characteristic of all Columbia products (Thomas, p. 74).[6] He began working with Capra immediately upon Capra's arrival at Columbia, and he shot Capra's first Columbia movie, *That Certain Thing*

The dehumanized mob: deep focus in *American Madness*.

(1928). Walker wrought an instant and important change in Capra's visual style. Up to the point of his association with Walker, the lighting in Capra's films had been strictly functional. His Langdon films generally lack any sort of sophisticated lighting setups. Even the speakeasy scene in *Long Pants* (1927) is flat as far as the lighting is concerned. But with Walker behind the camera, Capra began his first experiments with lighting, shadow, and mood.

A good example of this expressionistic experimentation occurs in *That Certain Thing*. Charles Senior had disinherited his son upon learning of Junior's marriage to the fortune-hunting "gold digger" that he believes Molly to be. Unfortunately, Molly has much the same opinion of herself. It is to her credit, then, that she decides to walk out of Junior's life, although in the larger movement of the film that is the wrong move to make. In any case, the scene we are concerned with takes place after Molly leaves the honeymoon suite at the hotel and returns to her tenement. It is raining heavily, and the night is cold and darkly foreboding. We see Molly in long shot as she walks towards the camera, coming into the tenement. She stops in the entry way, and we get a closeup of her as she stands there dripping wet and altogether miserable. We do not get the extreme back lighting that we will eventually see in *It Happened One Night,* but there is enough back lighting to illuminate momentarily some of the water in Molly's hair. This is set against the dark, shadowy background provided by the tenement doorway and the street beyond, and the effect is one that emphasizes Molly's feeling of dispair, her sense of bright hopes extinguished in the gloom of self-imposed guilt and rejection at the hands of the upper classes.

Capra continued to employ this type of expressionistic lighting and camera work throughout most of his career, and it is clear that he felt an instant affinity for Walker's camera and lighting techniques. Walker was the first cameraman to provide Capra with the option of employing such cinematic devices, and Capra was quick to take advantage and learn his lesson. Capra thus made Walker's technique his own. Hence, while it is true that Walker is greatly responsible for Capra's expressionist tendencies, it is also true that Capra continued this type of lighting approach even after he stopped working with Walker.[17]

A production still: expressionist lighting in *It Happened
One Night*, featuring Clark Gable and Claudette Colbert.

Capra's use of color is again consistent with his feeling for realism. His first color effort was *Two Down, One to Go* (1945), a war information film describing the procedure used to determine which soldiers from the Atlantic theatre would be transferred to the Pacific front and which would be allowed to go home. Color here was strictly descriptive and realistic. Capra continued this functional use of color photography in the Bell System Science Films (1956-58).

Capra's first color feature was *A Hole in the Head* (1959), and here too Capra saw color primarily as another device for maintaining the realistic illusion. For the most part, Capra refained from any Godard-like experiments with color, but there does seem to be an almost subliminal color correlation in *A Hole*

in the Head, setting warm colors (reds, oranges, browns) associated with the virtues of the family, against cold and hard colors (dark green, steel blue) that come to stand for insensitive self-centeredness.

Two shots serve to define this opposition of colors. The first follows a scene in which Tony Manetta (Frank Sinatra) and Shirl (Carolyn Jones) go out to the beach to talk instead of going to the airport to pick up Tony's brother Mario (Edward G. Robinson). Shirl tells Tony he is a kiwi bird ("they just sit around all day long flapping their wings, they can't get off the ground") and she challenges him to fly away with her, leaving his son and his responsibilities behind. He rightly balks at the proposition, and she runs out into the nighttime surf. Capra then gives us a panoramic long shot of the shore. The moonlight reflected off the waves and the sand gives a hard metallic appearance to the scene, cold and menacing.

This ominous shot contrasts sharply with the film's final image. Tony's plans to save his beachfront hotel have fallen through, and he asks his tightfisted though wealthy brother Mario to take Allie (Tony's son: Eddie Hodges) back to New York to live with Mario and his family. Just as Mario, Aunt Sophie (Thelma Ritter), and Allie are leaving, however, Allie jumps out of the taxi and runs along the beach to his father, who had been hiding behind a palm tree. Tony and Allie are then joined by Mrs. Rogers (Eleanor Parker)—who we presume will shortly be Allie's new mother. In the meanwhile Uncle Mario and Aunt Sophie get out of the cab to see what is going on. At the sight of Tony and Allie wrestling joyously in the surf, Mario grabs Sophie's hand and begins his first vacation in forty years, running along the beach to join the rest of the family. The final shot is another deep focus view of another beach, but instead of a solitary surfer we get the entire Manetta clan running into the warm orange sunset.

One of the reasons one doubts any sort of conscious intention behind the color scheme in *A Hole in the Head* is the lack of any such scheme in Capra's only other color feature, *Pocketful of Miracles*. Two colors predominate in *Pocketful*: red and white. Annie's apples are red; the walls of Queenie's speakeasy are red and white; the speakeasy furniture is red; Dave wears red and white suits; and so on for most of the details of the film. It is at first tempting to try to associate red with Prohibition decadence and white with the virginal virtues that Queenie strives for and Louise represents, but it simply cannot be done. Louise wears a bright red dress on one occasion, she attends the engagement reception in a pink gown, and there are other occurrences that negate a strict red/white color scheme. *Pocketful* is much more colorful than *A Hole in the Head* (though this may have something to do with the quality of the prints I have seen), and one can only conclude that Capra fell prey to a Minnelli-like fascination with color for color's sake. Without being obtrusive, *Pocketful of Miracles* is visually beautiful in the same way that *Meet Me in St. Louis* is beautiful, and the concern is not dialectic (though both films have their dialectics) but decor-

ative. It is as if Capra were saying "look how beautiful the world can be"; and from that point of view Capra certainly succeeds.

One final element of visual style remains to be considered: Capra's use of the Panavision screen. Capra shot his last two movies in the wide-screen process, and he apparently had no trouble understanding and utilizing the cinematic possibilities inherent in the wider frame. Generally speaking, we can say that he saw the Panavision frame primarily as a larger window on the world. It allowed him to put more people in the frame without crowding them together in a moblike fashion. A scene from the beginning of *Pocketful of Miracles* demonstrates Capra's typical use of the wide screen.

Dave the Dude (Glenn Ford) has just blown open the safe of his dead friend, Rudy Martin, and discovered that Rudy had been bumped off because of massive gambling debts. Queenie (Hope Lange) then comes in, thanks the Dude for his kindness in paying for her father's funeral, and gives him the deed to her father's speakeasy. Joy Boy (Peter Falk) informs her that the club is not worth a plugged nickel, and she offers to pay off her father's debt to Dave at the rate of the five dollars a week she can spare from her wages at the cafeteria. The shot here is a closeup that includes all three characters: Joy Boy at screen left, Queenie in the middle, and Dave the Dude at screen right. The point of the closeup is to emphasize Queenie's emotional integrity, but the wide screen allows Capra to include his realistic character in the action of the scene without cutting. Joy Boy is right there in the picture to express his exasperation at Queenie's financial naivete, and we do not have to look elsewhere to encompass this ironic reaction (as we do, for example, in *Meet John Doe*).

Similar economies in cutting were frequently allowed by the wide screen process, and this generally accounts for the relaxed tone of these final films. The rhythm of the cutting is much less frantic, and the feeling is one of cinematic ease and self-confidence.

Another effect of wide screen is to cut down on camera movement. Given the wider perspective, Capra is frequently able to follow a character's action without actually panning the camera. What tension we do find in the films is more a matter of character movement than camera movement. During Dave the Dude's final orgy of selfishness, when he refuses to have any more to do with Apple Annie (Bette Davis) and her schemes, the camera sits still. But Dave does not. He moves around, waving his arms, stomping back and forth, and the effect is similar to the tension Capra normally creates through cutting.

Beyond this decrease in cutting and camera movement, however, Capra's style in his last two films recalls that of his earlier efforts. The overriding stylistic concern in most of Capra's movies is the accurate rendition of the comic world. The plot action that takes place in that comic universe may demonstrate certain fantastic qualities, but the physical appearance of the comic world matches up with actual reality, hence providing a realistic context for the emotional realism that is Capra's primary goal. Thus, there is no inconsistency between the realistic and the fantastic, because the emotional reactions of the comic characters are what we might realistically expect of actual people were they to find themselves in such fantastic circumstances.

Such a stylistic balance between art and reality seems to be what André Bazin had in mind when he said that "the margin of loss of the real, implicit in any realist choice, frequently allows the artist, by the use of any aesthetic convention he may introduce into the area thus left vacant, to increase the effectiveness of his chosen form of reality" (II. 29).[15] Capra's "chosen form of reality" in this formulation is concerned with the accurate portrayal of human emotions, particularly as those emotions serve to embody comic oppositions between life and death, fertility and sterility, love and hate, and so on. With this as his realistic cornerstone, Capra is then free to employ any conventions, realistic or otherwise, to "increase the effectiveness of his chosen form of reality." Hence we can say that Capra is a cinematic realist as far as his visual style is concerned (*e.g.*, his penchant for realistic acting, his use of deep focus, moving camera, etc.), without forgetting the aesthetic conventions that determine the often fantastic dramatic structure of his films.

Capra with Clarence Muse.

NOTES

1. Frank Capra, *The Name Above the Title* (New York: Mac-Millian, 1971), p. 475. Unless otherwise noted, similar statements of fact have the autobiography as their source.

2. In *Signs and Meaning in the Cinema* (Bloomington: Indiana University Press, 1969), pp. 163-5, Peter Wollen proposes "a very elementary typology of styles. There are those which are individual and those which are collective, on one hand, and, on the other hand, those which are conscious and those which are unconscious" (p. 164). The weakest case for individual authorship would be, then, the unconscious collective style, in which the artist simply assumes the stylistic mode of the period. But even here, it seems to me, choice can be talked about, for an unconscious decision is as much of a choice and carries as much significance (perhaps even more) as a conscious decision to adopt such and such a stylistic manner. The question would be, then, why an artist found a collective style appropriate to his individual sensibilities. What was it about the collective Hollywood style of the late thirties (which Bazin describes in *What is Cinema?* I, pp. 23-40) that attracted such diverse personalities as Hawks, Capra, Ford, and Wyler? The answer would be another book, doubtless, but the issue of collective style could be raised and dealt with, I believe, without eliminating the notion of individual stylistic choices.

3. Raymond Durgnat, *Films and Feelings* (Cambridge: The M.I.T. Press, 1971), p. 34. See also Pauline Kael, *Going Steady* (1970; rpt. New York: Bantam Books, 1971), pp. 105-158.

4. Stephen Handzo, "Under Capracorn," *Film Comment* 8, no. 4 (1972): 9.

5. Richard Corliss, "Capra & Riskin," *Film Comment* 8, no. 4 (1972): 19.

6. Bob Thomas, *King Cohn* (New York: G. P. Putnam's Sons, 1967).

7. See the filmography for complete credit information and sources (pp. 235-247).

8. Capra is credited as a writer on *The Strong Man* (1926), *Flight* (1929), *Forbidden* (1932), *It' A Wonderful Life* 1946) and William Wellman's *Westward the Women* (1950).

9. Both the Buchman script for *Mr. Smith* and the Riskin script for *It Happened One Night* can be found in John Gassner and Dudley Nichols, eds., *Twenty Best Film Plays* (New York: Crown, 1934).

10. David Zinman, *50 Classic Motion Pictures* (New York: Crown, 1970), p. 52.

11. Richard Griffith, *Frank Capra,* New Index Series, no. 3 (London: The British Film Institute, 1951): 23.

12. See John Baxter, *Hollywood in the Thirties* (New York: Paperback Library, 1970), p. 140, to get the opinion of a critic who found the *Lost Horizon* sets effective.

13. William Pechter, *Twenty-Four/Times/A/Second* (New York: Harper & Row, 1971), p. 131.

14. Frank Capra, et al, "Frank Capra; 'One Man—One Film'," *Discussion,* no. 3 (Washington, D.C.: The American Film Institute, 1971): 9.

15. André Bazin, *What is Cinema?,* translated by Hugh Gray, 2 vols. (Berkeley: University of California Press, 1967 and 1971), I, p. 32.

16. See William T. Murphy, "The Method of *Why We Fight,*" *The Journal of Popular Film* 1, no. 3 (1972): 185-196.

17. Walker worked on 18 of Capra's 36 feature films, the last being *It's A Wonderful Life* (1946).

7

The Langdon Features:
The Strong Man and *Long Pants*

Most of the controversy regarding Capra has re-volved around the politics (naive or not so naive) in his films. His status as an auteur has seldom been questioned, although his value as a cinematic artist has not always been conceded. Recently, however, a minor auteur controversy has begun over the fea-ture films that Capra directed for Harry Langdon. Who was responsible for Langdon's success? Is Capra to be credited with creating the Langdon character, or should Langdon himself be acknowl-edged as a self-sufficient comic artist of the Chaplin or Keaton type?

Since the 1949 appearance of James Agee's "Comedy's Greatest Era," the standard notion has attributed Langdon's swift rise to stardom primarily to Capra's adept gagwriting, guidance, and direc-tion.[1] As Capra tells the story in his autobiography, Landgon was an unknown vaudeville performer when Mack Sennett signed him to a contract. Capra and the other Sennett writers were universally be-fuddled with their new charge, having no idea what to do with him. This all changed, suddenly, when Arthur Ripley chanced to remark that only God could help them with Langdon. This insight set Capra's fertile imagination to work, and the Chris-tian-innocent Harry Langdon persona was born. The team of Capra and Ripley (writers) and Harry Edwards (director) took over the Langdon two-reelers, and guaranteed their success by making

Harry Langdon: the Christian innocent.

sure that gags inappropriate to their conception of the Langdon character were not allowed. This tripartite guidance apparently turned the trick, for within two years Langdon left Sennett to form his own production company, with the Capra-Ripley-Edwards team still running the creative show.[2]

Langdon retained his position as a first-rate film comic as long as Capra remained with him. Harry Edwards left the team after the first Langdon feature, *Tramp, Tramp, Tramp* (1926). Capra then took over as director of the next two films, with Ripley heading the writing staff. After *Long Pants* (1929), Capra left (or was fired) and Langdon became his own director with Ripley still along as chief writer and adviser. Langdon's first self-directed effort was *Three's a Crowd,* and most writers see the film as the beginning of Langdon's downfall. The obvious conclusion to draw is that Capra was the crucial factor in Langdon's cinematic success. Capra

was the one member of the original team that Langdon could not do without. But as Richard Leary points out in his article "Capra & Langdon," it is possible to overemphasize the magnitude and nature of Capra's contribution, and to do so at the risk of forgetting Langdon himself.[3]

I suspect that we will never be able to determine precisely how much Langdon owes to Capra or vice versa. The nature of the collaboration was such that Capra had to accept limitations (although he probably did not see them as such) that he would seldom have to face again. In most of his films, Capra had complete control over scripts and casting, and his normal *modus operandi* saw him settling story line and character before he actually began casting. With Langdon the order was reversed. Capra already had his actor, and the actor already had a character, and

Do no evil: Harry assaults a fellow passenger.

the trick was to build a film around that characterization. The whole purpose behind the Langdon films was, furthermore, Langdon himself; to provide him with a cinematic vehicle for his, indeed, great comic talents. Langdon was, even in his vaudeville days, very much a child-man, and what Capra and Ripley did was to establish a rationale for an already existent character. This rationale was primarily a negative one, however: Harry could not do this, that, or the other thing. As long as he did nothing out of keeping with his essentially innocent childishness, Capra gave him great leeway in developing gag ideas into extended routines. Thus many of the character touches that we now associate with Langdon probably originated with Langdon himself. For example, one of Capra's "must nots" was that Harry must "think no evil, see no evil, do no evil" (Capra, p. 63). To the extent that Langdon's innocence was incapable of comprehending the concept "evil," this rule was never broken. There simply was no sense of morality (or reality) inherent in Langdon's character. But there is yet a profundity resulting from Langdon's complete amorality that Capra never seems to have consciously noticed. Langdon did evil, without any knowledge that it really was evil. Fortunately, Capra saw that it worked, even if he may not have fully understood how it worked, and he took advantage of this tendency towards amorality, making it the subject of *Long Pants*.

To the extent then that Langdon was Langdon before Sennett and Capra ever got their hands on him, and continued to be himself throughout his association with Capra, we must surely agree with those who rightly point out that Langdon was, like many other comedians, very much of a nondirector auteur. The force of Langdon's character provided a definite tone to his films. Everything that was done was determined by Langdon's abilities and characteristics. Capra clearly did not provide Langdon with a genius for pantomime, nor did he give him his flawless sense of hesitant timing, or the tight suit and the bowler hat; but Capra did, particularly in the feature films, provide Langdon with the kind of cinematic expertise that showed Langdon's talents to best advantage.

So what we are dealing with, then, in *The Strong Man* (1926) and *Long Pants* (1927), is really a case of complementary multiple authorship, but authorship of two different sorts. Langdon created (*i.e., was*) himself, and to the extent that the meaning of the films related to the kind of character he portrayed, they are indeed "Langdon films"; but Capra filmed the movies, and to the extent that the environment or context in which the Langdon character moved modified the meaning attached to that character, then we are talking about "Capra films." The thing to pay attention to, therefore, is the interplay of authorship, the way Capra-as-auteur utilizes Langdon-as-auteur to come up with films of unified sensibility and vision.

Both *The Strong Man* and *Long Pants* are about childhood. The former deals with Harry's search for an appropriate guardian. He is the archetypal infant seeking a parent. *Long Pants* is not so much about parents and children (although both are obviously there) as it is about adolescence and the pitfalls of juvenile romanticism. In both instances Capra takes the given of Harry's baby-face character and utilizes it in works that are demonstrably Capraesque, no matter how important the Langdon contribution might be. The Capra-formulated principle of the eternal infant protected by Providence underlies the plot structure and hence the meaning of both films. Harry-as-infant thus serves as the subject and the issue in both features.

This concern with Harry's childishness is evidenced in the opening sequence of *The Strong Man*. After a series of deep-focus, battlefield vistas (and a short conversation scene that tells us that Harry is in "No Man's Land"), we cut to a restricted medium closeup of sandbags, with a tin can sitting atop the pile. Dirt jumps all around the sandbags as the errant bullets of some offscreen sharpshooter miss their mark. The sharpshooter is none other than Harry himself, sitting nonchalantly to one side of the machine gun, absentmindedly firing it in whatever direction his fancy chooses. His mind seems to wander (and the wandering bullets serve as the visual correlative for his meandering consciousness) but every once in a while he remembers that can over on the sandbags, and again he points the weapon in that direction. He plays with the machine gun as if it were a toy, and when one toy fails to dislodge the offending can, Harry pulls out another toy, his slingshot, to finish the deed. But there is a war on, and the war does not stop to let Harry indulge his childlike fascination with his destructive

Harry the sharpshooter in *The Strong Man*.

toys. The enemy is near, and the enemy, *i.e.,* one overweight and slightly foolish-looking German soldier (Zandow), starts to take pot shots at Harry with his revolver.

Harry's response to the threat the German represents is restricted though not totally unawares: he does scratch the cootie on his knee rather than the one on his chest; but the general tenor of his reaction is that of a child ignorant of the disastrous possibilities he faces. Only Harry would attempt to fight off an armed enemy with a slingshot and hardtack, and only a David-like Harry with Providence on his side would succeed even momentarily. But God cannot watch over Harry continually, and it is clear that Harry must find some earthly source of guid-

ance and support if his childishness is to survive in a world of howitzers and aerial bombardment.

Harry seems to realize this need for guidance, and he is generally content to be Zandow's prisoner cum slave, even after the war is over. But the person Harry really longs to find is Mary Brown (Gertrude Astor), an American girl who loves him and who will properly care for him (as she does at the film's conclusion, picking Harry up after he trips over the rock in the street). Mary is clearly the right kind of girl for Harry, maternal and virginal at the same time, and the comic movement of the film will be to bring Harry and Mary together.

Two things seem to stand in the way of this comic conclusion: (1) Harry's innocence, and (2)

Innocence at hazard: Harry awaits Zandow's coming.

the cynicism (associated with the big city) that is always ready in Capra to take advantage of innocence. Here we have the first statement of a theme that was to become increasingly important in Capra's later work: you can seldom trust city slickers. Harry's first encounter with the world of city experience almost proves the death of him (physically as well as spiritually), and later in the film even the small town of Cloverdale, the ancestor of Mandrake Falls and Bedford Falls in later Capra films, is prey to big-city gin runners. In both instances, Harry manages to avoid the danger implicit in the situations, but he does so only at great risk to his innocent selfhood.

The first assault on Harry's selfhood is set in sexual terms, even though the object of seduction is not Harry but the roll of money in his jacket lining.

Pursued by a detective, Lily (Priscilla Bonner), a slick moll type, is forced to dump a large, ill-gotten bank roll into Harry's pocket while he stands on the corner, looking for Mary Brown. After the detective questions her and leaves, she again reaches into Harry's pocket, only to discover that the money is gone. A quick check, however reveals that the bank roll has slipped into the lining of Harry's coat. Lily therefore has to get the coat from him, so she tells Harry that she is "little Mary" (she had earlier overheard him questioning another woman about Mary Brown). Harry is overjoyed, and after a few very formal embraces, he grasps her hand, swinging it merrily to and fro as they walk down the street. Lily is all business, however, and she discourages any activity that might call attention to them, whether it be overexuberant hand

A child in oversized clothes: Harry is *The Strong Man*.

holding or popcorn crunching. She finally spirits Harry into a taxi, and, while Harry sightsees, she gropes behind him for the money. Harry suddenly flattens out against the seat, as if to protect his buttocks from what he perceives as the sexual advances of "little Mary." He takes a bewildered look at his snapshot of Mary, and then recoils again, crawling even deeper into his corner of the cab, as Lily again tries to take his coat off.

This pattern of sexual assault continues once Harry gets Lily up the stairs and into her apartment (she had "fainted" when Harry refused to accompany her up to her flat). Harry's frantic horror, if it had not been emphasized before, is visually underscored when Lily tries to remove Harry's coat while he sleeps fetuslike on the couch. As soon as she touches him, Harry awakes and begins to struggle. Most of this is shot from eye level and in full shot, but then Capra cuts to a shot looking directly down on the couch from immediately overhead. Harry appears like an insect pinned to a specimen board, spasmodically trying to escape. After further struggle and cajolement, Harry is forced at dagger point to kiss Lily (although by this point the kiss carries the emotional weight of rape). As she kisses him, she uses the dagger to slit open his coat and remove the bank roll. With this she collapses in exhaustion on the couch. Harry feels defiled, and he begs her not to tell anyone of his indignity.

One of the most striking aspects of the child-man Langdon character is his bifurcated sexuality: every personal encounter that actually hints towards physical sex, which excludes his relationship with Mary Brown, of necessity verges on incest. Harry is too much of a child, and every woman is too much of a mother. As James Agee put it, Langdon had an "instinct for bringing his actual adulthood and his figurative babyishness into frictions as crawly as a fingernail on a slate blackboard" (p. 81). This crawly friction is clearly at work in this scene between Harry and Lily. Harry seems to sense the discord between his own sexlessness and Lily's voluptuousness, and to realize that any initiation into the adult rites of sex would destroy him. Harry feels vitally threatened by the prospect of sex (and the knowledge of good and evil that accompanies it), but one senses Harry's anxiety as a larger fear of total engulfment (a world of expanded knowledge would surely engulf his childish innocence). Harry

clearly wants to return to the womb (note how often he assumes a fetal position), and yet he does not want to return (note his fear of sex) lest he should lose what little selfhood he has. He just wants to hold hands and munch popcorn.

We approve, I think, of Harry's determination to retain his innocence. There is a blissful assuredness to the life he leads that we certainly envy. Harry is a visual image for the notion that ignorance is bliss. We thus have an emotional stake in his ability to remain childlike in a predatory society. Rather than allow him to grow up, we would rather that the society be ordered with sufficient room for his innocent self. Clearly Capra as providential director had such an ordering in mind, and we understand that however hostile the immediate society may be towards Harry, the universe is governed by a beneficent Providence, one that will provide Harry with a sufficiently virginal helpmate in Mary Brown (note her connection with God via her position as the preacher's daughter).

If Harry's innocence is to remain unchanged, then something definite and drastic has to be done to reorder society. New York City is obviously too large and too far gone to change, so Providence arranges for Harry to get to Cloverdale, a small town still capable of protecting its small-town innocence. It is a place where Mary Browns can exist. The signs of this providential guidance are many. We know, for example, that God made that hill such that the road had to have a switchback so that Harry could roll down the hillside and descend with a stupendous crash right back into the Cloverdale-bound bus that he had been ejected from only a few moments earlier. But note also how appropriate it is that Harry should be brought to Cloverdale in the employ of boss McDivett. God moves in mysterious ways, and uses mysterious means. The octopus of self-indulgent immoral cynicism has spread its tentacles even into Cloverdale, drawn there by Cloverdale's innocence. But cynicism, like innocence, carries the seeds of its own destruction. McDivett is caught in a trap of his own making, surrounded by innocence without (Holy Joe *et al*) and assaulted by innocence from within (Harry).

This triumph of innocence over cynicism is not necessarily an easy one. It can happen in Cloverdale because Cloverdale is still under God's keeping (He seems to have given up on New York City). But

Harry returns to the Cloverdale bus.

here also we have a sexual threat, not directly to Harry, but to Mary Brown. McDivett (the local racketeer) makes it clear that he would like nothing better than to see Mary Brown as the star attraction in his Palace peep show (doing one of those crazy hula routines?). By so corrupting her innocence, he would get back at Holy Joe and his congregation, who continue to plague McDivett with their claims of morality. Were he to succeed in his plan to put Mary Brown on the bill, McDivett would succeed in depriving Harry of the guidance he needs to maintain his own potentially self-destructive innocence. McDivett is thus the dragon who threatens to violate Harry's dream princess, and by so doing McDivett threatens Harry's own innocent existence.

Here we should recall Richard Griffith's description of the typical Capra movie. It is, he says, a "fantasy of goodwill" in which "a messianic innocent, not unlike the classic simpletons of literature, pits himself against the forces of entrenched greed. His experience defeats him strategically, but his gallant integrity in the face of temptation calls forth the goodwill of the 'little people,' and through their combined protest, he triumphs."[4] Griffith tries to construct one sociological formulation that will encompass all of Capra's output. The films that most clearly approach this archetype are *The Strong Man* and *Mr. Smith Goes to Washington* (1939), but neither is, in fact, accurately described under Griffith's rubric. Harry is clearly not a social reformer. He never realizes the relationship between McDivett and Holy Joe. He never once betrays the slightest awareness that anything is wrong with the existence of the Palace bar, and he has no idea that his subsequent actions will lead to a reassertion of Sunday-school goodness. The final climactic fracas comes when a drunk insults Mary. Harry's brave (indeed, foolhardy) attempt to silence the ruffian is clearly a personal, not a political, act. Harry does not "pit himself against the forces of entrenched greed." He is rather unwittingly "pitted" by an overriding benevolent Providence against the forces of cynicism that threaten not only Harry's existence but Cloverdale's. Harry can perhaps be considered the answer to Holy Joe's prayers, but it is Providence that uses Harry, not Harry uniting in protest with the "little people." Indeed, the little people (except perhaps to the extent that they prayed) have nothing whatsoever to do with Harry's triumph: Harry single-handedly destroys the Palace. Only after the Palace has been leveled do the little people unite to chase the bad guys out of town. Similarly, Jefferson Smith does not triumph because of the support of the little people. His little people are either bought off or terrorized. Like Harry, Jefferson Smith experiences

Pitted against the forces of cynicism: Harry as providential agent.

a personal triumph of integrity, and Providence works the social miracle (with Jeff as a providential instrument), if a social miracle is worked at all.

Of course, the overall tone of *The Strong Man* is humorously lighthearted. Only on rare occasions do we sense the terror that accompanies Harry's innocence. We do not really doubt for a moment that Harry and Mary will be married and that the serenity of Cloverdale will return. God as a possibility occurs in all of Capra's movies (at least to the extent that God can be considered the very type of cosmic adequacy), but His presence is never more strongly felt than in *The Strong Man*. The strength of this presence is demanded by the weakness of the Langdon character. Capra much prefers his leading characters to be freer agents, more capable of handling things on their own, but when working with a character of Langdon's helplessness, Capra was forced to bring Providence into greater play if Harry's comic success was to be assured. Providence is thus Harry's real parent, and his search for Mary Brown is just God's way of putting him in the right place. Mary is obviously an agent of heaven, and for all of her blind optimism, she is guidance enough to see Harry through life in Cloverdale, where the largest threat to his selfhood is the stone he trips over in the street at the film's conclusion.

Perhaps more than subsequent Capra comedies, *The Strong Man* is a story that works "through to its own logical end."[5] Harry's helpless innocence separates him from the adult world of the spectator. We cannot see him as representing a real human being in the real world. We all certainly have our Harry-like moments, and the film clearly approves of innocence if it exists in a place like Cloverdale, but the film also recognizes that Cloverdales are few and far between. The meaning of the film resides not in any easily decoded social message, but rather in the kinds of deeply felt positive emotions it arouses. We are to approve of innocence, where we know that innocence can survive. We are to approve of integrity (Harry's innocence *is* a type of integrity). We are to approve of selflessness, for it is the selfless concern of Mary Brown that will keep Harry safe from harm. Most of all, we are to approve of the comic drive towards fulfillment that the film imagines, for that is a wish that we all share.

While *The Strong Man* generally endorses Harry's childishness, and does so in a comic structure that

Harry strikes a pose for Mary.

rewards Harry's integrity, *Long Pants* is concerned with demonstrating the folly of innocence gone berserk. It is the first and most definitive of the Capra romances (indeed, the film classifies itself in the opening sequence), demonstrating both the quest structure and antiromantic point that typify Capra's use of the romance form.

The structure of *Long Pants* has two major sections: (1) Harry at home, encountering Bebe, the dope-dealing vamp, his longing to leave Oakgrove, and his attempt to murder his fiancé, Priscilla; and (2) Harry in the city, Bebe's jail break, their trials with policemen, alligators, and gun-toting gangsters, Harry's brief episode in jail, and finally his return home. Capra's two major images, the home and the city, are thus set over and against each other, and the progress of Harry's adolescent wanderings from one milieu to the other serves to define the process of his maturation (although the limited emotional range open to Harry makes the leap in intelligence and maturity very small indeed, not large enough ever to take him fully into the realm of adulthood).

The nature of Harry's adolescent romanticism is clarified in the first of the two major sections. The furtiveness of the opening sequence, in which a set of disembodied hands surreptitiously takes books from the "romance" section of the library shelves, reflects both a terror of discovery and a childish love of the secretive. We then see Harry comfortably ensconced in his corner of the attic, pouring intently over his new cache of romantic literature (Byron's *Don Juan,* O'Neill's *Desire Under the Elms*). He pauses long enough to daydream (he sees himself as a romantic young prince who climbs the balcony of a gingerbread castle and kisses a princess), but he is aroused from his reverie by the sounds of laughter outside. He goes to the window, and sees a girl walking past. He whistles, meekly, to get her attention. She stops, and, apparently put out by the intrusion on her private thoughts, tells Harry that "little boys should be seen and not heard." Befuddled, Harry retreats into his garret.

Harry is obviously mortified by his failure as a lover. He wants to grow up, to grow out of the short pants that brand him as a "little boy." But he clearly sees growing up (*i.e.,* getting his long pants) exclusively in terms of his own romantic notions of sex. To grow up for Harry is to become the kind of dashing romantic prince that he was in his dream. He has no sense of adult responsibility or intelligence. The whirligig nature of Harry's romanticism is imaged in the ecstatic rings that Harry, the daredevil bicyclist, rides around the automobile of Bebe, his new-found heartthrob. For Harry to continue his romantic mode of perceiving the world means that he will continue to run around in circles (as he does, carrying Bebe around in a box) until he finally walks circles in a jail cell, betrayed by his own dreams. Harry has no real conception of life, and he therefore has no real conception of death. Hence, he can contemplate shooting Priscilla as a means of avoiding marriage. But note that killing her is, at least as he imagines it, a matter of heroic self-fulfillment. He stoically leaves her fairy-tale corpse lying in a luminescent fairy-tale heap, and there is no awareness of the reality of death. Harry is brought to that awareness in the shootout in the nightclub—when people are shot, they die, and they die horribly—and Harry is shocked into a more complete knowledge than his romantic conception would have permitted.

Harry's romantic daydream in *Long Pants*.

But it is ultimately Harry's innocence that saves him. He may get himself into the deepest trouble, and do so without realizing what is in store for him, but, as in *The Strong Man*, Providence clearly watches over him, and makes sure that, for all of the danger Harry faces, he will finally return home in answer to the prayers of Priscilla and Harry's parents. Evidence of Province's good work comes in the scene where Harry takes Priscilla out into the forest. Harry is to be wed to her that very afternoon, but the woman he loves, Bebe, the cocaine peddler, is in jail, and Harry cannot desert a damsel in distress. Harry thus has to scotch the wedding plans. At this point he could just run away (indeed, when all else fails he does run away). But he rather decides to disrupt the wedding by doing away with the bride. According to plan, then, Harry takes the unsuspecting Priscilla out into the woods to do the deed. The following comic sequence is one of the highlights of silent comedy.

Just before the ceremony, Harry appears at Priscilla's window, and asks her to take a "little walk in the woods." She is hesitant, though not alarmed, and she agrees to accompany Harry. Once they get among the trees Harry stops, points to something, and then attempts to walk away while Priscilla's attention is diverted. He tries this several times, and on each occasion she turns around before he gets far enough away. Finally she actually turns around and follows Harry, creeping along behind him as if

Whirligig romanticism: Harry rides circles around Bebe.

they were playing hide and seek. Harry is non-plussed, but he too hits upon the game gambit, and he tells her to hide her eyes and count. This time he finally gets far enough away, but he cannot get the gun out of his pocket. By the time he finally does fish the gun from his trousers, Priscilla, having finished counting, turns around, and Harry immediately drops the gun into a pile of leaves. He tells her once again to start counting (to five hundred this time) and he searches the leaves for the pistol. He comes up with a slightly pistollike piece of wood that has a rope tied to it, and just as Harry starts to aim this toy, a horse, tied to the other end of the rope, takes off running, sending Harry crashing to his leafy frustration once again.

Harry, determined to carry out his romantic mission, once again searches the leaves for the revolver, and he finally comes up with it. This time, however, he finds it nearly impossible to aim the weapon, and he is almost relieved when he looks up and sees a "no shooting" sign. He puts the gun in his pocket. Priscilla, in the meanwhile, picks up a horseshoe. Harry immediately takes it from her, thinking it will provide him with the luck necessary to complete his task, but, when he throws it over his shoulder, it rebounds off a tree and cracks him in the head, knocking him off his feet. Harry tries to get up after this latest indignity, but he earns only further frustration. He stands up under a low-hanging tree limb, jams his top hat down over his eyes,

In *Long Pants* at last: Harry before the wedding.

and falls once again. A second attempt to stand only bruises his crown once more and jams the top hat even tighter over his brow. While wandering around sightless, attempting to pull the hat from his head, Harry stumbles into a barbed-wire fence, and proceeds to painfully thrash about, getting more entangled with each effort to free himself. Finally, he manages to disengage himself from the wire, but he no sooner does than he steps into a bear trap. The bear trap is in turn secured by a chain to a nearby tree, and every time Harry attempts to pull his foot out of the trap, the tree comes crashing down upon his pate, knocking him once again to the forest floor. Harry finally sits forlornly on a log, until Priscilla comes to his rescue. Then she finds the gun, and she starts a joyous session of target

practice, shooting expertly at the newspaper she pins to a tree.

The point of this detailed description is not only to show that Harry is thwarted in every one of his many attempts to murder Priscilla, but to give an accurate impression of how completely frustrated Harry is by the time Priscilla releases him from the trap. For all of his effort, Harry just cannot do the murderous job. In fact it is the nature of Harry's romanticism that makes it impossible for him ever to carry out his purpose. It never occurs to Harry simply to pull the gun out and shoot her, no matter what she is doing or where she is looking. No, Harry has to do it just right, precisely after the fashion of the heroes he idolizes, and it is simply impossible for Harry to do it in that manner. Of course, that

The princely raiment Harry does not get.

impossibility is not so much Harry's fault as God's. That particular section of forest was obviously booby trapped so that Harry could never get around to pulling the trigger, even when he could find it. Harry is both an innocent and a romantic, and while the romanticism has to go, Harry's innocence must be protected. This is clearly what Capra had in mind, and we are to understand that Harry is basically good. God will therefore protect him, even from himself.

The second half of the film can best be seen as "the educating of Harry." He sets out on his romantic quest, and the romantic notions that were only dreams in the Oakgrove library are set against the reality of an urban, Sternbergian underworld. Instead of a towering, baroque castle, Harry gets a squat, granite prison, and warehouse-district back streets. Instead of riding a white charger, Harry carries a steamer crate. Instead of an imaginary dragon that falls before his knightly prowess, Harry gets a real-live alligator that is not the least bit concerned with Harry's knightly abilities. To the contrary, the alligator is not the vanquished but the vanquisher, and Harry is lucky to escape with but a few holes in his trousers. Instead of princely raiment and kingly revels, Harry gets stolen and oversized street clothes and crazy, nightclub chorines. Even the princess that Harry had set out to save turns out to be something other than what he had expected. To be sure, Harry seems, at first, quite oblivious to all of these disappointments, but this obliviousness does not last. The final climactic shoot-out brings home to Harry the danger he is facing.

Of course, it is the measure of Harry's innocence that he decides to leave Bebe even before the bullets start flying. Bebe comes back to the nightclub with Harry in tow, there to confront the singer (whose getup and deportment anticipate Dietrich's Lola Lola) who had turned Bebe in. The first indication of any unease on Harry's part comes as the two women exchange insults and accusations with very unladylike manners. Capra focuses on Harry's befuddled reaction to the spectacle, and provides a perfect visual image for Harry's disorientation. Harry had lifted his hat in polite greeting to the singer, and as the insults start Harry's hand seems to freeze in midair, with the hat still pointing in the direction of the singer. Harry's head, meanwhile, turns from side to side as he observes the women,

so that the vertical plane of Harry's head and the plane of his hat are out of line. The image is further developed when Harry's eyes start to move independently of his head, so that we get three confusingly different planes where we should have only one.

The extent of this confusion becomes clear after the catfight concludes. The singer has been vanquished, and she crawls out the door in an appropriately humble posture. Bebe then goes to get a drink (seen in long shot past Harry, who sits with his back towards us in the foreground). She then slinks hands-on-hips over to Harry, and sits down beside him, putting her arm around him as she does so. This is all too much for Harry. Confusion deepens to disbelief, and he gets up with a look of genuine shock and disappointment on his baby face. He tells Bebe, "I'm surprised . . . my goodness . . . I'm sorry, but we must part . . . I'm through." It is clear that Harry's romantic expectations were cruelly dashed in the fight. Ladies are supposed to be spectators at titanic conflicts, not participants in them. The confusion that first beset Harry when the

Hell hath no fury; and Harry's in the middle.

women started to trade insults is thus cleared up when they begin to trade blows. Any illusion that Bebe was a princess is thus dispelled, and Harry rightly decides to have nothing more to do with her.

But Harry cannot decide to leave just like that. His lesson is only partially learned. Now he knows that Bebe is not the heroine he thought she was, but he is, as yet, ignorant of the real danger involved in mistaking a dope dealer for a princess. The danger is, of course, death, and death inflicted specifically by gunshot, as Bebe and the singer's boyfriend shoot it out. This realistic awareness serves to balance the romanticism of Harry's attempt to kill Priscilla. He could do that because he did not know what death really meant, and God therefore shows him what death means so that Harry will never contemplate such romantically destructive stunts again. Harry learns his dreadful lesson. The terrified expression on his face as he sits between the corpses is eloquent testimony to the import and power of the lesson learned. Harry just sits there, frozen in time and space, while crowds run in and out of the room. Harry pays no attention. He just stares at the camera.

Harry thus gets his appropriate comeuppance. He learns that his romanticism can be dangerous, both for himself and for others, and should be avoided in favor of more realistic aspirations. The film concludes with Harry's release from jail (which, I might add, is left unexplained, as if God had just stepped in and ordered it), and his return home. The home becomes a symbol of major importance to the pattern of Capra's concerns, and, as in later films, the home here stands for a realistic and comic awareness that the small-town opportunities offer personal reward enough to satisfy basic human longings. Harry is not asked to give up love and marriage, because both are obviously waiting for him in Oakgrove. He is required, rather, to give up overly romantic and therefore unrealizable dreams of love and marriage, which only serve to destroy the values to be found in small-town good-neighborliness. Harry obviously belongs in Oakgrove with Priscilla (or in Cloverdale with Mary), and any attempt to leave bespeaks an immaturity that verges on insanity. Indeed, Harry's leaving does eventually find him in an almost comatose stupor, and hence we can understand his quiet joy at getting back to Oakgrove.

We can now see how the symmetry of the film, imposed by Capra, serves to create the meaning of the film, likewise imposed by Capra. The first half of the film begins with Harry sneaking into the library, and then into his attic. It concludes with Harry's attempt to murder Priscilla. The second half of the film repeats very much the same pattern. Instead of walking into the woods and encountering horseshoes and bear traps, Harry walks into the city to encounter alligators and policemen. The second part also concludes with a shoot-out scene, and the film ends where it began, with Harry sneaking back into the house. The thing to note, then, is the way a particular action in one half comments on a similar action in the other half. For example, Harry's furtiveness in part one, in which he seeks to avoid discovery, plays off against his furtiveness in part two, where he invites discovery. Similarly, Harry's trip to the city, where romanticism is seen for what it really is, a mask for decadence and self-indulgence, is contrasted to Harry's trip to the woods, where romanticism escapes unscathed, even if Harry does not. Neither trip is to be approved of, at least not in terms of Harry's motives, but we understand the moral utility of the second journey: it serves to undercut the romanticism that serves to motivate Harry in both cases.

Long Pants, then, like *The Strong Man*, is concerned with making life safe for the child-man Harry. The major difference between the two films is in the form the concern takes. *The Strong Man* is a comedy that senses the rightness of Harry's innocence (because his innocence never becomes dangerous to anyone but Harry himself) and works to change the hostile environment (*i.e.*, get the McDivett gang out of Cloverdale) so that Harry can exist in peace. *Long Pants*, on the other hand, is a romance that understands the dangers inherent in romanticism, (which we can define in Harry's case as innocence carried too far into the realms of sexual experience), and works to change the romanticism into something approaching maturity. The environment in *Long Pants* is sufficient (Oakgrove is not enslaved by city cynics), and hence it is the character that must be brought into line.

Both films are thus clearly the product of Capra's creative intelligence. They exhibit themes, concerns, and images that Capra was to explore throughout his career. They demonstrate the two major forms

The innocent gesture: Harry Langdon as the archetypal child.

that Capra's subsequent films would take (comedy and romance). Seen from the directorial point of view of an auteur critic, then, *The Strong Man* and *Long Pants* fit very comfortably into the Capra canon. Nevertheless, as film historians, concerned with understanding the dynamics of commercial success as well as the dynamics of creativity, we are free to conclude that Langdon played an immeasurably important part in creating the films we have been discussing. Langdon gave Capra a great comic talent to work with. He provided Capra with a set of character limitations that demanded cinematic ingenuity. He provided Capra with an icon of innocence that Capra could set against the symbols of worldly experience. But the element that made *The Strong Man* and *Long Pants* aesthetic as well as commercial successes was the unity of purpose and design imposed by Capra, a unity that seems to have eluded Langdon when he directed his own films.

NOTES

1. James Agee, "Comedy's Greatest Era," *Life,* 4 Sept. 1949: 70-88. Other orthodox film historians are Kalton C. Lahue and Samuel Gill, *Clown Princes and Court Jesters* (South Brunswick and New York: A. S. Barnes and Company, Inc., 1970), pp. 196-206; and Donald W. McCaffrey, *Four Great Comedians* (South Brunswick and New York: A. S. Barnes and Company, Inc., 1968).

2. Frank Capra, "Baby Face," *The Name Above the Title* (New York: MacMillian, 1971), pp. 57-80.

3. Richard Leary, "Capra & Langdon," *Film Comment* 8, no. 4 (1972): 15-7. Other critics who question the accepted view of the Capra/Langdon collaboration are Raymond Durgnat, "I Was a Middle-Aged Water-Baby," *The Crazy Mirror* (New York: Horizon Press, 1969), pp. 89-92; and Elliott Stein, "Capra Counts His Oscars," *Sight and Sound* 41, no. 3 (1972): 162-4.

4. Richard Griffith and Paul Rotha, *The Film Till Now* (1930; revised and enlarged 1949 and 1960, Middlesex: The Hamlyn Publishing Group), p. 452.

5. Northrop Frye, *A Natural Perspective* (New York: Harcourt, Brace & World, 1965), p. 47.

8

The Bitter Tea of General Yen

The Bitter Tea of General Yen (1933) seems at first the exception to every Capra rule. Capra does not like suicide, yet General Yen's suicide is treated with grace and respect. Capra does not like bigshots, yet the film's hero is a ruthless mandarin general. Capra does not like artificiality, yet artifice becomes a major theme. Above all, Capra does not like unhappy endings, and yet *Bitter Tea* has the unhappiest of all Capra endings. Even the visual texture of the film seems strangely Sternbergian, not at all the bright and sunny style we usually associate with Capra. But all of these surface exceptions only serve to reinforce a deeper Capra rule, and hence we can best understand *The Bitter Tea of General Yen* not as an out-and-out departure from Capra's main line of development, but rather as being the most hardheadedly realistic of all the Capra romances.

The collision of romance and realism is presented as a clash of personalities and cultures. Megan Davis (Barbara Stanwyck) is a romantic Capra do-gooder, a missionary from the finest old Puritan family in New England come to China to tame bandit generals and to rescue orphaned children. The bandit general she eventually sets out to tame and convert is none other than the notorious General Yen himself (Nils Asther): a pragmatic, suave, cynical war lord who envies those whom he kills. "Human life is the cheapest thing in China," we are told, and, after running over Megan's rickshaw boy, Yen answers her frantic assertion that the boy

might be dying by saying "He is fortunate. Life at its best is hardly endurable."[1]

What we have, then, is the typical Capra pairing of the romantic innocent and the defensive cynic. But unlike the romanticism of Frisky Pierce in *Dirigible* (1931), Megan Davis's romanticism at least has human concerns at its center. Her problem is that she is woefully unequipped to deal with the people she wants to help. Likewise, the cynicism of Yen is not simply an emotional pose, as is usually the case in Capra, but rather an almost stoical philosophy. Nothing in the film does anything to contradict the fact that "human life is the cheapest thing in China." As Yen tells Megan later, it is better to shoot prisoners, letting them die quickly, than it is to let them starve slowly and painfully because of a general famine. We may or may not agree with Yen's cold-blooded pragmatism here, but the point is that Capra places Yen in a universe where such a conclusion is not without foundation. The movement of the film, then, will be to temper the extremism of both Megan and Yen, and the tempering agent is love; but it does so against a social backdrop of foreign oppression and civil war that never really questions the basis for Yen's cynicism.

The romantic dream destroyed in the film is thus Megan's missionary zeal. The racial contradictions inherent in her big-brother philosophy overwhelm her, and she is forced to admit to love on Yen's terms. Yen, on the other hand, is not forced to give up his dreams of conquest: he chooses, rather, to

The Sternbergian style in *The Bitter Tea of General Yen*, featuring Barbara Stanwyck and Nils Asther.

conquer a strange and beautiful missionary than an overpopulated and strife-swept China. But "conquer" is not the right word here. Yen is a rare individual, sensitive and intelligent, and Megan is right to love him. Yen, like other inspired Capra fools, knows the risk he runs in granting Megan's request to spare Mah-Li (Toshia Mori), and he willingly runs it. He is destroyed by that decision (Mah-Li betrays him to the enemy) and ennobled by it, for while he loses his province and his life, he gains the love, freely given, of Megan Davis. That she loves Yen on Yen's terms is only to love him that much more. So, like Antony and Cleopatra, Yen and Megan Davis abjure a world not worth keeping for a love that seems to defy time.

Capra's approach to the racial issue in *Bitter Tea* is both humanitarian and hardheaded. He does not load the East/West opposition any more than necessary to get the point across that the missionaries, despite their perhaps admirable goals, are constitutionally unable to accept the Chinese as Chinese, rather than as potential converts.

Missionary racism at its worst is seen in the Jackson house, where Megan's wedding to Dr. Strike (Gavin Gordon) is to take place. She arrives after the incident with the rickshaw boy, and goes immediately upstairs to prepare for the ceremony. Mrs. Jackson's crass reference to marriage as "the slaughter," when real slaughter and suffering are going on literally at her own doorstep, is jarring. "What kind of humanitarian is this?" we wonder, and we quickly find out. As Mrs. Jackson (Clara Blandick) helps her get dressed, Megan questions her about the strange combination of brutality and

Yen (Nils Asther) invites a reluctant Megan (Barbara Stanwyck) to dine as Mah-Li (Toshia Mori) looks on.

civility that she observed in Yen (although Megan did not know who he was at the time). Mrs. Jackson replies: "Don't be fooled about his looking civilized. They are all tricky, treacherous, and immoral. I can't tell one from the other. They're all Chinamen to me."

A more flattering picture of the self-aware missionary is presented slightly earlier in the Jackson parlor. The Bishop, a China missionary for fifty years, says that he pities Megan for the hardships she will have to face in "dedicating herself to the service of mankind in China," and he goes on to relate his experience in preaching to Mongolian tribesmen.

Only last month I learned a terrible lesson. I was telling the story of the crucifixion to some Mongolian tribesmen. Finally I thought that I had touched their hearts. They crept closer to my little platform, their eyes burning with the wonder of their attention. Mongolian bandits, mind you, listening spellbound. But alas, I had misinterpreted their interest in the story. The next caravan of merchants that crossed the Gobi desert was captured by them and . . . crucified. That, my friends, is China.

One perceives in the Bishop's speech an uneasy sense of futility, as if he realized how out of place his teachings were, how incapable he was of making the Chinese feel the necessity of Christian salvation. His motives are honorable, he is compassionate where Mrs. Jackson is not, but his missionary hybris is still there, the underlying assumption that the Chinese are insufficiently human and that missionaries are there to fill the morality gap. Capra thus makes clear the limitations and false expectations of missionary evangelism. As the Bishop himself tells us, the China missionaries are only "a lot of persistent ants trying to move a great mountain."

The relation of romantic expectations to sex, religion, and racism is clearly set forth in Megan's movement from one lover to another. Dr. Strike, her childhood sweetheart and fiancé, is a romantic missionary, like herself, who postpones their long-awaited wedding to go save some stranded orphans. She gladly goes along, and, in the confusion of the muddled rescue attempt, gets separated from Strike and is herself subsequently rescued by Yen. Strike's willingness to put off the wedding is strange. Doubtless another of the many missionaries present at the Jackson house could have taken care of the orphans.

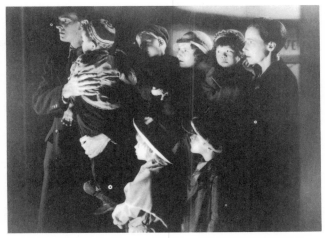

Saving orphans: Dr. Strike (Gavin Gordon) and Megan Davis (Barbara Stanwyck).

Yen gives Strike the phony safe-conduct pass as Jones (Walter Connolly) looks on.

Strike thus demonstrates a curious sense of self-importance and sexual repression, as if he were the only one who could rescue the children. In any case, before Strike can carry out his rescue mission, he first must go to Yen for a safe-conduct pass through the lines. Yen is understandably incredulous to learn that Strike left his own wedding to save the orphans (who are, after all, "people without ancestors"). Yen cannot give him a pass without divulging his own illegal presence in Shanghai, so that the document he finally does give Strike reads as follows: "This fool prefers civil war to the loving arms of his bride—General Nobody." The pass (written in Chinese characters that Strike does not understand) is, of course, useless, and the end result of it is that Yen will give up his civil war and, indeed, his life for a single moment in those same loving arms. Thus Yen and the sensual opulence that surrounds him stand as exact opposites to Strike and the sensual negligence characteristic of his sexually repressive missionary mind.

Megan is thus caught in the middle, between the sexual martyrdom of life with Dr. Strike and the timeless elegance of life with General Yen. Her sexual choice, one man or the other, is hence a racial and cultural choice as well, and the film's most striking sequence is an extraordinary dream that reveals both Megan's deep, sexual desire and her racial disgust for Yen.

Megan has just refused for the third and last time to dine with General Yen, and she walks out onto the balcony and sits down so that she overlooks a willow garden and stream. Soldiers and women are pairing off in various corners of the garden. The moon is full and casts a hazy light through delicate clouds. Megan falls asleep in her ornate wicker chair while watching these sexual goings-on, and, as she drifts off, we see a full shot of her bedroom door superimposed on a closeup of her face. Both images dissolve in a wave effect, and the dream proper begins.

Megan cowers on her bed while someone batters her bedroom door down with a rifle butt. As the door disintegrates, we get a closeup of the intruder. It is a grotesquely madeup General Yen, a Hollywood version of the dirty, lecherous Oriental; greasy hair, eyes at a bizarre slant, pointed ears, fingernails that curve inches away from the fingertips, his body cloaked in a loose-fitting, androgynous, black silk robe. The normal image of Yen in his general's uniform is briefly superimposed (as Megan's subconscious mind makes the connection), and then we get an almost Buñuelian medium closeup of Megan on the bed, shot from the waist of the intruder, so that the curved fingernails curl around the edge of the picture, all pointing to and framing the frantic Megan, as if she were caught in the web of some diabolical insect.

The Oriental demon is then about to ravish his prey, hulking over Megan on the bed, pressing her into the mattress, caressing her breasts with his elongated thumbs, when in comes the white knight to the rescue. Through the balcony window leaps a man in Western dress: white pants, white fedora, white shirt, black tie and jacket, and a black Lone Ranger mask across his eyes. The rapist turns on the knight, and raises his long dagger to strike. The weaponless hero cracks him a right to the jaw. The intruder slides to the opposite side of the room, as if he were falling downward, and he disappears as he makes contact with the wall.

At this Megan reaches up and takes her savior in her arms. He removes his white hat. She gently caresses his face and removes the mask from his eyes. Her Occidental savior is a smiling and very humanized (yet clearly Oriental) General Yen. In ecstasy, she slowly pulls him down on top of her. Then we cut to a closeup of Megan, with the background whirling around behind her, the visual expression of subconscious disorientation. We cut back to Yen and Megan on the bed, the image dissolving into a closeup of Megan asleep in the wicker chair. She awakes with a very disturbed look on her face, as if she were, herself, aware of the dream's implications. She looks out at the soldiers and the women in the garden, and then her head turns to the right as she hears someone speak behind her. It is Yen, in full Mandarin regalia, not the pure black suit of the dream, but an ornately decorated royal robe, and wearing a bejeweled cap with an ostrich plume in the crown.

The dream thus reveals Megan's desire to love Yen, and the racist terms in which she wishes to express that love. She wants his Western gallantry without his Eastern barbarity. But, as Megan learns, there is no "Western" gallantry that can be easily separated from Yen's "Oriental" callousness, because Yen's real sensitivity and civility are a matter

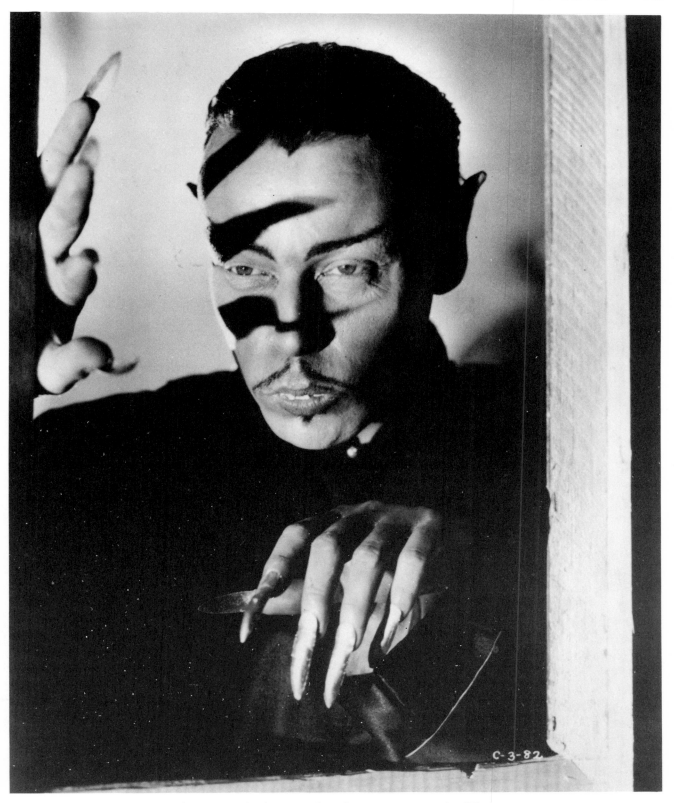

The Oriental demon: the dream sequence in *Bitter Tea.*

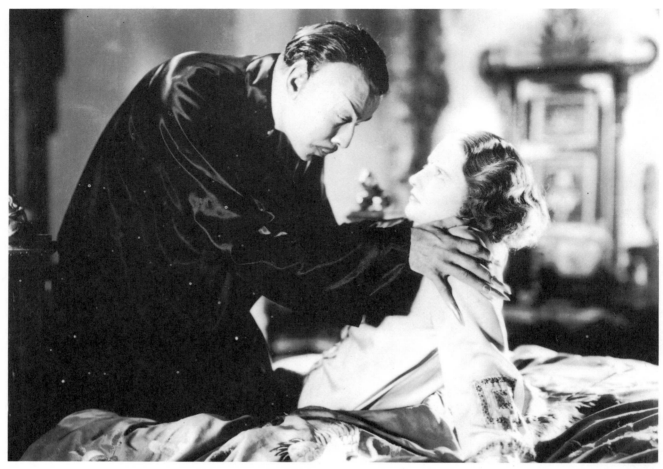

The demon and his prey.

of his Easternness. It is the racist in Megan that assumes that good qualities are by definition "Western" and that bad qualities are by definition "Oriental." She has to learn to accept Yen for what he is, and not try to remake him into what she thinks he ought to be. She has to face the facts of her own racism, realize that her naive missionary assumptions are completely out of tune with the facts of the brutal universe she inhabits, and only then can she devote herself completely to the one thing that really matters in her life, her love for the Chinese warlord.

The romanticism that is destroyed, then, is a missionary sense of moral absolutes that provides all answers to all questions, and that gives those in possession of "truth" the moral right and imperative to spread the word and damn as subhuman (as Mrs. Jackson does) those who reject it. This is replaced by the realistic existentialism of Yen, who realizes that power is what counts, power both to create and to destroy. Yen's moral development is hence along this creation/destruction axis. At the film's beginning Yen is concerned primarily with destruction, and his "they are better off dead" attitude towards rickshaw boys and captives presents no moral obstacle to his actions. His downfall comes when he decides, for once, not to kill somebody, and allows Mah-Li to live. His final act, killing himself, seems at first another destructive act, but seen in the context of the film's concern with artifice, it is in fact the final creative act.

In Yen's bitter universe the only human value is created value, the value of beautiful objects and emotions, which are, by the nature of their rarity and fragility, precious. Yen sees his relationship with Megan as being a created object, a thing fragile and, in worldly terms, transitory. Even sex is seen as a form of artifice. The film's visual dimension has presented the question of artificiality continually, if unobstrusively, throughout the film. The ornate summer palace with all of its rich appointments and *objets d'art* is contrasted with the burning cities of the film's first section. It is a created garden of tranquility in the midst of chaos, and its artificial nature, and the relationship of nature and sex to artifice, are both made clear in the scene following Megan's dream.

Yen tells her that it is the season of the "cherry-blossom moon," a time when "young and old, rich and poor, sick and sound, pay their homage to the god of love." Megan gets upset (doubtless at the suggestion that she too may be thinking of love) and demands to know when she will be released.

Yen promises to return her to Shanghai, but only when it is safe to do so. In the meantime, he offers to make her stay as pleasant as possible, and expresses the hope that they can improve their acquaintance. She doubts she could become familiar with a man who "ruthlessly slaughters helpless prisoners in one mood and, in the next, shows such a tender reverence for the beauty of the moon." Yen rightly points out that her absolutist attitude is that of a "true missionary." Men are either all good or all evil, she thinks, and she cannot imagine any degree of moral complexity beyond the simple either/or dichotomy. Yen knows that she believes the Chinese incapable of love, and asks her:

Have you ever read our poetry, Miss Davis? Do you understand our music? Have you ever seen our paint-

After the dream: Megan and Yen, with the willow garden in the background.

ings, of women walking among fruit trees, where the fruit trees look like women, and the women look like fruit trees? There has never been a people more purely artists, and therefore more purely lovers than the Chinese.

This is shot past Yen to a medium closeup of Megan, and she gets progressively more upset as Yen becomes more eloquent. She insists that Yen leave. He does so, but expresses the hope that she will accept his third invitation and join him at dinner. As he walks away she cannot help glancing back at him over her shoulder, almost despite herself.

During this conversation we get occasional shots of the moon over the willow garden, but something new has been added to the scene. We have not one delicate moon, but several, and the additional moons are Chinese lanterns. The whole package of nature, artifice, and sexuality thus comes together. To be a lover is to be a poet, and the poet creates an artificial beauty that is identical with natural beauty, because beauty, in the universe of General Yen, is simply not natural. Women may look like fruit trees, and fruit trees like women, but they do so only in a painting. Even the "natural" willow garden looks like a painting, and in fact it is, for the harmony of mote, trees, and lanterns is an artificial one, created by architects and Oriental gardeners.

Megan subsequently decides to go down to dinner, ostensibly to meet another American at the palace, Jones (Walter Connolly), the General's financial advisor, and to try again to persuade Yen to release her. Her first thought, however, having once made the decision to dine with Yen, is for her appearance, and she complains about her dress. Mah-Li offers to take care of her dress for her, and we get a busy sequence of servants bringing in a bathtub, water vessels, several Oriental gowns (Megan chooses a luxuriously bejeweled one), and finally an ornately carved makeup box, which Mah-Li opens, telling Megan, "I see you are in need of powder and paint." Megan replies "perhaps I am," as if painting were the most natural thing in the world for her to do, and she sits down before the box. We get medium closeups of her applying makeup, full shots of her admiring her dress, and a superimposed image from the dream in which Yen takes her in his arms. Immediately after this dream image, however, Megan looks at herself with dis-

gust, as if she realized the sexual motivation for "powder and paint." She then wipes the makeup off, and changes back into her plain, Western garb.

Megan is thus drawn to Yen and everything that he respresents. But she still clings to her missionary sense of the absolute, and her missionary superego catches her each time she is tempted to surrender to the gracious artificiality of Yen and his summer palace. But Capra is as evenhanded with Megan as he is with most of the other missionaries, and she can cling to her ideals as long as she does because they still have a ring of truth to them. Capra allows Megan the full expression of her creed, and permits her to confront Yen and his ideals directly.

At dinner Yen learns of Mah-Li's treachery and determines to have her life. Megan finds this out finally (she does not pick it up at dinner: Mah-Li has to tell her directly), and goes immediately to Yen to protest. She finds him in his bedroom, and pleads in the name of Christian mercy for Mah-Li's life:

Can't you forgive her? She's only a child. You can always do so much more with mercy than you can with murder. Why don't you give her another chance? Oh, I know you feel that she has deceived you, and sold information to your enemies, perhaps even been unfaithful to you. All that's dreadful. And if it's true you have a certain justification in wanting to crush her. But I want you to think of all those things, and then forgive her. I don't know how you feel about Mah-Li . . . I mean, whether you love her . . . well . . . as a lover, but that's of no importance. I want

After dinner: Mah-Li, Megan, Yen, and Jones.

you to see the beauty of giving love where it isn't merited. Any man can give love where he's sure it's returned. That isn't love at all. But to give love with no thought of merit, no thought of return, no thought of gratitude even, that's ordinarily the privilege of God, and now it's your privilege. Oh General, with all you have within you, your superior brain, your culture, how can you be so blind to spiritual greatness? Do this thing I ask you. Do it for me. Do it even blindly if you must, and I promise you . . . I'm so sure of it . . . I promise you that for the first time in your life you'll know what real happiness is. You'll know that I . . . (she breaks off weeping).

Even Yen, who has only scorn for missionaries, is moved by her sincerity here. Were this speech in any other Capra film we would recognize it as being close to Capra's own brand of Catholicism, and representing, even as it does to some extent here, his own view of the place of mercy in the world. But this is not another Capra film; it is, rather, the one Capra film that takes place in an amoral universe. Even in films like *Mr. Smith* (1939) and *Meet John Doe* (1941), where the evil potential in mankind is presented with striking cinematic and emotional force, there is always the sense that the universe is benevolent, even if the populace is not. You can always go back to your boys' camp or retreat to a roadside motel with the assurance that being the right kind of person will enlist Providence on your side. In *The Bitter Tea of General Yen* this sense of benevolence seems largely missing. It is as if Capra had decided to experiment: "what would the world be like without an active providence?" And he answers that it would not be very pleasant.

All of which is not to say that Capra is not sincere in *Bitter Tea*. It is simply that the "worst of all possible worlds" that has always been a potential in most Capra films is permitted to become a reality in this one. Capra does not let this bleak universe get too close to home, keeping it in a far-away setting with strange characters unlike his familiar "little people," but the fact remains that Capra clearly felt some deep emotional affinity with Yen and Megan, and the measure of that affinity is the almost ruthless honesty with which he undermines Megan's simple-minded, missionary brand of Christianity.

Thus Megan's speech, however sincere, is undercut and colored by two facts: (1) her sexual feelings toward Yen, and (2) what we already know about missionaries. The sexual overtones in Megan's speech are made more clear by the visuals. The scene is Yen's bedroom, both Yen and Megan are wearing nightclothes (Megan's robe is very silky and sensual), and as she becomes more impassioned Megan moves closer to Yen, almost as if to embrace him. She is subconsciously aware of all this. The only time she really breaks stride in her almost too perfect speech is the one time she has to deal with sex (*i.e.,* Mah-Li's relationship with Yen). Megan then reaches an almost sexual climax of missionary zeal, and she breaks off weeping, unable to control her emotions. Her final unfinished sentence is, "You'll know that I . . . " and we know that the concluding phrase would be "I love you." If Yen grants her request in the terms of Christian mercy wherein she wants him to grant it, he will have become the kind of person she could openly love. But of course, Yen does not grant it in the terms she wants it. He pardons Mah-Li not to demonstrate Christian mercy, but to demonstrate how foolish Megan is to ask mercy for Mah-Li. He lets Mah-Li go on the condition that Megan become responsible for her loyalty. Thus should Mah-Li break her vow of obedience, Megan is to answer to Yen.

Yen is playing with a loaded deck in all this. He knows that Mah-Li will betray him again (as she in fact does), and he knows that Megan will remain missionary enough to honor her word (thus becoming another martyr for Christendom). But, as we discover, Yen does not really want her love on those terms either. He grants Megan's request primarily to demonstrate the falseness, not necessarily of her ideals *per se*, but of her unrealistic attitude towards those ideals. Neither mercy nor Christianity is attacked for itself. Rather, the film is concerned to show how people can be disastrously simpleminded about such ideals, applying them indiscriminately in every case without attending to the reality of the immediate everchanging situation. It is not a simple world and simplistic idealism has little place in it. As Yen tells Jones, he is "going to convert a missionary," and what he converts her to is his own self-aware brand of sensitive existentialism.

As expected, Mah-Li does betray Yen: his treasure train is stolen, his troops desert him, and he is left alone in the empty palace, with only Megan and Jones for company. Megan discovers that all of her blithe assumptions about Mah-Li's goodness were

Megan comes to plead for Mah-Li.

false, and she goes to Yen to pay what she thinks will be the forfeit of her honor. But Yen does not want that. The dialogue at this encounter is important and worth quoting in full (we get the typical Capra cutting, from full shots, to medium shots, to closeups as the emotional and dramatic intensity build):

> YEN: You didn't think I meant a conventional thing, did you? Did you think that General Yen could accept anything that the heart did not freely give? Oh no. That opportunity has been open to me ever since you came here. It was your life you put up as a forefeit for Mah-Li's loyalty.
> MEGAN: My life?
> YEN: Yes, what else did you think I meant? (She stands up, almost backing away from Yen.) I see. You are afraid of death as you are afraid of life. You want me to send you back to your Dr. Strike.

He speaks the same meaningless words as you do. He has everything you want. You would like to be able to boast to him that the great General Yen, whom everybody feared, was destroyed because he was fool enough to hope. Well, why don't you go? Go on to him.

> MEGAN: You've taught me a terrible lesson.
> YEN: Yes, but to be able to do good works one has to have wisdom. You depend too much on your beauty, and also on the fact that you are so young, young and pale as a lotus blossom which blooms at night. Oh torture, real torture is to be despised of someone you love. Bargain or no bargain (embraces her), province or no province. Do you know what I expected to do tonight? I was coming to your room to kill you, and then follow you to some celestial garden, where there is no General Yen and no Megan Davis, just you and I. (She turns and runs away: profile closeup on Yen.)

Megan runs back to her room. She takes up the

Megan arrives to pay forfeit for Mah-Li's treachery.

bejeweled gown that Mah-Li had given her, opens the makeup box, and changes from her Western dress into Oriental attire. She weeps as she applies the powder and paint. Intercut are scenes of Yen slowly and silently preparing, in a calmly deliberate, almost ritualistic fashion, the "bitter tea" for his suicide. But before Yen can lift the cup to his lips, Megan reappears, not as a missionary, but as a "young and pale" lotus blossom, a woman from a Chinese painting. She silently puts a pillow behind Yen's back, spreads a blanket across his legs, and kneels weeping at his feet. As she presses herself against him she says, "I had to come back. I couldn't leave. I'll never leave you." Yen pulls out a silk handkerchief to dry her tears, says almost absentmindedly "silk, China gave the world silk," and slowly drinks his bitter tea.

The emotional integrity of this sequence is so overpowering that one hesitates to break it up, even in describing it. The full weight of the film's imagery is felt immediately, and the pure aesthetic beauty of the scene is overwhelming. But pretty pictures just for pretty pictures' sake is not the point. Pretty pictures mean something in this film, and the celestial garden that Yen talks about exists, if only for a moment, in the picture of Yen and Megan together. The one perfect, precious moment of artifice arrives, and Yen leaves the world a richer man than ever Jones could have made him.

But given Yen's suicide, we could argue *The Bitter Tea of General Yen* as tragedy rather than as romance, in the same way that most critics see *Antony and Cleopatra* as tragedy. But in neither work do we get a real sense of tragic loss. Tragic heroes normally give all that they have to give, and find it somehow lacking. Oedipus gives the people of

The celestial garden: Yen and Megan together.

Thebes all that his great integrity commands, and while he does in fact alleviate the immediate problem of the plague (and hence succeeds in social terms), he clearly loses in personal terms. His assumptions about his place in the universe (*i.e.,* as the son of Polybus and as *tyrannos* of Thebes) prove false, and for this metaphysical blindness he suffers physical blindness and exile. Yen, on the other hand, is proved false in nothing. He is in tune with his own brutal universe, and his death is a matter of clear choice, not metaphysical necessity. He trades his province for one moment of perfect tranquility, and that moment is worth every province and treasure trove he could ever have accumulated.

But in another sense Yen does not die at all, and hence the whole matter of loss becomes of little importance. Capra's usual benevolent Providence,

which is suppressed throughout the film, seems almost to reassert itself in the final moments. It is not the active Providence that saved Jeff Smith, but rather a passive private benevolence, which maintains a celestial summer palace for those like Yen and Megan who manage to achieve even a brief moment of felicity on earth, as if happiness once achieved becomes of its very artificial nature eternal.

Yen, of course, suggests this notion of timeless happiness in his final moments, but it is reinforced in the film's final scene, when an inebriated Jones and a now stoically serene Megan are on the boat back to Shanghai. Jones rambles on drunkenly about the events of the past week.

I bet your week in China seems like a lifetime. Well, maybe it is at that. Yen once told me . . . Yen's dead ain't he . . . great guy. I don't think you'll marry Strike. I got a hunch you're going back to America. Yen once told me you could crowd a lifetime into an hour. Yah, into a drink. Great guy . . . great gambler . . . told me he couldn't lose. The joke was certainly on him (closeup on Megan). He lost his province, his army, his life. Maybe not. Maybe the joke's on us (back to medium closeup of Megan and Jones). Maybe you will marry Strike at that. Yen was crazy. He said we never really die. We only change. He was nuts about cherry trees. Maybe he's a cherry tree now. Maybe he's the wind that's pushing that sail. Maybe he's the wind that's playing around your hair. Ah, it's all a lot of hooey. I'm drunk. Just the same, I hope when I cool off the guy that changes me sends me where Yen is. And I bet (closeup on Megan) I'll find you there too.

The camera tracks in slowly during this speech from full shot to medium closeup on both Jones and Megan. There are but three cuts, and the general tone is one of achieved tranquility. We are of course free like Jones to say that Yen's belief in immortality is "a lot of hooey." But the presentation of the scene seems to counteract Jones's litany of "maybe" with a sense of transcendent assurance. Even Jones comes to believe in Providence, despite himself.

The primary devices for establishing this sense of certainty are background music and skillful acting. Capra is, as usual, sparing in his use of background music. Most of the music in the film is made by people in the story, so that there is a "naturalistic" explanation for its presence. Truly expressionistic background music, however, is used primarily as a matter of extraordinary emphasis on mood and emotion. We hear this kind of music during Megan's dream sequences for example. But the music we are concerned with here is the theme that begins when Jones says that Yen was "nuts about cherry trees."

The theme itself is a hauntingly melodic combination of Western string and Oriental flute sounds, calm, lyrical, and ethereal. It is heard first when Megan comes to Yen's bedroom to pay the forfeit for Mah-Li's treason. Yen acts the gracious host, offering Megan a glass of brandy and putting a record on the phonograph while he explains the fact that Chinese portraits are painted only after the death of the subject. The record he plays is Yen's theme (as we might term it), and here its presence can be naturalistically explained.

The second time we hear the theme is just before Yen's suicide. Megan has changed into her Oriental robe, and as she returns, standing in the doorway of Yen's study, the music starts again. As in the first instance, the theme is associated with death and sexuality, but here it is clearly an artificial and expressionistic device, the aural expression of the love that joins Megan and Yen. Thus, while the music itself is "unreal," it serves to embody emotions that are clearly present and actual.

The final occurrence of the theme is the last scene of the film. Jones's suggestion that Yen might be in the wind that plays about Megan's hair, and her clear-eyed and straightforward expression, coupled with the presence of the music, clearly validates the feeling that Yen is somehow present. Megan surely believes he is there, and Stanwyck conveys that certainty by maintaining a Garbo-like inscrutability of demeanor (*Bitter Tea*—1933, predates *Queen Christina*—1933). Stanwyck's face is a wonderfully expressive blank that is filled in, Kuleshov-fashion, by the context of the scene. Jones believes that Yen is present, the music reinforces our sense of that presence, and the culminating closeup on Megan's face serves to underline the emotional reality of Yen's being. The music no longer has a naturalistic explanation, but the supernatural equation that binds Yen and Megan together in love has, as its product, this ethereal theme. Where the music exists, Yen and Megan exist, and the borders between the real and the unreal, the natural and the supernatural, are transcended by the emotional purity of love tempered by worldly brutality.

Artificial beauty thus overrides and encompasses mundane reality. Megan's original romanticism, out of tune with the verities of worldly existence, is destroyed and replaced by an existential romanticism that encloses and goes beyond her initial, limited moral viewpoint. Value is too fragile and precious and complex to be codified as a set of moral absolutes. Value is created moment by moment by committed individuals. And on rare occasions, when created value approaches perfect artifice, harmonious, elegant, deeply felt, we find that Providence still exists as a spiritual reality, endorsing human action when human action does justice to the existential complexity of the universe, and rewarding right-acting individuals with a spiritual existence transcending time and space.

Strife-swept China: no place for emotional honesty.

The primary difference between *The Bitter Tea of General Yen* and the rest of the Capra canon is thus a matter of setting. Yen's world not only looks different, but it is different. Yen and Megan are typical Capra characters, overcoming romantic barriers and finding personal fulfillment in the emotional integrity of love freely given, but the physical world has no place for their kind of emotional honesty. There is no Mandrake Falls to retreat to, and the only way Yen can preserve their love is to take it beyond the physical universe, into the providential realm of artifice and immortality. Capra never returned to this kind of universe, though he came close in *Meet John Doe* (1941) and *It's A Wonderful Life* (1946), and we can only speculate that Capra needed a strong scriptwriter like Edward Paramore before he could fully brave the terrors of this Sternbergian cosmos. World War II raised similar issues of social and emotional brutality (note that *Meet John Doe* and *Wonderful Life* bracket the war), but Capra never again initiated this exact set of concerns with the same precise directness.

NOTES

[1.] All references are directly to the dialogue in the film.

9

It Happened One Night

It Happened One Night (1934) is today generally acknowledged as Capra's most important film, if only for its influence on the subsequent history of Hollywood comedy. It was the first and most definitive of the "screwball comedies," sophisticated mixtures of folksy wit and urbane cynicism depicting the intellectual battle of the sexes. But *It Happened One Night* was not the first (nor would it be the last) of Capra's films to demonstrate these qualities of humor and intelligence. It was, rather, the one that brought these comic qualities to their most perfect fruition. Its public reception and its continuing reputation as a film masterpiece attest to this perfection. Repeated viewings of the film only reinforce the impression that not a single millimeter of film was wasted. Everything serves Capra's comic purpose, and as a comedy, *It Happened One Night* is an achievement of the highest order.

Critics were slow to acknowledge this achievement at first, and even when they jumped aboard the bandwagon of popular acclaim, they were hard-pressed to explain its popularity. The best of these early critics, William Troy, saw the film in the picaresque tradition of Fielding and Cervantes, and to the extent that he thus places the movie in the tradition of literary comedy, he comes closer than any other critic to understanding the dynamic of the film's appeal.[1]

Sociologically minded critics even today generally tend to acknowledge the film's greatness, and then to pass quickly over it to get at more clearly

The picaresque tradition: Clark Gable and Claudette Colbert on the road in *It Happened One Night*.

"significant" films (*i.e.*, those that lend themselves to a "relevant" social reading). But the significance of comedy, as we have noted, is sexual before it is moral (in that comic morality is a function of sexuality), and moral before it is political (in that comic politics is a function of comic morals). *It Happened One Night* is clearly one Capra comedy that generally steers clear of political considerations, and it can successfully do so because politics is no prerequisite for comic success. *It Happened One Night* is a moral fable very similar in its concerns to earlier Capra films. The measure of its success is

Capra's ability to fit the comic form perfectly to the issues at hand, and to have the issues at hand completely fill the comic form.

It Happened One Night's most immediate ancestors are *Platinum Blonde* (1931) and *Ladies of Leisure.* (1930). From *Platinum Blonde* Capra took the comic triangle of rich girl/poor girl/reporter. But here Ellie Andrews (Claudette Colbert) plays both female roles simultaneously, and hence the complication of her character (which we will discuss presently). This complication of the female role requires a corresponding complication of the male counterpart, so that Clark Gable's Peter Warne, while cut from the same cynical cloth as *Platinum Blonde*'s Stew Smith, is yet even more contradictory and defensive. Stew's moral confusion is symbolized by his contradictory preceptions of two indeed contrary women, but Peter's confusion results from his contradictory preceptions of one woman, who simply refuses, for the most part, to fit the comfortable stereotypes he assigns to her.

It is this relation of stereotypes to selfhood (and the various possible confusions of the two) that Capra first seriously explored in *Ladies of Leisure*. In that film, Barbara Stanwyck plays a "lady of leisure," Kay Arnold, who maintains a self-deprecating yet aggressive stance towards herself and reality. She is a "gold digger" who does not want to be a gold digger, so that she despises both herself and the kind of people (mostly rich playboys) who are attracted to her. The crisis of the film comes when Jerry Strong, a rich playboy tired of being a rich playboy, falls in love with her and starts treating her like the kind of person she wants to be rather than the person she thinks she is. Kay decides, after much *Sturm und Drang,* that Jerry (who loves her) is obviously much too good for her (since she is just a gold digger) and she attempts suicide. She is saved, convinced of her own self-worth in the process, and she and Jerry live happily ever after. The concern of the film, then, is to convince both Jerry and Kay that love transcends and transforms false stereotypes: she is not a gold digger and he is not a playboy. They are rather comic lovers who belong under the stars in Arizona (stars are a major image in both *Ladies of Leisure* and *It Happened One Night*) far away from the penthouse-pleasure-palaces of New York City.

In *It Happened One Night* Capra again concerns

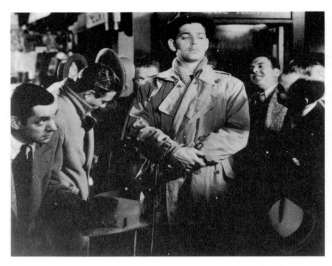

Clark Gable as Peter Warne, a reporter tired of reporting.

himself with such issues as self-assertion and self-respect. Peter Warne is a reporter tired of being just a reporter. He is a poet at heart, searching for the kind of emotionally involving story that he eventually finds himself caught up in. He is fired from the paper because he submits his copy in blank verse (although we should assume that blank verse is the one poetic straw among many that broke the editor's back). Peter is no fool, however, and he needs the story to win his job back: even poets have to eat. But he needs the story for emotional as well as financial reasons. Even if he remains just an uninvolved outsider, the story of the rich girl and the aviator is romantic enough to engage his sympathy.

Like Stew Smith, then, Peter Warne is a romantic posing as a cynic. He has been "sucker enough to make plans" before, has been hurt, and has withdrawn into cynicism for self-protection, convinced that the world can never match up to his romantic expectations. Here we see the difference between Peter and his predecessor in *Platinum Blonde*. Stew's cynicism is simply a part of his reporter's persona: we never know the reason for it, and we do not need to know, because his cynicism is not really an issue. If anything, he is all too willing to become romantically attached, and in his eagerness he attaches himself to the wrong woman. But cynicism and its origins and consequences in love are the central issues in *It Happened One Night*. Peter has allowed his own extremist brand of romanticism to betray his emotions and to alienate him from himself. He has been deserted by one woman, and he assumes that any woman who shows an interest in him will likewise abandon him. He therefore assigns the "spoiled brat" label to Ellie as a means of distancing himself from her. She is only a story to him.

But Ellie becomes much more than just a story, and indeed she is more than just the spoiled brat that Peter assumes her to be. She is a complex human being whose vulnerability is the result of a cynical brand of categorization very much like Peter's. Like Peter, Ellie's father (Walter Connolly) makes extreme assumptions about her personality. Where Peter sees her as a spoiled brat, her father sees her as a defenseless princess. In both cases the expecta-

tions are self-fulfilling prophesies. Treating her like a spoiled brat tends to make her act like one. Treating her like a defenseless princess only invites attack by false knights like King Westley (Jameson Thomas). The film is concerned, then, to break this cycle of false expectations and destructive consequences. Peter must learn that Ellie is not a spoiled brat, but a human being of deep emotional integrity. Likewise, her father has to learn that she is not defenseless, but that she is, given the chance, capable of making her own decisions and fighting her own battles. All of this is complicated by the fact, however, that Ellie is herself, at first, only dimly aware of her own personality. She too has to discover what emotional integrity is and what it

Claudette Colbert as Ellen Andrews: a spoiled brat or a fragile princess? Her father, Alexander Andrews (Walter Connolly) has the question on his face.

demands. She too must not only discover her ability to fight, but develop as well the intelligence to recognize the enemy when she sees it.

As I noted earlier, *It Happened One Night* repeats the comic triangle of rich girl/poor girl/ reporter from *Platinum Blonde*. The complication of Ellie's character is evidenced by the fact that she plays both female roles simultaneously. She is at once the spoiled brat who blithely assumes she can have anything she wants, whether it be a chocolate bar or an aviator, and at the same time she is a plumber's daughter who dreams of eloping with her dashing prince and fleeing the clutches of the evil dragon. As we might predict, it is the plumber's daughter in Ellie that we seem most attracted to. Her qualities of humor and exuberance can only find expression on the road, away from her city mansions and yachts. But the fact remains that we cannot draw any absolute lines between one persona and the other. When Ellie rightly gives the hungry boy their last dollar, it is the rich girl who does it. Capra does not romanticize money in the film (even the stargazing Peter Warne needs money before he can propose), and he knows that poor people do not have money to give away like that. We tend to overlook this complication in Ellie's personality. Being rich allows Ellie to be self-assertive in a way that Capra admires. We make the same mistake of simplification and categorization that Peter, Andrews (Ellie's father), and finally Ellie herself commit when we assume that Ellie-as-poor-girl is the actual heroine, when it is actually Ellie-as-Ellie who convinces us of her own worth. It is this tendency to oversimplify, to assume that reality will match one's own misguided expectations, that is the major villain in the film. Extremists never come off well in Capra, and the film shows how such extremely simplistic assumptions are out of tune with the facts of existence. People are too complex to be easily categorized, and the comic movement of the film demonstrates how one goes about getting past categories to people, shedding false assumptions, and moving on to support renewed relationships.

The basic plot of *It Happened One Night* is fairly uncomplicated. Ellie, recently married to King Westley, is caught by her father before the marriage is consummated. Ellie flees her father at first opportunity and takes the bus to New York City to join her aviator husband. Peter, a fellow bus pas-

senger, recognizes her, and agrees to get her to New York undiscovered in return for her exclusive story. Peter and Ellie fall in love. Mistakes of judgment and timing, however, jeopardize their relationship, and it is only when Ellie learns the truth at the last moment that she flees King Westley and the remarriage ceremony to join Peter in the autocamp.

The propelling force behind this slight plot, the one that lends the film its vitality, is "recognition." On the surface level of the intrigue plot, it is vital that Ellie *not* be recognized. She has to get to New York undiscovered, if only to spite her father and his sleuths. On the deeper comic level, however, it is vital for both Ellie and Peter that they do come to truly recognize themselves and each other, so that the vitality evident in their relationship can be fostered rather than destroyed.

The process of the film, then, is one of education (much is explicitly made of Peter's role as professor). Peter and Ellie learn about selfhood and about each other, and they learn to go beyond the false stereotypes that obstruct such self discovery. Every incident in the film serves to define and reveal character. Even the gags, however improvisational some of them might be, are designed to tell us something about the characters involved. Of course, there is a discrepancy of awareness between ourselves as viewers and Peter and Ellie as characters: we can see both sides of the wall of Jericho, while each of them can see only what occurs on his own respective side. We are thus aware of their mistakes before they are, and we can understand, even if they cannot, that their difficulties arise literally from mistaken identities.

What we get, then, is a *Comedy of Errors* structure in which sterotypes are mistaken for individuals. Just as Shakespeare's characters must discover themselves anew before the play is resolved, so must Capra's characters come to a renewed awareness of selfhood before the film concludes. And just as Shakespeare's characters almost always find themselves in marriage, so must Peter and Ellie come to understand that proper self-perception can best be obtained within the context of the openness and vulnerability of marriage. Hence the process of learning is likewise a process of loving. The "walls of Jericho" are thus both perceptual and sexual barriers that must be made to fall.

The progress of the love between Peter and Ellie is described and its nature is defined in three successive "bedroom scenes."

The first is the justly famous initial autocamp scene about walls, stripping, doughnuts, Westley, and brains. Peter has just unilaterally "married" Ellie to stem the chatterbox patter of Shapely (she tries to thank Peter, but he says he did it for himself: "his voice gets on my nerves").[2] A bridge ahead of the bus is washed out by the heavy rains, and the passengers are forced to seek shelter in a nearby autocamp. Ellie waits at the camp office while Peter dickers with the manager. Peter finally yells at her to come out of the rain and as she passes by the manager on her way to the cottage he says, "hope you and your husband rest comfortable." Taken aback by this, Ellie turns this way and that, indecisively looking first at the cabin and then back at the office, and finally seeks refuge in the cottage, persuaded by the rain and Peter's further summons.

The lengthy conversation between Peter and Ellie that follows is alive with the kind of sexual wit characteristic of "manners" comedy. The idea of seduction underlies everything that is said. Ellie assumes that Peter is another Shapely, a bit more sophisticated perhaps ("clever, these Armenians"), but after the same thing. Peter is likewise aware of the possibilities inherent in the situation, and his fast talking is, like the string and blanket wall of Jericho, an attempt to forestall any sexual interest. He wants to get to bed and to sleep as quickly as possible before

Peter's strip routine.

anything can happen. He thus uses the threat of sex (his strip routine) to prevent sex (by making Ellie run for her modesty). But the very level of the wit, the earnestness behind the frivolity, betrays the very real attraction between the two of them. The nonchalant manner in which he tells her that they are registered as Mr. and Mrs., as if it were of no sexual consequence, only reveals how consequential it really is. When she replies "What am I expected to do—leap for joy?" he says "I kind of half expected you to thank me," which is curious in light of his previous unwillingness to accept her thanks after saving her from Shapely. He wants Ellie to like him, and yet he does not want to like her too much himself. She is, after all, "just a headline."

And it is not just the wit that carries the sexual connotation of the scene. The physical situation, *i.e.,* beds in a motel room, is obviously sexual enough as is, but Capra reinforces this sexuality through the use of Joseph Walker's diffuse back lighting that lends a very sensual quality to the image itself. Once Peter has turned the lights out, the only illumination is moonlight through the windows. And these windows do more than just let in moonlight: they are awash with rain. The water that slides down the glass panes serves as both a filter that lends much of the iridescence to the lighting and as a symbol of sexuality. It is as if the water were caressing the earth and the cabin and the window, and by so doing it urges a sympathetic flow of affection in Peter and Ellie.

So to this point in the scene we have learned

Seeking shelter in the autocamp.

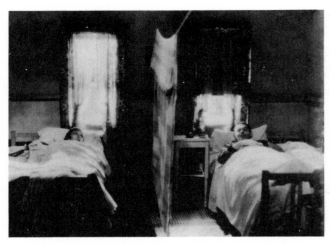

The Walls of Jericho: *It Happened One Night.*

several important facts. We know that both Peter and Ellie are thinking about sex (recall his disturbed reaction to the lingerie Ellie slings over the wall). We know that Peter is not and never will be a Shapely. He clearly respects Ellie's integrity as a sexual being. His reluctance to get emotionally involved in no way precludes the kind of physical relationship that Shapely proposes (although Shapely is clearly bluffing: he is too much of a family man to go past the patter stage). Given the fact that Peter is attracted to Ellie, it is to his credit that he does not think of forcing himself on her. He may be thinking of getting involved, surely, and he fears what that may bring; but there is no thought of physical involvement without emotional commitment. Thus for all of Peter's cynicism, his reluctance to give way to his emotions, we know that his basic notion of love is a proper one. His problem is not a matter of not knowing how to love, but rather of not being willing to love knowing the emotional risk necessary. Ellie senses this honesty on Peter's part (he is obviously unlike other newspapermen she has met), and she knows that however much he needs her for copy fodder, he will never betray her integrity as a feeling human being (no matter how stuck-up or snobbish he thinks she may be). Of course, Ellie cannot come right out and say that she trusts him, but saying, "Pleased to meet you, Mr. Warne," particularly the way she says it, carries much the same meaning.

After a brief glimpse of the frantic Andrews urging his pilot to give the plane more gas, the autocamp scene continues as we see Ellie awaking at the sound of an airplane (presumably her father's) overhead. A good night's sleep has certainly improved Ellie's disposition (and it has also eliminated for the moment any worry about sex). Ellie's bright mood is matched by the flood of sunlight through the windows, but Peter still seems exasperated, more than being in a simple hurry would require. The only time he slows up his patter is when he comments upon how little Ellie is and how cute she is with her hair mussed. The delight he takes in telling her that the "showers and things" are outside is a further revelation of his defensive stance. He is starting to treat her like a spoiled brat so that he will not have to deal with her as a real woman. But this only indicates his growing interest in Ellie. He even gets slightly jealous when he sees her talking to Shapely outside.

When Ellie returns from the "showers and things," we get the famous doughnut scene. And the thing to note here is not primarily that Ellie does not know how to dunk doughnuts, although that is not unimportant, but that Peter uses the doughnut ploy as a means of changing the subject. Peter would like to think that he is the poor man teaching the rich young thing how to live (and doughnut dunking is, with piggyback riding, one of the primary activities of life), but he is in fact avoiding the issue that Ellie represents. In a few moments of conversation it becomes clear that (1) Ellie is not the kind of spoiled brat that Peter thinks she is. She is, rather, a bird in a gilded cage who has finally had the courage to escape (even if she has not really learned all there is to know about flying). As she tells Peter, "People who are spoiled are accustomed to having their own way. I never have. On the contrary, I've always been told what to do and how to do it and when and with whom." We also learn that (2) Peter refuses to acknowledge the truth of Ellie's assertion. He insists on playing the teacher role himself, and refuses to learn anything from Ellie lest he become involved with her. And we can understand why he works so hard at ignoring her. It is because he does not really ignore her at all. He realizes that she is, like himself, a bird "that cries in the night," one that longs to escape the tedium of existence in a run-around world, one that longs to fly to far-away places. This only strengthens the attraction between them, and Peter

The doughnut scene.

has to work all that much harder to keep her at arm's length.

Peter's reluctance to learn in this scene (and in the film in general) is matched by Ellie's eagerness to learn. Once she decides that Peter is not going to victimize her she readily gets into the spirit of the trip. She is glad to learn how to dunk doughnuts. She enjoys going to the end of the washroom line where she is free to stick out her tongue. She enjoys singing crazy songs on the bus. She enjoys being thrown on the floor when the bus runs off the road. In general, she enjoys being an ordinary human being. If she was once the center of her own universe, she was trapped by her own satellites. She much prefers her liberty as one free being among many, capable of aligning herself with whomever she

chooses rather than with the trolls and ogres her father chooses for her.

Ellie's ability to learn quickly when necessary is also evidenced in this first bedroom scene. Immediately after Ellie tells Peter that she would "change places with a plumber's daughter any day," her father's detectives show up (reason enough to want to be somebody else's daughter). Ellie is at first flustered, but as soon as Peter sits her down and starts to muss up her hair and clothes she gets the idea, and in the subsequent domestic quarrel she almost outperforms Peter himself. She has wanted to be a plumber's daughter, and given the chance, she is pretty good at playing the role. But note that it is Peter who gives her the role to play: he is the auteur of the scene. He is doubtless correct to push

Make-believe marriage in *It Happened One Night*.

the conversation into a quarrel and thus put the detectives on the defensive, but we nevertheless understand the appropriateness of the scene as it develops to the real concerns of the actors who play it. Peter would surely like to be Ellie's "protector," but he fears that she would turn out to be a coy flirt who attracts big Swedes. Ellie, likewise, would like to be protected by Peter, but she fears that he will be heavy-handed and oppressive, like her father, and her temper tantrum here as the plumber's daughter is a parody of the original quarrel with her father at the film's beginning. Peter is rightly impressed with her abilities ("Got a brain, haven't you"), and he playfully suggests that they start a "two-people stock company." He has let his defenses down momentarily, but when Ellie suggests that they do "Cinderella, or a real hot love story"

Peter nixes it as "too mushy." That is precisely the kind of story he would like to play the lead in, but, for all of his desire, he fears it as well. Nevertheless, the better he gets to know Ellie, the more he lets his desire overcome his fear. His next telegram to the editor describes the story as getting "hotter and hotter," and, in the context of the immediately preceding scene, we understand that "hot" refers to the "Cinderella quotient," the degree of Peter's emotional involvement with Ellie.

Further evidence of Peter's growing attachment to Ellie comes in the second bedroom scene in the hay field. As Ellie tells him, he has become "terribly disagreeable lately," and the more disagreeable he becomes, the more he reveals his concern for her. He obviously cares whether she sleeps comfortably or not (note the care with which he makes her bed of straw) and he obviously cares whether she is hungry (he goes to get the carrots). His anger when his ability as provider is questioned only reveals how much he really longs to be her lifelong protector. Ellie simultaneously learns to depend on Peter, as it becomes clearer to her that Peter is indeed an acceptable bodyguard, one who, unlike her father's hirelings, cares for her emotional as well as her physical well-being.

The change in Peter's feelings toward Ellie is measured both by word and deed. Peter now calls himself a "prize sucker" for "taking a married woman back to her husband," a task that should be perfectly normal, except that Peter is now attracted to the woman and would rather she never got back to her husband. And to a great extent, Ellie now shares the same desire. She no longer wants to go back to King Westley. Her telling Peter that he "can leave anytime" only indicates how much she does not want him to leave. Lest there should be any doubt in the matter, she gets hysterical the moment that she perceives he is gone. She may be all alone in the woods, but the intense nature of her reaction indicates more than simple fear of the dark. There are farmhouses in sight, and we already know that she is courageous enough to flee her father and swim from the yacht to the shoreline. She is actually afraid that she will lose Peter, and while she is not yet ready to throw herself into his arms without a pretext, she clearly wishes he would find some excuse to take her in his. The atmosphere is clearly charged with the same kind of sexual energy that

A production still of the "haystack" scene.

we saw in the first bedroom scene. We have the same kind of lunar back lighting, and the rain of the first scene is replaced by dew on the haystacks. Even the setting itself, a newly mowed field, suggests plenitude and fertility. Peter and Ellie are both clearly aware of this sexual potential, and when Peter comes over to cover her with his topcoat, there is no question that they both wish that King Westley and New York and Alexander Andrews would disappear altogether so that the two of them could start all over again right there in the haystacks. Peter once again resists temptation, but nothing can contradict the growing strength of their attraction for each other. Peter's faraway gaze into the misty distance and Ellie's single, glistening tear evidence their mutal desire to succumb to the temptation of love.

Their mutual desire becomes an open secret in the next bedroom scene. Ellie insists that they stay at an autocamp for the night, even if they are less than three hours from New York. "Who ever heard of getting in at three o'clock in the morning," she says, playing the spoiled-brat role. But she clearly plays the role in order to spend one more night with Peter (she knows that her father has publicly agreed to abide by her marriage with Westley). Peter, apparently obtuse about her ruse, seems lost in his own thoughts, which revolve not around the fact that they have one more night together, but that tomorrow Ellie will be back in her husband's arms. The urgent repartee of the first bedroom scene is replaced with long moments of silence broken by occasional labored one-liners. Only when the wall is again raised, and they have both gone to their separate beds, do they open up to directly confront the issue of love.

Ellie sits tensely on the edge of her bed, unable to relax or lie down. She nervously rubs her arm as she tells Peter he "could make some girl wonderfully happy." Peter admits that he has thought of love, but he cynically insists that the right kind of girl ("somebody that's real—somebody that's alive") can never be found ("They don't come that way any more"). Throughout Peter's ensuing speech we get shots of Ellie as she reacts to both the hope and hopelessness of Peter's dream paradise. The visual setup is just the reverse of the first bedroom scene. Now Peter is in the bed screen left and Ellie in the bed screen right. The movement of the

scene is similarly reversed, to reveal love rather than conceal it. Where most of the first bedroom scene was concerned with the fear of sex, this scene is concerned with the desire for love. Peter's speech is worth quoting in full (it begins on a closeup on Peter):

> I've even been sucker enough to make plans. You know, I saw an island in the Pacific once. Never been able to forget it. That's where I would like to take her (MC on Ellie). But she'd have to be the sort of a girl who . . . well . . . who would jump in the surf with me, and love it as much as I did (MC on Peter). You know, nights when you and the moon and the water all become one (MC on Ellie), and you feel that you're a part of something big and marvelous. That's the only place to live. Where the stars are so close over your head you feel you could reach up and stir them around (MC on Peter). Certainly I've been thinking about it. Boy, if I could ever find a girl who's hungry for those things (cut to MC on Ellie as she comes around the blanket to his bedside).

There is a musical and poetic quality about Peter's speech that makes it stand out from the rest of the film. The film's imagery of moonlight and water and stars and sexuality comes to the resonant diapason of sensual longing. The editing serves not only to reveal Ellie's reaction to Peter's vision of paradise, but to specify her rightful place in that vision. It becomes clear by the sequence of cuts that Ellie is the "her" that Peter should take to his island. She is the woman that Peter should "become one" with. She is the one who should be stirring those stars with him. She realizes that she loves him, and that her place is with Peter and not with Westley. She tells him so, momentarily breaching the wall of Jericho, and thus she reveals herself as a fellow dreamer and lover.

Yet this breach in the wall does not last long. True, Ellie has made her commitment. What had been unspoken is now a matter of open emotional fact. But Peter's immediate reaction is to squelch emotion, and he sends her back to her side of the wall. She is still a married woman, and Peter's first thought is for that obstructing reality. But his thoughts do not stop there. He knows he is faced with a choice between risk and certainty. He can either accept the vulnerability that love requires, and hope for the emotional rewards love can bring; or he can rely on the certainty of Ellie's legal re-

Resisting temptation in *It Happened One Night*.

lationship with King Westley. If he takes her back to her husband, and never sees her again, he cannot be hurt any more than he already has been. He makes his choice: he will take the risk and follow the romantic yellow brick road. He whispers through the wall, asking her if she really meant what she said, would she really go with him? She is asleep and does not answer. Peter does not let her being asleep stop him, however. But note how he decides to handle the occasion. Rather than waking her and telling her what the situation is, he decides to play prince charming, riding off in the night to bring the talisman back before daybreak so that he can awaken his princess with a triumphant kiss. The result of this decision is near-disaster, as it leads to a complicated series of errors and false assumptions that almost destroy the newfound and newly recog-

nized love between Peter and Ellie. Once again Peter is too romantic for his own good. The remainder of the film works, on a plot level, to reunite the lovers, and thematically to demonstrate the necessity for honesty and realism in love rather than the folly of secrecy and romanticism.

When you ask for trouble in Capra you usually get it, and Peter gets more trouble than he bargains for (although one suspects he is realist enough not to be greatly surprised when reality steps in to thwart his romantic schemes). Ellie does in fact wake up before Peter's return (and while she is forcibly awakened, that in no way revokes the possibility that she could have awakened of her own accord for any number of reasons, or that Peter might easily have been prevented from returning on time no matter how soundly she slept). Believing

Ellie despairs and calls her father.

that she has been abandoned, Ellie despairs and calls her father. Papa, King Westley, and a full complement of motorcycle police then come to pick her up. In the meantime Peter sells his story for the money he thinks he needs to accompany his proposal. But his sexual elation (he tells the secretary that "all women are beautiful") is ironically undermined as we realize that the very source of his jubilation has been cut off: Ellie has gone back to King Westley. She has made what is in fact a false assumption as to Peter's motives and actions, and on the basis of this error she climbs back aboard the endless and pointless social merry-go-round represented by King Westley and his crew.

Thus, at the very moment when Peter thinks to tear down those walls of Jericho, another wall, the freight train at the crossing, draws away to reveal that the walls of Jericho no longer have meaning. He sees Ellie leaning on King Westley's shoulder, looking coldly and pointlessly at the back of the front seat, and once again Peter's dream is shattered (or so he thinks). He now assumes that Ellie has "taken him for a buggy ride" (as he tells her father later). He now has proof positive that Ellie in particular and women in general cannot be trusted: they will use you and desert you every time.

This too is a matter of mistaken identity. Peter does not recognize that Ellie's cold mask of indifference is not "natural," as he thinks it is, but is, instead, unnatural, bespeaking a sense of sterile hopelessness. Ellie is ready to remarry King Westley in a lavish public ceremony just for the sake of getting married: "It doesn't matter how, or where, or with whom," she says. But it does matter. We know (as Peter knows, even if he will not admit it to himself) that Ellie is "alive" and "real" (to use Peter's own terms), a women of deep emotion and commitment and honesty. Peter lets his renewed cynicism completely cancel out the knowledge he has so laboriously gained. The consequence of this error is comic disaster. If Peter is allowed to continue in his ignorance, the comedy will end with the marriage of Ellie and King Westley, a false marriage that represents aimlessness, indifference, self-indulgence, and pettiness rather than a true marriage representing comic rejuvenation, fertility, and community.

To this point I have said little about the danger represented by King Westley. He is largely a stick

Looking suave and slightly greasy: King Westley (Jameson Thomas).

figure whose primary job is to look suave and slightly greasy. But he is, despite his infrequent presence, an important symbol. He is the false bird that Ellie tried to fly away with. He is a headliner and fortune hunter (he is easily bought off), who never seems to fly anywhere. When Ellie tells her father that she has chosen to go through with the marriage to King, despite the fact that she loves someone else, she tells him she does it for the sake of stability: "I'm tired, father, I'm tired of running around in circles. He's right, that's what I have been doing ever since I can remember." But we know that she is mistaken here. Marrying King Westley and his whirligig autogyro will only continue the circularity of her existence. King Westley thus serves to embody the spirit of the "three-ring circus" (as Peter describes it) that characterizes the self-indulgent social milieu that Ellie has been trying to escape.

The proper way for Ellie to escape is, of course, to marry Peter, to wed the "whipperwill who calls in the night" and fly to that Pacific island that Peter talked about (or at least to a cozy autocamp away from the craziness of the big city). What stands in the way is, as I noted earlier, the cynical tendency to extreme oversimplification (which is an easy sin to commit, given false information). Peter assumes that Ellie is a self-concerned heartbreaker who uses men for emotional kicks but then drops them when kicks verge on commitments. She rides her merry-go-round and cannot stop for anyone. This is clearly

Ellie at the center of her cynical merry-go-round.

a false evaluation, but for those involved it is convincing. Ellie clearly accepts this image of herself. Peter is right, she thinks. She is a spoiled brat and hence he was right to leave her when he did. She feels herself of no consequence as a human being, and thus it is of no consequence whom she marries. Like Kay Arnold in *Ladies of Leisure,* she assumes that she is no good, and that Peter is therefore much too good for her. To be sure, when she discovers that Peter wants to talk finances with her father, she changes her opinion of Peter: he becomes another fortune hunter like King Westley, but that in no way changes her very low evaluation of her own self-worth. We thus have two mistaken identities to straighten out: (1) Peter's picture of Ellie, that she in fact shares; and (2) Ellie's picture of Peter.

Getting things straightened out is deceptively simple, relying, as it does, on Peter's haphazard last-second decision to see Andrews at the Andrews mansion. Once that decision is made, however, the rest follows fairly easily. Peter and Ellie have already done the real work of learning to know each other, and all that need be done is to demonstrate the falsity of their cynical extremist assumptions.

Ellie's hitherto ogrelike father is the one who orchestrates this demonstration. Andrews is another in a long line of rich, cigar-smoking Capra fathers. And like many of his Capra kindred, he is capable of comic rejuvenation. We know that for all of his mistakes, he genuinely loves his daughter. The horrified look on his face when he slaps Ellie in the opening sequence attests to this concern. He is disgusted with his own behavior. His whole demeanor during the search is not one of a father concerned with maintaining any sort of family image (as was the father in *That Certain Thing*—1928), but rather that of a father sincerely worried about his daughter's safety and happiness. He is, after all, correct to label Westley a fake from the beginning, and it is to his credit that he stagemanages Ellie's escape at the end. But note that instead of telling her what to do, he asks her. It is her choice whether she goes through with the marriage. Andrews provides her with the option.

He can give her this option, because, unlike Ellie and Peter, he knows what both of them want. Peter thinks that Ellie wants King Westley, and Ellie thinks that Peter wants the reward. But Andrews knows that they want each other, and once he finds out he does what he can to bring them together. He makes Peter admit (to himself) that he loves Ellie. He makes Ellie conscious of Westley's essential silliness. Note, however, that his extremist mode of command is gone: he tells neither lover what to do or how to do it. Rather, he gives them information, understands them well enough to allow them their freedom (he does not raise any objection during the wedding ceremony), and he is enough of a comedian to know that freedom is all they need. We never do find out how Ellie finds Peter after fleeing the wedding, but it does not really matter. She is resourceful enough to find him once she sets her mind to it.

The film then concludes with one final bedroom scene. The walls of Jericho finally fall at the blast of a child's toy trumpet (heralding children to come?), and the emotional energy heretofore devoted to avoiding sex is released in a celebration of comic fertility (even Andrews celebrates, if only by long distance telephone). At long last the barriers of cynicism, false perception, and false information are completely overcome, and we rightly share the joy of the event. The thing to remember, however, is not this final burst of good feeling, but the manifold dangers that stood in the path of this comic *kômos*. Critics who condemn the film as a "pretty indefensible affair" that takes place in a "social and economic vacuum" are quick to point out what they consider the escapist nature of this conclusion.[3] But the point to make is that Capra escapes nothing. He makes us acutely aware of the pitfalls that are found on the road of everyday emotional existence. He did not need the added baggage of Depression social issues to make us aware of life's dangerous possibilities. Life is dangerous enough as is. People are more than capable of crippling themselves without the aid of economic chaos.

Even so, the film is not without its social comment. But it is a sort of social comment that can be easily overlooked by those unfamiliar with comic conventions. *It Happened One Night* varies significantly from those conventions in two important regards. To begin with, the pattern of the comic journey is usually that of escape and return (*e.g., Midsummer Night's Dream, As You Like It*), leaving untenable circumstances long enough to gain self-awareness and self-respect that can then be brought back to help rejuvenate the original society. Secondly, once that return takes place, the comedy normally concludes with a social festivity, a dance or wedding feast. Note, then, that Peter and Ellie do not return to society, they leave it; and their celebration is not social, but private. Ellie, in fact, flees a classic full-dress wedding ceremony because it clearly represents a stifling sort of fake festivity, a caricature, a solemn dedication to social sterility rather than social health. The usual Capra implication is clear: the society of the rich is beyond rejuvenation and is to be avoided whenever possible. Only a rare man like Alexander Andrews can be wealthy and humane at the same time. King Westley is the norm, the personification of fortune-hunting foolishness, and it is his very sort of self-indulgence that the film can be said to attack. Such an attack is oblique, and not very pointed (*i.e.,* it lumps most of the rich together under one heading), and yet it is more of an attack than most of his critics give Capra credit for. But such social satire is clearly not the heart of *It Happened One Night,* which deals, for the most part, with more lasting problems of emotional interaction and integrity. Such personal issues are the dialectical substance of the Shakespearean sort of comedy, and *It Happened One Night* is clearly a masterpiece of comic emotional realism. For those who would have it otherwise, there is probably no answer; but for those who are capable of looking past ideology to humanity, the film is richly mature, complex, and rewarding.

NOTES

1. William Troy, "Picaresque," *The Nation,* 14 March 1934: 314.

The full-dress wedding ceremony in *It Happened One Night*.

2. All references are directly to the dialogue in the film. A script for *It Happened One Night* is readily available [see *Twenty Best Film Plays,* edited by John Gassner and Dudley Nichols (New York: Crown, 1943), pp. 1-59] but it differs greatly from the finished movie.

3. Robert Stebbins (pen name of Sidney Meyers), "Mr. Capra Goes to Town," *New Theatre, May* 1936, rpt. in *American Film Criticism,* edited by Stanley Kauffmann (New York: Liveright, 1972), pp. 334-5.

10

Mr. Deeds Goes to Town

As Stephen Handzo points out, *Mr. Deeds Goes to Town* (1936) "continues to dominate discussion of the films synonymous with Capra's name."[1] It is a deceptively simple film, and many previous critical misunderstandings of the movie in specific and of Capra in general can be traced to this deceptive simplicity: it is fairly clear, after all, who the villains and heroes are. Few, for example, have questioned the status of Longfellow Deeds as Capra's populist spokesman and all-around rural St. George. But while we are ultimately correct to see Deeds as representing the sort of properly oriented and motivated personalism that Capra usually approves, he only becomes such a representative after a long series of misadventures and potentially disastrous mistakes.

We can best approach the complexity of *Mr. Deeds* by considering the way Capra handles the contrast and conflict between the country and the city. Capra continually plays one against the other (*i.e.,* Deeds goes to *Town*), and it is through this interplay that the point of the film becomes clear.

Places are as important in *Mr. Deeds* as they were in *Platinum Blonde* (1931). Longfellow (Gary Cooper) is as out of place in his newly inherited city mansion as Stew Smith was in the Schuyler palace. But the alternative for Mr. Deeds is different. Rather than retreating to an uptown flat, Mr. Deeds has Mandrake Falls to go home to. The vestigial green world of the Schuyler gardens is thus only a halfway hothouse for Deeds. He can walk in Central Park with Babe (Jean Arthur), or take off his hat and rub the rain into his brows on his own palatial front porch, but Mandrake Falls, Vermont, still beckons as a realized pastoral ideal, waiting to shelter its hometown boy. The sun shines strong and bright in Longfellow's Vermont village (we seldom see sunlight in the city, which is illuminated by street lamps and neon signs instead), and the hometown folk evidence a strong sense of community in their own eccentric fashion, seeing Deeds off at the station when he leaves for New York City to take control of his late uncle's estate. The town's status as a symbol for fertility is further emphasized by the sexual connotations associated with its name: the mandrake root has long been considered an extraordinary aphrodisiac.[2]

Tied into this rural green world imagery is the kind of innocence that Deeds thinks he has found in "Mary" (better known as ace reporter Louise "Babe" Bennett). Her initial concern for Deeds is a professional one. She is the best reporter on the newspaper staff, and she is determined to get the scoop on the "cornfed bohunk" (as the editor describes Deeds). She gets things started by "fainting" on the sidewalk in front of Longfellow's house (recall a similar scene, with another "little Mary," in *The Strong Man*—1926). She plays upon his inherent sense of responsibility, and the chivalric Deeds does not disappoint her. He picks her up and

The all-around, rural St. George: Gary Cooper as Longfellow Deeds.

The ace reporter (Jean Arthur) and her editor (George
Bancroft) in *Mr. Deeds Goes to Town*.

asks if he can help. She tells him she has been job-
hunting all day (finally finding a job, by the way)
and Deeds impulsively hails a taxi to take them to
dinner. He clearly sees her modest poverty as a re-
freshing respite from the constant carping of city
favor seekers, and he wants to learn more about her.

It soon becomes evident that Babe feels guilty for
stringing Deeds along. She quickly understands that
his motives are honest concern and a desire for com-
panionship. Hence she feels appropriately ashamed
of herself for taking advantage of him. This doubt
first becomes manifest at the restaurant when Deeds
beckons the violinist over to their table. Capra cuts
among medium closeups of Babe (with the violinist
in the background), Deeds (watching Babe), and
Babe (watching Deeds watch her). Babe can see

The cafe scene in *Mr. Deeds.*

the selfless happiness on Longfellow's face, the pleasure he takes from the pleasure he gives, and her duplicity troubles her greatly, enough to bring about a brief change in her expression. Her reporter's mask drops for a moment, and we see a disturbed, confused human being underneath. The thing to note, however, is the speed with which Babe perceives Longfellow's integrity, and the corresponding swiftness with which she feels distaste for the role she plays. She has known him only for the length of a taxi ride, but even in this short time she comes to admire and respect him.

We know then that Babe has the same capacity for honest emotion and romantic concern that is Longfellow's hometown hallmark (indeed, as she tells him in the park, she was raised in a similar small town by a father who took her fishing and who played in the town band). But Longfellow is ro-

mantic to the extreme, and the film sets out to temper his overdeveloped sense of the melodramatic. The degree of this overdevelopment is made clear in the sentimental proposal poem that Deeds hands to Babe as they stand in the rain on her tenement steps (recall how Capra uses rain as a symbol for sexuality). Babe reads in an emotional whisper:

> I've tramped the earth with hopeless beat,
> Searching in vain for a glimpse of you.
> Then heaven thrust you at my very feet,
> A lovely angel, too lovely to woo.
> My dream has been answered, but my life's just as
>   bleak.
> I'm handcuffed, I'm speechless, in your presence
>   divine.
> My heart wants to cry out, if it only could speak.
> I love you, my angel, be mine, be mine.[3]

The girl that he knows as Mary represents an angelic

Madonna-like purity that Deeds has never found, not even in Mandrake Falls. He has remained a bachelor because he could never find a girl who could live up to his overromantic expectations. He seizes upon Babe as the object of his fantasy because, in the context of the big city, she seems an innocent "lady in distress" (as he puts it), a victim of the moochers that Deeds has already learned to dislike. Of course, Deeds does not know what is going on. It is not heaven that thrust her at his very feet, but her editor's promise of a month's paid vacation if she gets the story on Deeds. Nevertheless, Longfellow's great disappointment in her results less from what she actually is than from his fantastic notions of what she should be. Deeds clearly demands too much of her, and his romantic mistake is

to assume that actual angels exist in an unangelic world.

Deeds is thus something of an innocent, although he is generally too levelheaded, commonsensical, and shrewd to fit anything approaching the Harry Langdon stereotype. The speed with which he perceives the snobbism of the opera patrons and the literati bespeaks a quick intelligence, one not unaware of subtle cruelty and greedy self-centeredness. Deeds's innocence, then, is not ignorance. He knows that there are moochers in the world, and he generally knows how to handle them. His mistake will be to assume that all men (rather than some men) are moochers simply because the woman he has put on a pedestal proves to be more human than divine. But this momentary (though potentially disastrous)

Longfellow confronts the Opera Board.

intellectual lapse is not the general Deeds rule. He may write sentimental, greeting-card verse and play tuba in the town band, but he is much more self-aware and sensitive than Dickson was in *American Madness* (1932). Dickson's financial romanticism is his ordinary state of mind, while Deeds's romantic interlude is still only an interlude. Deeds begins in Mandrake Falls, knowing right from the start that money means trouble (recall the way he hesitates over the mouthpiece of his tuba when the lawyer breaks the financial news). At the film's end we have no doubt that he will return to Mandrake Falls with Babe as his new bride. Hence the comic journey in *Mr. Deeds* is not one that tests the major premise of Longfellow's life, but rather one that reaffirms his basic intelligence despite his momentary fling at big-city idiocy.

The "basic intelligence" of Longfellow Deeds is the kind of commonsense populism that critics like Jeffrey Richards delight in pointing out.[4] Like many Capra heroes, Deeds refers to Lincoln and Thoreau. But his real hero is Ulysses S. Grant. Mary takes him to Grant's Tomb (seeing it was one of the reasons that he decided to come to the city in the first place). The night is dark and foggy, and the tomb is a very unmonumental rotunda with just a few simple columns. Babe asks him if he is disappointed ("to most people it's a washout"), and he says it depends on what you see. She naturally asks him what he sees in it, and he replies:

I see a small Ohio farm boy becoming a great soldier. I see thousands of marching men. I see General Lee with a broken heart surrendering. And I can see the beginning of a new nation, like Abraham Lincoln said. And I can see that Ohio farm boy being inaugurated as President. Things like that can only happen in a country like America.

This kind of populist patriotism is surely characteristic of Capra, and I would not want to deny that. But note that despite the romanticism of the "any boy can become President" motif, there is yet a strong sense of the historical struggle required to put Ohio farm boys into the White House. Grant is perhaps the least idealized (or idealizable) of the populist gods that Capra could have chosen here, and the use of Grant as a symbol for Deeds's Mandrake Falls ideals is in keeping with Deeds's own brand of aware realism: it is a measure of Long-

fellow's commonsense belief in the common man that he picks a farm boy like Grant for his folk hero.

Deeds thus represents the country term of the city/country dialectic. He represents a rural intelligence and sensibility, and the film's conflict arises from the friction between Longfellow's country self and the foreign-city environment. But the city in and of itself, even if it seems to be populated only by self-seeking cynics like the crooked lawyer, John Cedar (Douglas Dumbrille), is not altogether responsible for Longfellow's misfortune. In fact, Longfellow's sort of comic romanticism (and I will define this formal relationship presently) is equally the villain in the film, and if city cynicism triggers Longfellow's romantic sensibilities (and is thus partly responsible for his agony), they were Longfellow's sensibilities to begin with, as much a part of his country-boy persona as his more admirable qualities of intelligence and honesty.

Longfellow Deeds is, in fact, too much a rural comic hero for his own farm-boy good. Once he meets Babe, he sets his heart on wooing her and winning her, making her the heroine in his own private comedy. Deeds is thus romantic about being comic. He rightly senses the developing love between Babe and himself, and within the context of city cynicism, he banks all of his faith on the success of that love. Deeds adopts a romantic stance towards his own status as a comic lover, and when he

At home in Mandrake Falls: Longfellow (Gary Cooper) with Cornelius Cobb (Lionel Stander), Mrs. Meredith (Emma Dunn), and John Cedar (Douglass Dumbrille).

learns that Babe has not told him the entire truth from the beginning, when he learns that the comedy is not developing precisely as he had imagined it, he despairs, believing that there is no comic value to be had anywhere. Of course, Longfellow is right to attach importance to his relationship with Babe. She is, in fact, the person he has to find before he can really find himself. But he is wrong to insist that she fulfill his expectations. She is not the mythical spring princess of Longfellow's fantasy, but a real human being, vulnerable and vital like Deeds himself, and he has to learn to accept her for what she is, not for what he wants her to be.

Thus another important theme in the film, one that cuts across and goes beyond the original country/city antinomy, is awareness, and the way expectations can cloud preception. Capra sets up a comic structure, a set of conventional expectations, in order to reflect upon the conventions themselves. For example, at one level Capra clearly intends to show the city as being essentially inferior to the country in matters of life style, ethics, and so forth (an ancient comic motif: see *The Acharnians* by Aristophanes). It is easier to be a good man in Mandrake Falls than it is in New York City. But at another level, Capra demonstrates that such a strict city/country split is an insufficient analysis of the real world. To be truly aware of actuality is to know that there are good people in the city (Babe, Mac-Wade, Cobb, the judges) and bad people even in Mandrake Falls. Indeed, the most damaging and dangerous witnesses at Deeds's trial are the Faulkner sisters (Margaret Seddon and Margaret McWade), nice, little old ladies from Longfellow's

The Faulkner sisters (Margaret Seddon and Margaret McWade): "everybody's pixilated."

hometown who are, in their own charmingly deceptive way, as self-centered and self-important as the worst city cynic. Given the opportunity, the Faulkner sisters are, like the equally charming Brewster sisters in *Arsenic and Old Lace* (1944), not at all unhappy to help put Longfellow out of his misery (he is "pixilated" after all).

In many ways, then, the film is Capra's *8½* (Fellini—1963), a film about vision and creation. It is a film by a sentimental poet about a sentimental poet that shows how overdone sentiment can cloud perception. Once Deeds lets his romantic expectations muddy his normally clear-eyed vision, he falls prey to a simplistic and self-indulgent sort of either/or thinking that does not do justice to the complex nature of reality. For example, once Longfellow learns of Babe's deceit (*i.e.*, she admits writing the "Cinderella Man" stories) he wrongly assumes that all men are moochers, that everyone is out to take advantage of him. He even suspects the unemployed farmer (John Wray) of being just another moocher, greedy for a handout. Thus Deeds becomes a cynic himself. Just going back to Mandrake Falls, as he is about to do before the hunger-crazed farmer breaks into his mansion, is therefore not enough. If he goes back to Mandrake Falls without learning that cynicism is not a viable stance, he is likely to take an advanced case of the disease right back to Vermont with him. What has to be maintained and fostered in the face of cynicism is a realistic faith in the ability of men to handle their own lives in a humane and honest manner, and that faith can only be maintained by those who have a realistic awareness of the complex nature of life in the world. Either/or thinking is incapable of comprehending that complexity, so what is needed is both intellectual honesty and spiritual constancy: perceiving problems accurately and dealing with them appropriately.

Therefore the rock-bottom issue in *Mr. Deeds Goes to Town* is the necessary interdependence of awareness and faith. One must be aware of the validity, utility, and necessity of faith in the adequacy of the universe, the ability of men to deal honestly and often successfully with the problems they face; and one must have faith that awareness, a willing vulnerability to the facts of existence, will not prove absolutely overwhelming and debilitating.

Thus we see Deeds and his faith come into the city. They test and are tested by the self-centered city vultures. Some of those vultures become aware of the goodness within themselves by seeing the goodness in Deeds. Both Babe and Cornelius Cobb (Lionel Stander)—Deed's press agent—see the essential rightness of Longfellow's comic faith. In the meanwhile, Deeds lets his romanticism get the better of his shrewd realistic senses. His romantic either/or extremism easily trips him into a pit of cynical despair. He loses all sense of proportion, and betrays his better self. It is ironic that at the moment of his deepest *angst*, as he sits staring Bartleby-like into the shadows of his insane asylum cell, Babe is actually giving him every reason not to give up, every reason to believe in the power of honest integrity to renew people. But his despair prevents him from knowing the good he has actually done. He simply does not give Babe the chance to explain.

Deeds undergoes a series of moral crises before he returns to his common sense and regains his comic equilibrium. The first one is his discovery of Babe's duplicity. His fairy princes turns out to be a flawed human being and a Pulitzer Prize winner as well. His last illusion is shattered, he despairs, and decides to leave. He is prevented when the farmer comes in waving a gun and denounces Deeds for feeding doughnuts to horses rather than to hungry people.

The second crisis is his arrest and confinement. When the farmer confronts him, Longfellow realizes that, practically speaking, too much money is the root of all of his troubles. It is not enough to throw the opera crowd out of his house (as he does), but he has to get rid of the bait that draws the cultured rats to his door. His troubles began when he got the twenty-million dollars, and he is intelligent enough to figure out that getting rid of trouble means getting rid of the newly acquired fortune. But note how he decides to do it. His populist ideals are rejuvenated for the moment by the farmer. Clearly the best way to dispose of his riches is to underwrite as many rural homesteads as possible, family farms where family virtues can grow and prosper. Deeds throws himself into the task with a certain frenzied energy. The loss of Babe has destroyed his good humor, but the bare bones of his ideals are still intact.

Unfortunately, Longfellow's good intentions only serve to create more trouble. His deceased uncle's crooked lawyer cannot bear the thought of parting

A blank stare and bare walls: Longfellow in his cell.

A production still: the farmer (John Wray) breaks into Longfellow's mansion.

with such a lucrative account, so he digs up some distant relatives and files suit, claiming that Deeds is insane (he would have to be to give away twenty-million dollars to a bunch of farmers) and unfit to administer the Semple fortune. Deeds is caught by "catch 22," and hence the depth of his despair. The one thing that he must do to redeem his Mandrake Falls soul is the one thing that he cannot do without being accused of insanity and locked away. His road to salvation seems blocked, and he sees no way out.

The third crisis is the climactic courtroom scene. Deeds has obviously decided that it is not in the nature of things for him to go free (although this is clearly a false assumption). His resolve grows stronger with every nitwit witness that Cedar (the lawyer) presents against him. As Babe tells the judges, Deeds has been hurt every time he has opened his mouth, and he sees no reason to subject himself to any further humiliation. Why should he sanely defend his sanity when Cedar insists that sanity is stark, raving imbecility and presents authoritative witnesses to prove it. What has to happen, and does happen, before Deeds finally realizes his mistake, is that Babe, MacWade, Cobb, and finally the farmers have to demonstrate the falsity of Deeds's self-deprecating stance. Deeds has to be made aware that his basic personal faith in the common man is justified no matter how crazy or fanatic some men might be, and once he does so, his faith and intelligence are more than enough to convince the court of his sanity.

But note that the issue is not, as most critics simplistically assume, a social question of whether or not Deeds can defeat corrupt city sophisticates (we know he can if he sets his mind to it), rather it is the personal-moral question of whether he wants to defeat them or not. Deeds has let his extreme romanticism cloud his preceptions, and he has decided that it will avail him nothing to protest the faithless, heartless way of the world. But that is simply not true. Given the situation (*i.e.,* trumped-up charges and impartial judges), Deeds can not only preserve his own liberty but help thousands of other people to achieve economic self-sufficiency. Babe and Cobb show how faith has changed their lives, and the farmers call Deeds to fight for the sake of that faith. Deeds thus gets the proof he needs that morality is still viable and he quickly sets about to destroy Cedar's case.

But if this description of the film's concern is accurate, as I believe it is, what function does the courtroom scene itself serve? Once Longfellow has decided to defend himself, and the immediate personal issue is settled, the remainder of the courtroom confrontation could be seen as extraneous. But it is not extraneous at all, and if the thematic issue is settled, the comic plot still requires that the ritual *agon* be completed and the victor rewarded.

What we have then is an almost Aristophanic debate between the principles of good and evil. Cedar is allowed to present his hair-brained case first that he might be shown up for the fraud he is when Longfellow finally takes the stand (and recall that whoever speaks first in an Aristophanic *agon* is norm-

Babe pleads with Longfellow to defend himself.

ally the antagonist, the one who represents false principles). Deeds is thus allowed a forum for his golden-rule ideals, ideals that have been implied but never given full expression previous to Longfellow's speech. Deeds is also given the opportunity to be his folksy self, to demonstrate his qualities of wit, humor, concern, and compassion. Being a rejuvenated Longfellow Deeds is being truly human, and there is a generosity about his humane concern that gives the lie to Cedar's mealymouthed greediness.

It is also in the courtroom scene that political issues are allowed to surface for the first time. But even here they are generally avoided. Cedar may protest that it is un-American to give away money, but Longfellow Deeds rightly replies that it is not a matter of political ideology but simple human responsibility. Those who have money should help those who do not. This certainly smacks of *noblesse oblige,* but note the context in which it occurs. As Deeds says, his money was making him miserable, messing up his life, and given the fact that he wants to rid himself of his fortune, he is presented with a choice: give it to the farmers who need it, or give it to the likes of Cedar who do not need it but nevertheless lust after it. In this situation, *noblesse oblige* is simply a matter of common sense and compassion, not politics. The film makes it clear that such generosity is, as the judge tells us, "most uncommon," and while Capra might have hoped that Deeds would inspire some of the nations haves to share their plenty with the have-nots, he was not under any illusion that they would.

Given this sort of realistic awareness, an awareness that few critics have been able to perceive, Capra is entitled to maintain his belief in the relative superiority of rural life. Capra is clearly aware that simplistic thinking can lead to false perception. But *Mr. Deeds* is not a simplistic film, and hence Capra earns the right to his populist conclusion: concerned personalism of the Deedsian sort is indeed better off in Mandrake Falls. The city has a way of bringing out the worst, even in good people, and reinforcing their mistakes by perverting their vision.

What we have, then, is a package of basic ideals, represented by Longfellow Deeds and the people who support him, set over and against the cynical grubbiness of slick, city materialists. Deeds believes in the ability of men to be humane towards one another. He believes that people are more important than money. He believes that families should be permitted to grow and prosper without fear of hunger and destitution. Such beliefs are neither unrealistic nor ideologically suspect, for they are predicated on a comic faith in the universe, a faith that constructive action, fertile rather than sterile, is possible. It is this faith in the utility of human action that is shaken when Deeds is arrested and put on trial. It is this faith in the integrity of life that is vindicated when Deeds overcomes his enemies.

Once we have properly understood this issue of faith in *Mr. Deeds Goes to Town,* we can properly understand its status as a Depression-era film. The Depression certainly called the faith of many people

Deeds rides in triumph.

into question, not simply their faith in the free-enter-prise system, but their larger faith in the possibility of meaningful existence. With thousands of "good" people out of work and in the breadlines, people questioned the moral utility of being "good." It is at this basic level of trust in the universe and in other people that *Mr. Deeds Goes to Town* operates. It is clearly dealing with a contemporary issue, but the issue is not the Depression *per se*. The issue is rather a deeper, moral question that the Depression raised. Hence, attempts to see *Mr. Deeds* as being Capra's recipe for instant economic recovery have missed the point of the movie. It is not a film about Longfellow Deeds, the social reformer, attacking a corrupt capitalist system. It is rather about Long-fellow Deeds, the comic hero, and his attempts to maintain his personal integrity in the face of moral cynicism. To the extent that such cynicism can be traced to wealth and the systems that produce wealth, we can relate it to the historical milieu of American capitalism. But in fact, the film does not attack the economic system (Deeds himself is a part-owner of a tallow works back in Mandrake Falls), but rather people who let any system corrupt their moral integrity.

The film is realistic in that it recognizes that no amount of Deedsian goodness is going to change the people like Cedar who generally run the city show. Goodness alone is not going to fix a crippled economic structure. Goodness can, on the other hand, redeem people who are essentially good at heart anyway (even city folk like MacWade and Cobb), and when luck gives a good man like Deeds twenty-million dollars, we can expect him to do good deeds with it. But this is not a solution to the Depression. Capra is not saying that the problem will be solved when the rich give away their wealth. In Capra's sense of the word, Deeds is not rich; he only has a lot of money. Richness is a state of mind that people with money normally succumb to (and Deeds faces this threat), but the Longfellow Deeds who gives up the world's goods for the sake of his soul is neither a rich man nor a political reformer. He is a comic hero. Thus *Mr. Deeds Goes to Town* is not a right-wing or Republican film (as critics like Durgnat and Griffith suggest), but rather a deeply comic film in which the moral fertility of awareness and faith is celebrated and renewed.[5]

NOTES

[1] Stephen Handzo, "Under Capracorn," *Film Comment* 8, no. 4 (1972): 8.

[2] Set Machiavelli's comedy, *Mandragola*.

[3] All citations are directly from the dialogue in the film.

[4] Jeffrey Richards, "Frank Capra and the Cinema of Populism, *Film Society Review* 7, no. 6 (1972): 42.

[5] In addition to Griffith and Durgnat (refer to Chapter I, notes 1, 6, and 10), see also Graham Greene, *The Spectator*, 28 August 1936: 343; Mark Van Doren, "Second Comings," *The Nation*, 13 May 1936: 623-4; and Robert Stebbins (pen name of Sidney Meyers), "Mr. Capra Goes To Town," *New Theatre*, May 1936, rpt. in *American Film Criticism*, edited by Stanley Kauffmann, (New York: Liveright, 1972), pp. 334-5. Greene describes *Deeds* as having "as grim a theme as *Fury*; innocence lynched as effectively at a judicial inquiry as in a burning courthouse," but he goes on to point out that Capra's ending, unlike Lang's, "is natural and unforced." Sidney Meyers generally agrees with Greene's reading, seeing in the film "the salutary implication, if not recognition, that the world is a place of sorrows where the great multitudes of men suffer for the excesses of the few" (p. 335). Van Doren argues an opposing point of view, and he takes Capra's wish fulfillment to task: "The weakness of the film is not that [Deeds] rises at last in defense of himself, but that his defense succeeds—the implication being that New York henceforth will honor such men, whereas we know of course that it will do nothing of the sort as long as it consists of people like ourselves" (p. 624).

11

Mr. Smith Goes to Washington

I argued in chapter 3 that the comic dynamic is essentially the same in all of Capra's comic films. Even Capra's political films revolve primarily around the kinds of personal issues characteristic of comedy. We have seen how *Mr. Deeds Goes to Town* (1936) is best understood not as a political tract or as a treatise on New Deal economics, but rather as a comedy of personal morality. Similarly, while *Mr. Smith Goes to Washington* (1939) is obviously concerned with the democratic process and the corruption of that process, it remains a film that focuses first and foremost on the emotional and moral issues that face the central characters.

The personal-moral issue (faith versus cynicism) that was the heart of *Mr. Deeds* is repeated and expanded in *Mr. Smith Goes to Washington*. The relatively apolitical *Mr. Deeds* follows the lead of earlier Capra films in distrusting the wealthy and the moral attitudes that normally accompany wealth. *You Can't Take It With You* (1938) is the first film where the relationship between big money and big government is made explicit. But *Mr. Smith Goes to Washington* is the first film to explore and expose the deep nature of the bond that can (and usually does) exist between financial and political power. It is not simply a matter of grafting political issues onto the moral structure of the *Mr. Deeds* prototype, however. Capra and Sidney Buchman do a splendid job of synthesizing the moral issues of the deep structure with the surface political questions, so that *Mr. Smith* goes quite beyond the relatively re-stricted social vision of *Mr. Deeds,* without losing for a moment the effective comic force of the former film.

Mr. Smith Goes to Washington is concerned very deeply with freedom, the political freedom of Jefferson Smith (James Stewart) to be naive and idealistic, as well as the sexual freedom of Clarissa Saunders (Jean Arthur) to be open and loving.[1] Both freedoms are jeopardized by the self-seeking and sterile combination of economic and political power symbolized at its worst by the unholy alliance of the fat-cat cigar-chomper, Jim Taylor (Edward Arnold), and the once moral, but now bought-and-paid-for "Silver Knight" of the Senate, Joseph Paine (Claude Rains). The personal and political issues are thus inextricably intertwined: as long as Saunders sees dollar signs instead of capitol domes, as long as she believes that the principles of greed and corruption represented by Taylor and Paine run the world, she allows herself to be run by those false principles, and she cannot take the risk (a risk we have seen before in Capra) of loving Jeff Smith. Thus, while we cannot say that Saunders is kept from Jeff by the direct opposition of Paine (as Birdie was kept from Eddie by the direct opposition of Morris in *The Younger Generation* —1929), we can say that it is the oblique opposition of Paine, in that he fosters and reinforces her sterile attitudes, that keeps Jeff and Clarissa apart.

The comic necessity for bringing Smith and Saunders together is made clear midway through the film

The bond between financial and political power: the Senator (Claude Rains), the Newspaper Magnate (Edward Arnold) and the Governor (Guy Kibbee) in *Mr. Smith Goes to Washington.*

when Jeff outlines his plans for a Willet Creek National Boys' Camp. Jeff and Saunders are in his office late at night, and while Clarissa (in her role as secretary) takes notes, Jeff describes the spirit he wishes to embody in his bill:

> Liberty is too precious a thing to be buried in books, Miss Saunders. Men should hold it up in front of them every single day of their lives and say "I'm free, to think and to speak." My ancestors couldn't. I can. And my children will.[2]

We cut from Jeff to a closeup of Saunders as Smith says "my children," and the juxtaposition makes it clear where those children are going to come from. There is a comic rightness to the union of Jeff and Clarissa that belies the chance nature of their acquaintance. It is almost as if fate (in the form of a flipped coin) had decreed that Jeff and Saunders should marry. Saunders is clearly moved by Jeff's description of the "tall grasses" and "lazy streams" found in his western paradise, and she clearly longs to leave the dark tunnel of her cynical life for the light of Jeff's small-town idealism. The comic movement of the film, then, is towards overcoming the bondage of cynicism that prevents the marriage, thereby achieving the kind of political and sexual

James Stewart as Jeff Smith and Jean Arthur as Clarissa Saunders.

freedom for Jeff and Clarissa that will foster their love and thus insure the future generations who will enjoy the hard-won liberty.

The opposition of cynicism to idealism thus forms the major conflict in the film (as it did in *Mr. Deeds*), and the interrelationship of one to the other is personified in a spectrum of major characters. Jefferson Smith is at one end, the bird-calling Boy Ranger-idealist who just naturally climbs on sightseeing buses and sends pigeons home to mother. He is, like Longfellow Deeds before him, a natural man from the fertile rural frontier of civilization whose courage and natural intelligence are in tune with the "green world" he lives in (recall his heroism in the Sweetwater forest fire). At the other end is Jim Taylor, a ruthless party boss who literally owns and operates the home state as a personal con-

cession from the capitalist gods. In the middle we find Saunders and Paine, moralists turned pragmatic realists who have allowed personal ambition to suppress their ideals. Of course, Saunders has a lesser piece of the graft action to worry about, and her morality always seems closer to the surface. Her cynicism is less self-seeking than Paine's, and as the film progresses, it becomes clearer that she is more concerned with defending her emotions than her pocketbook. As Jeff's sure defeat becomes more nearly reality, she becomes more fearful of seeing Jeff hurt. She may not be able to prevent their dropping Jeff out of a balloon, but she does not want to be around when he hits. She is, she says, "squeamish."

In many ways Paine is just as squeamish about seeing Jeff hurt as Saunders is. His real respect and

Jeff Smith: the bird-calling Boy Ranger.

Clarissa and her cynical sidekick Diz (Thomas Mitchell).

affection for Jeff are never called into question. He may reluctantly do everything in his power to destroy Jeff, but it is always evident that Paine actually admires Jeff's honesty and idealism. Even when he lectures Jeff on the fine arts of political compromise, we never sense that Paine totally believes what he says. He says what he has to say in order to get Jeff out from in front of Taylor's steamroller. And it is Taylor's power, and Paine's own Presidential ambitions, that trap Paine in the situation where his choice is either to destroy Jeff Smith or destroy himself. But in a sense, to destroy either is to destroy both, for Jeff represents what Paine once was and should still be. To destroy Smith, then, is the last step between Paine and complete damnation. Smith is, in effect, the good angel opposite Taylor's bad angel, and Paine is Faustus, caught in the middle.

This identity between Smith and Paine is made clear in the scene we just discussed where Paine tries to convince Jeff to keep his nose out of the Willet Creek affair. He tells Jeff that it is a man's world, and that Jeff should go back to his boys before he gets hurt. It is a hard, brutal world where you must "check your ideals outside the door like you do your rubbers," Paine tells him, and he goes on to compare Jeff to himself:

> Thirty years ago I had your ideals. I was you. I had to make the same decision you were asked to make today. And I made it. I compromised, yes, so that all those years I could sit in that Senate and serve the people in a thousand honest ways.

And we know that Paine is, in part, correct here. He was a Jefferson Smith, and he fought side by side with Jeff's father for "lost causes." But he made his first compromise, and we know why: despair. He does not trust the people. "I've had to compromise, had to play ball. You can't count on people voting. Half the time they don't vote anyway. That's how states and empires have been built since time began."

But note what Paine has compromised: his integrity. He employs the rhetoric of legitimate give-and-take politics to justify a political swindle. Taylor, with Paine's full knowledge and under phony names, is buying land that he plans to sell to the government at an enormous profit as soon as a Paine-sponsored bill, which authorizes purchase of the very same land, is passed. Such greedy self-serving schemes cannot be characterized as "compromise," at least not in the Websterian sense that Paine intends it (and recall that Jeff literally sits at Daniel Webster's Senate desk).

There is thus an enormous gap between Paine's rhetoric and his action, but what counts here is Paine's motivation. He is uncomfortable from the beginning with Taylor in general and the Willet Creek swindle in particular. His rhetoric sounds as hollow to his own ears as it does to Jeff's and ours (note Paine's masklike expression as he speaks). He goes along with the scheme only for fear of jeopardizing his political future. Thus it is despair of honest politics rather than a desire for personal profit that

The dual focus of *Mr. Smith*: Paine and Jeff on the Senate floor.

motivates Joseph Paine. Of course, Jeff is prey to the same despair, and it takes a guardian angel like the morally rejuvenated Saunders to bring Jeff back to his comic senses. But when Jeff stands on the Senate floor to launch his filibuster, he does so in the name of the very people that Paine has written off.

Paine is thus what Jeff could be were he to lose his populist faith. But Jeff does not lose it: he is not simply a younger version of the cynical Paine, and this difference between the two is emphasized visually at the same time that Paine verbally attempts to convince Jeff of their similarity. The scene is a typical Capra conversation, filmed in medium closeup with occasional full closeups cut in on the dialogue. Most of what we see, however, is Smith and Paine in profile, Paine leaning against his desk screen left and Smith standing tall at screen right. Paine is surrounded by pictures of political pals and dignitaries (including one of Taylor, hanging just over Paine's head) that serve as an appropriate backdrop for his lecture on real politics, while Jeff stands against the stark background of the office door he has just barged through. Indeed, the door frame serves as a dividing line running right down the center of the screen. On the one side is Paine outlined by the evidence of his collusion, on the other Jeff Smith, unadorned and uncompromising. Jeff can still stand tall without leaning on his desk or his past. There is thus an important difference between the two men. One has long ago stepped across the line of despair, selling his principles in the process, and the other still stands firmly for what he believes in. Of course, Jeff's faith is tested, and Jeff comes near to failing that test. But the point is that he doesn't fail. With Clarissa's help, he comes back to continue the struggle. The difference between the two men is thus not only a matter of time but experience: what they have done with their time and what they have let time do to them. Paine may once have been an inspired fool, but the death of Jeff's father (shot in the back by mining interests) apparently wised him up. But note how he wised up. Instead of going back to tell his people the truth (as Jeff planned to do), he sold out altogether and joined the very sort of machine that he

had previously fought. Where Jeff can still lead Boy Rangers, Paine can only follow men like Taylor.

And the major point to make by this detailed comparison between the two men is that it is as much Paine's film as it is Jeff Smith's. As in *You Can't Take It With You,* we have a dual focus, concerned both with the comic lovers and the comic obstacles. Smith wins his moral battle and the love of Saunders when he decides to go back to the Senate and fight it out, despite Paine's charges of corruption and graft. Thus the major question in the film's final minutes is whether Paine can be saved from himself. It is not a matter of Jeff becoming like Paine (although that danger was present for a moment), but of whether Paine can become like

Taylor (Edward Arnold) and his cronies gang up on Jeff.

Jeff Smith. Can Paine divorce himself from the cynicism of Taylor and reassert his moral identity along with Smith and Saunders?

Much depends, then, on our interpretation of the closing minutes of the film. Who wins? and how do they do it? What kind of political implications are to be found? What kind of statement does the film make about political power? The answers to these questions are apparently difficult (witness the critical confusion), and many a scholar has followed Griffith's lead in concluding that it is the victory of the "little people" and their ideals over the corrupt "Taylor-made" politicians who run the show.[3] But the fact of the matter is that the "little people" do not win the battle. Rather, it is lost by the Taylor machine at the last minute because one exceptional man, Joseph Paine, finally redeems himself and speaks the truth. The "little people" are, in fact, either brutally crushed or bought off, and the moral victory of Smith and Paine is attenuated by the vision we have of the corruptibility of the people.

To be sure, I have argued that Jeff Smith is a populist, and I will not deny it. But Capra is a populist filmmaker who does not wholeheartedly believe in the people. Capra says we should believe in them, yet he knows that doing so means running great risks, even perhaps crucifixion. And the point is not so much that Jeff wins, but that he almost loses, almost gets crucified. After endless hours of speaking in the name of the people, Jeff finds that he has been deserted by the people. All of those denunciatory letters and telegrams nail him hard to the cross. Photographed from slightly above, Smith reaches out his arms, clutching telegrams in both fists, as if to say "My God, my God, why hast thou forsaken me?"

And Jeff's anguished question is answered: he has not been forsaken. The one man who has safeguarded his rights all along, the Vice President (Harry Carey), gives him a smile of encouragement. It is enough. Jeff is not licked yet, and he goes over to confront Paine, throwing Paine's own idealistic words back in his face:

I guess this is just another lost cause, Mr. Paine. All you people don't know about the lost causes. Mr. Paine does. He said once they were the only causes worth fighting for. And he fought for them once, for the only reason that any man ever fights for them.

"My God, my God, why hast thou forsaken me?"

Because of just one plain, simple rule: "Love thy neighbor." And in this world today, full of hatred, a man who knows that one rule has a great trust.

* * *

You all think I'm licked. Well, I'm not licked, and I'm going to stay right here and fight for this lost cause even if this room gets filled with lies like these, and the Taylors and all their armies come marching into this place. Somebody'll listen to me . . . some . . . (he faints).

Smith demonstrates his hard-won sense of realism here: you cannot win a lost cause, and he knows that, barring a miracle, his cause is indeed lost. But he has had providence on his side all along (his being appointed resulted from an almost miraculous coin toss), and the miracle that he needs is provided: Paine repents and confesses.

But what does this kind of political miracle mean? Are we to infer that miracles will become a common enough occurrence to solve all of our political problems? Is that what Capra is telling us? Must we agree with Otis Ferguson when he says that "the main surviving idea is that one scout leader who knows the Gettysburg Address by heart but wouldn't possibly be hired to mow your lawn can throw passionate faith into the balance and by God we've got a fine free country to live in again."[4] Obviously not, Griffith and his critical crew notwithstanding. Capra makes it abundantly clear that political miracles are still miracles. They happen only on rare occasions and for rare individuals (and Jeff Smith, Paine himself tells us, is a "rare

Jeff confronts Paine.

man"). But Capra also implies that we must all strive, as a matter of comic necessity, to assert the kind of simple and naive political morality embodied in Jefferson Smith if a comically viable society is to continue. It is not just a matter of oppression but sterility. The kind of society that keeps apart the Jeffs and Clarissas will eventually choke on its own success and everything, people, ideals, and institutions, will die. The way to champion the lost cause is to have your children, build your boys' camps, and continue to oppose the Taylors in the hope (and it is a hope) that some generation, if not this one the next one, will rise up and overthrow the Taylors. This is not to say that you should sit back and let the Taylors run the show. What it does say is that like it or not, the Taylors of the world *do* run the show, and that comic heroes will have to give everything they have just to keep from losing what little piece of the green world they have man-

aged to protect. Willet Creek is only Willet Creek, an obscure little stream in a nameless western state, but you fight for it because that is what you have to do.

In light of this analysis it is hard to accuse Capra of naivete. Jefferson Smith may be naive, although he learned his first, ugly, political lesson early when his father was murdered by mining corporations, but Capra is not so naive as to tell us that all the Smiths of the world need do is blow a few bird-whistles and corruption will disappear in a poof of sentiment. The world does not work that way. But neither is he saying that we all need be political sophisticates. If Capra is antiintellectual, it is because he is aware of the way people routinely misuse their intellects. If you can rationalize leaving your ideals at the doorstep like rubbers, then you had better look closely again at the relationship between reason and morality. Capra's simple, golden-rule morality is an attempt to discover a common moral denominator that can unite those "little people" into the kind of political solidarity that will give them the power to deal with the corporate bosses and hence control their own lives. That in itself may be a naive goal, but it is as sophisticated as Capra ever needs to be given his use of the comic form, and far more sophisticated than Capra's critics give him credit for.

Mr. Smith Goes to Washington, then, is Capra's most successful attempt at dealing with politics within the comic framework. He achieves a level of moral sophistication that does full duty to the political reality without attempting the kind of detailed political analysis that would obstruct the essential comic movement. Capra was clearly aware that he had excelled himself, for the film evidences a stylistic confidence far beyond the low-key perfec-

tion of *The Bitter Tea of General Yen* (1933) or *It Happened One Night* (1934). Both of these earlier films were intimate achievements, concerned very much with minute observations of personal, emotional reality. Accordingly, Capra could let his camera dwell longer on a single mood or gesture. In *Mr. Smith*, on the other hand, Capra expands his field of vision. We see a greater use of long shot and montage, and a higher editing frequency, all calculated to present a larger world with the same sense of acute observation that has always been Capra's forte.

And it is this stylistic precision that makes the film the masterpiece it is. Every shot carries an emotional charge. *Mr. Smith* is actually no less intimate an achievement than *It Happened One Night*; but where the latter shows us Peter and

Long shot in *Mr. Smith*.

Capra as portrait artist: shooting a closeup on Jean Arthur.

Ellie falling in love across a breakfast table, *Mr. Smith* shows us Jeff and Clarissa falling in love across (and, metaphorically, despite) the cavernous expanse of the Senate chamber. Thus, while the film does demonstrate an expanded field of vision, the world viewed is still a world of intense emotional action. The images that stay most in the mind are of emotional or agonized faces: Jeff on the Senate floor, Saunders in the Senate balcony when she is sure that Jeff has been defeated, Paine at his desk while Jeff reminds him of his own idealistic past, and so on through a catalogue of great character portraits. As Graham Greene put it, Capra took a delight "equal to that of the great Russians" in the human face, and his style in all of his films pays particular attention to human emotion as revealed by facial expression.[5]

Thus, *Mr. Smith* is of the same stylistic mode as Capra's earlier efforts. Capra's primary concern is with the way people feel about themselves and each other. The issue in *Mr. Smith* hinges upon such self-evaluations. Is Saunders right to see herself as a self-centered cynic? Is Jeff right to see himself as a worthless, bird-calling fool? Is Paine right to see himself as Taylor's political servant? These are the questions that the film explores, and the answers to these questions, taken together, constitute the film's meaning.

To put it briefly, the point of the film is that people are free to reject such diminished images of their own self-worth. People can assert their emotional and moral integrity no matter how oppressive the political situation may be. But such personal assertions are not necessarily political solutions. Personal integrity is surely seen as a necessary qualification for ethical political behavior, but one ethical politician does not make the political system altogether viable or trustworthy.

But we need not belabor the political issue. Even a critic like Stephen Handzo, who ultimately distrusts Capra's political vision, willingly admits the irresistible "verve" and appeal of the film. The only mistake in such a reading is that the critic makes the same sort of self-deprecating assumption that Capra warns against in *Mr. Smith*. The critic sees himself as seduced by a "virtuoso whirlwind" style into accepting something that is ultimately unacceptable (Handzo, pp. 11-12). But we need not make such assumptions. *Mr. Smith Goes to Washington* has much that is honest, valid, and legitimate to tell us about human adequacy and emotional integrity. The film is about emotional honesty, and Capra presents it with emotional honesty, and accordingly we need not apologize for finding *Mr. Smith Goes to Washington* a moving and vital cinematic experience.

NOTES

[1.] Stephen Handzo makes a similar point in his article "Under Capracorn," *Film Comment* 8, no. 4 (1972): 14. His section on *Mr. Smith* is particularly good.

[2.] While a script is available for *Mr. Smith* [in *Twenty Best Film Plays,* edited by John Gassner and Dudley Nichols, (New York: Crown, 1943), pp. 583-651] I quote directly from the dialogue as it is in the film.

[3.] Richard Griffith and Paul Rotha, *The Film Till Now* (1930; revised and enlarged 1949 and 1960, Middlesex: The Hamlyn Publishing Group), pp. 452-3. Griffith describes *Mr. Smith* as "the classic example" of his "fantasy of goodwill" formulation.

[4.] Otis Ferguson, *New Republic,* 1 Nov. 1939: 369-370.

[5.] Graham Greene, *The Spectator,* 5 Jan. 1940: 16.

12

Meet John Doe

Meet John Doe (1941) offers a strained and strangely ominous conclusion to the populist trilogy. William Pechter points out that the progression from *Deeds* (1936) to *Smith* (1939) to *Doe* is one of increasing pessimism, requiring ever greater miracles to solve increasingly insoluble problems.[1] But the pessimistic fact is that the greater miracle needed in *Meet John Doe* is not provided. Long John (Gary Cooper) does not overthrow or expose financier-politician D. B. Norton (Edward Arnold) the way Jefferson Smith (however providentially) overthrows the Taylor machine in his film. The greatest miracle that Capra could honestly muster (and he tried several) is to save John Doe from suicide. The corporate bosses are not defeated, only inconvenienced, and the populist solution, the implied resurrection of the John Doe Clubs, can only be seen as a tenuous possibility, given what we already know about the political clout of the Nortons and the political fickleness of the people.

We can best understand the progressively increasing pessimism of the trilogy films in light of their increasing similarity to the Langdon films: decreased hopes and a greater need of providential guidance are a function of decreasingly adequate, decreasingly mature comic protagonists. Long John Willoughby is clearly the least intelligent, the most Langdon-esque of the three populist heroes. His decision to go along with the Norton-promoted circulation stunt is motivated less by any evil design than by hunger and the wish to get back into baseball. He is child-ishly ignorant of the ramifications of his actions. Longfellow Deeds was not only shrewd enough to stay out of breadlines, but smart enough not to sign any contracts without thinking them over first. Jefferson Smith, for all of his idealistic naivete, has the intelligence necessary to stand up and fight in the Senate. But Long John Willoughby gets disgraced and cut off before he ever gets his mouth open. His most eloquent action would have been suicide, but there is little doubt that Norton would have silenced him even in death (Norton could easily have intercepted the letter John mailed to the newspaper).

The structure of *Meet John Doe* is basically that of the comic journey, a pattern Capra had used in the Langdon films (1926-1927) and more memorably in *It Happened One Night* (1934). But *Meet John Doe* has two comic journeys, and the necessary intersection of the two clarifies the film's basic drive towards the symbolic fertility of a comic conclusion.

The first journey, the roundabout wandering of Long John and The Colonel (Walter Brennan) in the general direction of the Columbia River country, is seen as insufficiently comic. The Colonel (the prime mover in this northward trek) is too cynical, too antisocial, more concerned with escaping responsibility than accepting it. Capra has a certain degree of admiration for The Colonel's free-wheeling, individualist creed: his speech about the danger of becoming a helot (one of a lot of heels) rings with the sort of antimaterialist fervor that

The Langdonesque hero: Gary Cooper as Long John
Willoughby in *Meet John Doe*.

Capra obviously approves. But when The Colonel condemns love and marriage as just another unnecessary entanglement, he goes beyond the comic limit. Marriage is a comic necessity, and The Colonel's irresponsible cynicism is as dangerous from one side as Norton's fascist brand is from the other.

The second journey, Long John and Ann (Barbara Stanwyck) crisscrossing America to promote the John Doe ideal of concerned good-neighborliness, recalls *It Happened One Night*—two people, on the road together, learning about life and each other as they move from town to town. This movement overtakes and replaces the first movement, as John chooses Ann rather than The Colonel as being the more comically proper companion.

There is thus a sense of appropriateness to the John/Ann match recalling the rightness of the Harry/Mary couple in *The Strong Man* (1926). Both John and Ann display a certain childish naivete, a divine innocence at once self-centered and unassuming. Long John is a bush-league pitcher with a bum wing, down and out, and willing to tell a lie or two if it gets food in his gullet and the promise of a sawbones for his arm. Ann Mitchell is another of Capra's cynical female reporters, but her cynicism, too, has a childlike quality to it. She supports her mother and two sisters, and she is understandably enraged when she gets sacked in a Norton-ordered drive to boost circulation. When told that her copy has too much "lavendar and lace" and not enough "fireworks," she angrily dashes off a "the-whole-world's-going-to-pot" suicide letter to the editor and signs it "John Doe," without any

On the road again: Long John and The Colonel (Walter
Brennan) at a roadside diner.

further idea in mind than to blow off some righteous
steam. Of course, she is not unintelligent, and when
she sees what a furor John Doe and his promised
suicide have created, she quickly decides to take
advantage of the situation. But the thing to note is
that we do not have, on her part, any of the consciously evil intent that the Taylor machine had in
fishing for a stand-in stooge Senator in *Mr. Smith*,
or that Cedar, Cedar, Cedar, and Budington had in
their hope to find another easy touch who would
let them continue their control of the Semple fortune in *Mr. Deeds*. Ann is simply tired of being
poor (and it is easy to be poor when your mother
gives away all your money to help the less fortunate). Ann wants to get the kind of financial secu-

rity necessary to support her family, and if she has
to play publicity games to do so, it does not bother
her. She is unaware of Norton's real intentions (although she is aware that he wants to make a political splash), and she even comes to believe the John
Doe ideal (taken from the philosophical musings
in her late father's diary), despite the minor sub-
terfuge that got the movement started.

So the problem in *Meet John Doe* is, as it was in
Long Pants (1927), a matter of growth and maturation. Long John and Ann are kindred spirits,
children at heart, who must grow up both sexually
and morally if the tender vitality of their developing relationship is to survive in a cynical world.
Between them, John and Ann symbolize both per-

Getting the movement started: Connell (James Gleason) briefs John on the details of the deception.

sonal and social fertility, and the comic movement of the film is to bring them closer together, to make them see the necessity of their union.

But growing up is largely a matter of imitation, trial, and error, modeling behavior after those who are older, more authoritative, more successful, and then seeing if that type of action is appropriate to one's self and one's picture of the world. The two major models in *Meet John Doe*, embodying the normal Capra opposition of idealism and cynicism, are D. B. Norton and Dr. Mitchell.

Norton is a financier-politician with ambitions for the White House. Ann works for a Norton paper (one of many Norton publishing or broadcasting ventures), and he quickly sees in Ann's relatively innocent publicity stunt a means of expanding his own power base. Norton already has his own blackjacket-paramilitary force (clearly patterned after Hitler's S.S.), as well as the backing of industrialists and labor leaders, but as yet he lacks popular support. Presented with the opportunity, then, Norton exploits Ann and Long John, using their naivete and the naivete of the people they appeal to for his own oppressive purposes. But the most dangerous thing about Norton is his apparent kindness. He has a rich man's assurance and grace that Ann finds understandably attractive. She does not see him (as we do) at the head of his own private army, and accordingly we can comprehend how easily even an essentially good person like Ann

Norton (Edward Arnold) gives Ann (Barbara Stanwyck) a raise and some fatherly encouragement.

can be taken in by Norton's fatherly demeanor.

Opposed in spirit if not in fact to Norton is Ann's real father, the late Dr. Mitchell, a kindly physician who devoted his life to serving the common people. He becomes a factor in the film when Ann, at a loss for words to put into John's first radio speech, seeks her mother's help. Mrs. Mitchell (Spring Byington) tells her daughter that people will not listen to "complaining political speeches." What they want to hear is "something simple and real, something with hope in it."[2] She then gets her husband's diary and gives it to Ann as a source of inspiration. Ann respects her father greatly, and she takes his populist maxims to heart, writing truly impassioned populist speeches for John to deliver.

And it was this populist philosophy that offended many critics and reviewers when *Meet John Doe*

first appeared. The film was, for the most part, well received (although it did not figure in the Oscar running) and most critics applauded it as a "brave protest against the present state of civilization."[3] But a significant and influential minority of reviewers felt that Capra had finally gone too far in the direction of simpleminded sentiment. Otis Ferguson complained that the film "talks too much to no purpose and in the same spot."[4] John Mosher in *The New Yorker* declared that "Capra's love for the common man, the average man, the dope, the punk, passeth all understanding."[5] And finally Edgar Anstey in *The Spectator* condemned *Meet John Doe* as a "nauseating modern vulgarization of the New Testiment . . . a shocking exploitation of false sentiment."[6]

Such critical response is not without foundation.

Long John learns about the "little people" in *Meet John Doe.*

The Santa Claus socialism of John's first radio speech, particularly his appeal to the spirit of Christmas, is difficult to take. But Capra was clearly aware of this difficulty. He clearly intended the naive John Doe ideal to be simpleminded and childish. The point of the film is not to be found (as some critics assume) in its set speeches but in its action. Capra has characters mouthing the John Doe ideals primarily that those ideals might be tested and tempered in the context of human struggle. Ideals are nice in a diary, but what do they mean in actual practice?

Of course, Capra does not totally undercut the John Doe creed. The whole point of the ending is to emphasize the validity of populist morality. But that validity is as much a function of the characters who hold those ideals as it is of the ideals themselves. Long John and Ann begin their journey with the John Doe ideal as a given, and what they must achieve together is a realistic, mature awareness of the place of morality in an often hostile universe. What counts, therefore, is not just the ideals, but how the characters learn to feel about those ideals in the course of their emotional and intellectual lives.

What we have then is a process of parallel maturation going on in both of our comic lovers rather than the sort of intersecting development that we saw in *Mr. Deeds* and *Mr. Smith*. The Jean Arthur character in both films has the example of a Jefferson Smith or a Longfellow Deeds to live up to. But Long John and Ann have no living model for properly moral behavior. Dr. Mitchell is dead, and Norton lacks any sense of idealism. What Long John and Ann have to learn is the right way of putting ideals to work in their lives. Norton (alive but immoral) and Dr. Mitchell (moral but not alive) thus serve as extremes of action and idealism, and John and Ann have to create a workable and self-aware third term for this moral dialectic.

So the problem is not one of becoming the kind of person you know you ought to be, but of discovering what you ought to be while in the process of becoming it. This somewhat directionless groping in the moral dark accounts, I think, for the sense of hesitancy in the film, the feeling that too much has been improvised and too little has been directed with a knowing hand. Capra has admitted problems in directing the film, but his major difficulty was with the ending. He could not come up with a fully satisfactory solution to the plot problem he set forth. The hesitancy, however, comes in the beginning of the film, and it is not so much a fault as it is the subject of the film. Of course, the ending does present problems, and we will discuss them presently, but the problems with the ending are a matter of plot, not pacing.

The first indication we get that Long John is in love with Ann comes in the almost surreal phantom baseball game in Long John's posh penthouse. Long John is the pitcher, and his potato-playing sidekick, The Colonel, is the catcher. The Colonel offers little tidbits of misanthropic advice as if they were signals for the next pitch. But they are not so much baseball signals as danger signals. The Colonel clearly sees (even if John himself does not yet) that John is getting caught up in something more than just a publicity stunt: he's getting caught up in love. He tells John that he is "stuck on the girl," and continues, saying "that's all a guy needs, to get hooked up with a woman."

The phantom baseball game.

The first inkling of any sexual or ideological maturation on Ann's part comes in the scene when she primes John for his first radio speech. She tells him that she has fallen in love with the character in the speech she has written (John is visibly affected by this). Her imaginary John Doe "turned out to be a wonderful person," and Ann pleads with John not to let her down (shot mostly over John's shoulder to a closeup on Ann):

If you'll just think of yourself as the real John Doe. Listen, everything in that speech is things a certain man believed in. He was my father, John, and when he talked people listened. And they'll listen to you, too. Funny, you know what my mother said the other night? She said to look into your eyes, and I'd see father there.

The Santa Claus socialism that comes out in John's subsequent speech clearly indicates the kind of personal morality Capra is considering in the film: faith in the essential goodness of the common man. As usual, Capra is too intelligent simply to let it go at that, however, and the remainder of the film shows the cost of that belief. In any case, this kind of concerned good-neighborliness hinges on a Deedsian faith in the universe, the belief that things will turn out all right if the John Does of the world all get up on their feet and start pulling together. This too has an adolescent ring to it (and the tone of that ring will change through the course of the movie), but it is appropriate as Ann's first step in the direction of faith (recall that Ann wrote the speech).

But note, however, that this ideological step is a sexual step as well: she literally loves her father for his ideology. This rough equation of the real John Willoughby with the once-real Dr. Mitchell and the imaginary John Doe puts Long John at the center of Ann's sexual attention. If he can be enough like the dead father ideologically, he stands to be Ann's living lover sexually. But she is still operating in a fantasy world of imagination, divorced from her cynical reality as publicity-stunt woman for D. B. Norton. John has to become an actual embodiment of an acceptable morality, but to do so means running the risk of crucifixion. The wide-eyed, good-Samaritan character in the speech is sufficient in imagination, but it is quite a different matter when this fantasy comes up against the reality of Norton's black-jacket troopers. Ann has to learn that her imaginary lover will not do. Not only must he be flesh and blood, but he must be aware of the sins the flesh is heir to, aware that being a trusting "Joe Doakes" is not enough in a universe full of D. B. Nortons. This is something both John and Ann must realize before they can become partners in a viable comic marriage.

The relationship of father figures to sex and morality is made clear later in the film when Ann prepares for the trip to the John Doe convention. She admits to Charlie (one of John's bodyguards) that she has treated John like a heel. She goes into her bedroom to pack, and John enters to tell her of a dream he had the night before. John sits down in the doorway, watching her fold her clothes on the bed in the background (camera shooting past him to pick Ann up in full shot), and he recounts the story of the "crazy dream" in which Ann is about to marry Norton's nephew.

The dream itself is an *It Happened One Night* in little. John chases the childlike Ann (growing older and bigger as she runs) across the rooftops, and he catches up with her just as her nightie becomes a wedding gown and just before she begins to recite her marriage vows with Ted Sheldon (Ron La Rocque). As in the earlier film, the connection between morality and sexuality is evident. It is comically immoral for Ellie to wed King Westley, and it is just as immoral for Ann to marry Ted Sheldon. John is both Ann's father and the justice of the peace in the dream, and hence he represents both sexual and moral authority. He makes it clear that marrying the wrong kind of person is, in the childlike terms of the dream, an offense punishable by spanking. To marry a rich man means sterility, cynicism, and playing the kind of power games that rich men always play in Capra. Thus Ann's sexual choice is a moral choice as well. Proper morality means devoting yourself to the kind of romantic knights-in-armor values that John-as-father describes, and that means marrying the kind of person who believes those values.

The dream makes it clear that the distinctions among John Doe, John Willoughby, and Ann's father are breaking down in John's mind: he is becoming the kind of knight he describes ("the man you marry has got to swim rivers for you, he's got to climb high mountains for you, he's got to slay dragons for you"). He grows from a self-center-

Ann begs John to continue the John Doe campaign.

ed child to a person maturely concerned with his responsibility towards others.

Further evidence of this comes later in the restaurant. John asks Ann how many people he has talked to since they got started, and goes on to describe the way he feels about those thousands of people:

I never thought much about people before. They were always just somebody to fill up the bleachers. The only time I worry about them is if they . . . when they didn't come in to see me pitch. You know, lately I been watching 'em when I talk to 'em (closeup on Ann: she looks down guiltily). I could see something in their faces. I could feel that they were hungry for something, you know what I mean? Maybe that's why they came. Maybe they were just lonely and wanted somebody to say hello to. I know how they feel. I been lonely and hungry for something nearly all my life (closeup on Ann, even more upset).

John was hungry when we first met him, but the hunger he talks about here is obviously a spiritual one. He is mature enough now to recognize the relationship between spiritual hunger and the John Doe role he has been playing. He has begun to believe his own speeches, and to take seriously the "love thy neighbor" ethic. What this means is that John recognizes a responsibility towards all those neighbors: they are no longer just bodies in the bleachers. Note too that this social awareness is coincident with his sexual awareness. He is no longer just "stuck" on a woman and playing phantom baseball games. He is thinking marriage, and will be proposing to Ann via her mother (he's still too shy to talk to Ann herself) within the next scene or two.

The key incident in the final maturation of both

Connell calls Norton a fascist skunk.

Ann and Long John is the confrontation in Norton's mansion after Connell (James Gleason)—the editor of Norton's newspaper—informs John in a fit of patriotic virtue that Norton is actually using John to front a fifth column movement. Norton is a fascist skunk, says Connell, trying to establish a fascist dictatorship and extinguish the lighthouse ideals of democracy in the fog of totalitarianism. John does not believe the accusation: Norton has "been marvelous about the John Doe clubs." He cannot conceive of Norton or Ann being involved in the kind of power grabbing scheme that Connell describes. He seizes the speech and angrily marches up to Norton's palace to find out if Connell's assertions are true.

John arrives in time to overhear Norton divide up the political pie among his influential guests and expound his own fascist plans for America. "These are daring times," says Norton, "we are coming to a new order of things. There's too much talk been going on in this country. Too many concessions have been made. What the American people need is an iron hand." Immediately upon finishing this little diatribe Norton turns to toast Ann Mitchell as "the brilliant and beautiful lady who is responsible for all this." At this point John walks into the room and asks Ann whether she wrote the speech (which nominated Norton for President on the John Doe ticket). She replies: "Yes, I did John, but I had no idea what was going on." Given what he has seen and heard John is perhaps justified in not believing her, and he asks about "that nice bracelet" that brands her in his eyes as a "dough grabbing dame" (to borrow Connell's term) who will do anything for a price. At this point John has had all but one of his illusions shattered, and that one, his faith in John Doeism, will be crushed at the rally when the bitterly disappointed John Does villify and humiliate him.

Ann too has an illusion shattered: it is no longer possible for her to ignore Norton's real intentions. She in fact "had no idea what was going on," and it was because she did not want to know. But now she knows. She has to make a moral choice between John and Norton, and make the choice she does. John rips into Norton for wanting to squash "the one worthwhile thing that has come along," and tells Norton that he cannot do it. "Well you go ahead and try," John challenges Norton, "you

John confronts Norton and his henchmen.

couldn't do it in a million years with all your radio stations and all your power, because it's bigger than whether I'm a fake, it's bigger than your ambitions, and it's bigger than all the bracelets and fur coats in the world." Ann chimes in "You bet it is John," and we know that she has finally awakened to her responsibility.

But both Ann and John still have a final lesson to learn. Norton's radio stations and political power *are* enough to kill the John Doe movement. Full maturity, for Long John and Ann as it was for Jeff Smith and Saunders, will be the realistic awareness that power counts, and that worthwhile ideals must be fought for with the full knowledge of the odds against success. To be moral and mature means being right, and fighting for that right, no matter what the chances for victory. To be immoral and immature is to be unaware (as both Ann and John were unaware) of the evil that faces you, for evil unopposed will triumph all the more surely.

John finally learns what he is up against when the John Does turn on him at the rally. He sees how quickly "love thy neighbor" can become "scorn thy neighbor," but he does not give up on the ideal itself. Like Jeff Smith, John is prepared to give all he has (including his life) to testify for his simple philosophy. But suicide is also anticomic. Dead heroes are sterile heroes, and it will be the measure of Ann's commitment that she can talk John out of killing himself.

The ending of *Meet John Doe* presents a great

In the rain at Wrigley field: the John Doe convention.

many difficulties. To begin with, Capra filmed five different conclusions, and four of the five were actually released. The ending as it now stands was suggested to Capra in a fan letter, and while it generally works, Capra is, to this day, dissatisfied with it.[7] But it is the ending we have, and for all of its awkwardness, it is clearly the right ending, taking into account all that has gone before and offering as much of a solution as is possible given the progress of the plot to that point.

The question is whether or not John will jump, and for what reason will he jump if he does? What will his death mean? What will it accomplish? He clearly views self-destruction as an expression of ultimate sincerity, and from his point of view it is, but suicide is just as clearly a gesture of futility. He will accomplish nothing beyond his own destruction, and the probable destruction of Ann as well. Certainly he would not rejuvenate the John Doe movement through his sacrifice, because Norton would doubtless hush things up. There is no question that Norton has power enough to squelch John's letter to Connell. John's decision to jump is based on two false assumptions: (1) that he cannot communicate his concern or demonstrate his integrity in any other manner but suicide, and (2) that the woman he loves, the person he trusted above all others, is in fact just another helot. Like Longfellow Deeds before him, Long John is acting on false information in deciding to end his life as a mode of protest. John feels deserted and betrayed by Ann, just as Deeds felt betrayed by Babe, and in both cases the

The John Does with their savior—before the crucifixion.

appearance of betrayal is more than erased by the fact of love freely given. Both Deeds and John assume they have nothing more to live for than the last-ditch integrity to be found in protest by suicide, but both are clearly wrong. John has quickened the conscience of Ann, just as Deeds renewed the faith of Babe, and that in itself is evidence enough that action short of suicide is possible.

Central to the saving of Long John, then, is making him aware that Ann loves him. Were he to die without that knowledge, his death would be forever tainted with the irony of mistaken motives: doing the right deed for the wrong reasons. But John is made acutely aware of his mistake when Ann throws herself sobbing into his arms, imploring him not to kill himself. She tells him what she could never tell him before, that she loves him, that she

is aware of the danger represented by Norton, that together with him she is willing to fight to preserve the John Doe ideals (ideals for which she is herself greatly responsible). But note the way in which she communicates her concern. "We can start clean now," she tells him, "just you and I. It'll grow John, it'll grow big, because it will be honest next time." If the connection between politics and sex were not made clear before, it is made explicit here. John is the father of the John Doe clubs, and with Ann as his partner they will give new birth to the movement.

Ann's appeal is thus not simply a sexual one. She appeals to a whole set of interlocking John Doe concerns and responsibilities. Sex is thus a part, an important part, of the John Doe gestalt. It is an ethic based on families (much is made of Ann's family in particular through the course of the movie). It is also an ethic based on golden-rule Christianity. Christmas chimes are ringing. The world is celebrating the coming of the first John Doe, the one who died so that Long John could live. It is a populist ethic, because the spirit of Christmas is kept alive in all of the John Does. And finally it is an ethic of resistance, because it demands a constant struggle to insure that the Nortons are never unopposed.

The single most troublesome aspect of the ending is the presence of Norton and his crew on the city-hall roof. In the first ending Norton is converted to goodness just as Paine was in *Mr. Smith.* He has to be on the roof to be converted, and hence his presence is easily accounted for in the first version. But Capra realized that the conversion of Norton would strain probability beyond its ability to bend, and he rightly decided that Norton would have to remain damned. He represents evil in the world, and thus he has to remain as a Manichaean balance to goodness. But if this is true, why does he make the climb to the top of city hall to stop John from jumping? He has already made sure that John's death will have no effect, so what does he care whether John jumps or not?

What we have, I think, in the present version, is the result of Capra's weariness with the film. He reshot the ending, but he did not reshoot the scenes leading up to the conclusion. The entire sequence of Norton and his Christmas tree and the carolers lends an out-of-place Dickensian aura to the ending, as if Norton were a soon-to-repent Scrooge. But why should he feel guilty, as he clearly does (note the way he checks his wristwatch), about John? This concern for John's welfare is clearly, within the plot as we now have it, the reason for his trip to the city-hall roof. The tone of voice he uses in imploring John not to jump further evidences this concern. Without question, we sense a spark of John Doe goodness in Norton. Thus if Capra tried to get rid of this sympathetic side to Norton, he clearly did not succeed.

But, of course, Capra could not reshoot the entire film every time he came up with a new ending, and I think we can understand the necessity for Norton's presence, whether or not the plot device used to get him to the roof is completely satisfactory. It is crucial to the effect of Ann's last-minute appeal that both the John Does and Norton be right there. They

Ann hurries to the city-hall roof.

serve an iconographic function. John is faced with a choice between adult responsibility, which means living to continue the fight, and adolescent histrionics, which entails an immature (because unaware) belief that nothing short of death will have any effect. Ann refers once to Norton and his pals ("It isn't dead or they wouldn't be here . . . they kept it alive by being afraid") and once to the John Does (Christ "kept it alive in them"). After Ann finishes speaking she collapses into John's arms. Then the John Does beg John not to commit suicide (although he has obviously already decided not to jump). The import of their action is not to save John, but to save themselves through confession. As Bert (Regis Toomey) says, they lost their heads and acted like a mob. Then we cut to a subjective pan shot of Norton and his lackeys taken from John's point of view. If he still has the slightest doubt about not jumping, a good long look at Norton confirms his decision to live and continue the struggle against evil. There is thus an almost ritualistic formality to this final sequence. Characters embody responsibilities, ideals, and principles (both good and bad), and the final dancelike movement sees John, with Ann in his arms, and the John Does, departing as a community of responsibility, leaving Norton and his boys to ponder their fate in the isolation of their cold night. Thus the John Does have to be there to leave with John and Ann, and Norton has to be there so that he can be left behind (like Morris in *The Younger Generation*—1929).

Growing up in *Meet John Doe* can therefore be seen as a matter of awareness and acceptance: being aware of evil in the world and accepting the responsibility of each individual to combat evil; being aware that the lack of responsibility breeds hatred and isolation and accepting the responsibility to combat ignorance and the forces that prey on ignorance with self-aware determination and Christ-like compassion. Such a description of the film's point carries us far beyond the initial, simpleminded John Doe ideals. We are no longer talking about Santa Claus and the sentimental spirit of Christmas. We are talking about oppression, exploitation, and the necessity of resisting oppression whenever and wherever it occurs.

Meet John Doe is not, therefore, a simpleminded "Sermon on the Mount with a drawl" (Ferguson, p. 405). Capra puts his "fantasy of goodwill" to the test of experience, and the resulting artistic statement is complex, ultimately mature, and politically aware. But moral complexity does not necessarily make engaging cinema. *Meet John Doe* is less successful than the other trilogy films because it lacks a firm sense of directorial control. Capra literally did not know where he was going with the film, and while the movie's argument, as it finally stands, is generally consistent, the explication of that argument lacks the sort of significant detail

and directional purpose that characterized *Mr. Smith Goes to Washington*. Furthermore, the lead characters (particularly the Stanwyck character) are not as sympathetically engaging at the film's beginning as the central characters in the other trilogy films. We are not sure that we should like Ann Mitchell, and while she ultimately redeems herself and our sympathies, she does so very late in a very long film. Long John Willoughby is more appealing, more Langdon-like, and his fortune matters to us from the very start. But it takes two people to form a comic marriage, and accordingly, we feel less concern for the Ann/John match than we did for the Jeff/Clarissa pairing in *Mr. Smith*. Our concern certainly develops through the course of the film, but there is still a nagging lack of intensity. We expect more from Capra than he delivers in *Meet John Doe*, and the film disappoints less for what it is than for what we hoped it would be.

NOTES

1. William Pechter, *Twenty-Four/Times/A/Second* (New York: Harper & Row, 1971), pp. 126-8.
2. All references are directly to the dialogue in the film.
3. Philip T. Hartung, "Capra and Doe's Little Punks," *The Commonweal*, 28 March 1941: 576.
4. Otis Ferguson, "Democracy at the Box Office," *The New Republic*, 24 March 1941: 405.
5. John Mosher, "Meet the Messiah," *The New Yorker*, 22 March 1941: 80.
6. Edgar Anstey, *The Spectator*, 10 Oct. 1941: 355.
7. For information on the ending of *Meet John Doe* see Frank Capra, "Five Endings in Search of an Audience," *The Name Above the Title* (New York: MacMillan, 1971), pp. 294-308; and "Mr. Capra Goes to College," an interview with Capra by Arthur Bressan and Michael Moran, *Andy Warhol's Interview*, 1 June 1972: 25-31.

13

It's A Wonderful Life

It's A Wonderful Life (1946) is the first of Capra's retrospection-period films, and it can best be understood as the mirror image of *Mr. Deeds Goes to Town* (1936), approaching the same problems and issues from a different stylistic and historical viewpoint. *Mr. Deeds* combines Capra's comic and romantic concerns, and the result is a comedy with romantic overtones about what happens when the hometown boy strikes it rich and hits the big town. The issue in *Mr. Deeds* is Capra's normal opposition of cynicism and romanticism, but it is expressed and solved within the context of the Depression and the New Deal. *It's A Wonderful Life* likewise mixes comedy and romance, but the result is a Capra romance with comic shading, concerned with what happens when the hometown boy does not strike it rich and never gets to the big city. Bedford Falls is Mandrake Falls revisited ten years and a world war later, and the threat of cynicism that is usually confined to the big city is seen at work in the very heartland of Capra's populist America. The issue of faith in the universe thus remains constant across the two films, but *It's A Wonderful Life* was made in a postwar universe, and the film reflects upon the effects of history on the lives of provincial Americans.

As is usual with Capra, however, the general issue is worked out primarily in personal terms, focusing on the personal history of one romantic dreamer. Capra's romance plot is thus set in the midst of Capra's rural comic landscape, and Capra's point is that nobody can escape moral issues by sitting on the provincial sidelines. Time and history wait for no man, regardless of his place of residence. World wars happen, cops and cab drivers are drafted to fight on foreign shores, and each man is required to consider both the value of his experience and his experience of values.

A few critical misconceptions should be cleared away before going on to discuss the film in detail. Most critics treat *It's A Wonderful Life* as somehow atypical of Capra, markedly different from his previous work in terms of form and content. Three problems account for this misunderstanding. First, previous critics have not made the distinction in film form between Capra's comedies and his romances, and hence they cannot put in perspective the fact that *Wonderful Life* looks unlike Capra's comedies. Of course it looks different: it is not comedy at all but romance, and Capra has been making romances off and on since 1927 (*Long Pants*).

The second problem involves the time scheme in the movie, which in the context of Capra's political period films seems strikingly unusual. Capra normally focuses on a short and crucial period in the lives of his characters, and thus the thirty some years covered in *Wonderful Life* seem remarkable. But again, knowledge of Capra's entire canon reveals that Capra had used a similar time scheme in *The Younger Generation* (1929), a film that fol-

It's A Wonderful Life: Mary (Donna Reed) and George
(James Stewart) on their wedding day.

lows the twenty year rise of Morris Goldfish from
paper boy to art importer. Thus, Capra has always
been interested in the past and its importance in the
present (*e.g.,* the importance of dead fathers in *Mr.
Smith*—1939 and *Meet John Doe*—1941), so that
his presentation of the past throughout the film is only
a slight variation from his normal approach, and
it represents no real thematic change at all.

The final problem concerns the presence of Providence personified and the device of the celestial
narrator. Providence has almost always played an
important, if implied, part in Capra, and Capra's
decision to make Providence an explicit factor by
involving George Bailey's guardian angel directly in
the action of the film is again primarily a matter of

Capra doing what he has always done rather than
doing something really new. The celestial narrator
(St. Joseph) is a little harder to handle. Capra has
always been a great storyteller, but he has always
been an invisible narrator whose presence was felt,
though never made explicit. In *Wonderful Life,*
however, the metaphor of the director as the all-
knowing and all-seeing diety is boldly asserted for
the first time. We are literally told the story from St.
Joseph's point of view, and St. Joseph's sympathetic
attitude partly determines how we feel about George
Bailey (James Stewart). George is surely likeable,
and we do not feel manipulated by Capra's use of
the explicit narrator, but the fact remains that the
presence of the narrator is something new.

What we are to make of this narrative presence is unclear. Stephen Handzo attributes it to a lack of confidence on Capra's part, evidencing a retreat into the comfort of the comprehended past and away from the uncertainty of the postwar present. The film's style certainly reveals a high degree of urgency on Capra's part, editing frequency and general noise level approaching the norms of Capra's political films, and we cannot help feeling that Capra experienced some deep sense of personal involvement. In fact, the film has a clear, autobiographical bent to it, reinforced by references both to earlier Capra films and to Capra's own life (*e.g.*, the George/Potter struggle recalls Capra's disputes with Harry Cohn: see Handzo for further biographical detail).[1] But personal involvement is not, *a priori*, a measure of artistic failure on Capra's part

(as Handzo implies). If anything, Capra is to be praised for turning his own concern with the value of his experience into a work of art that we all can share. Indeed, the narrator can be seen as Capra's attempt to get closer to his audience, to communicate in a more direct manner with the people. The film is about community and shared experience, and Capra's use of the narrative device encourages us to participate more fully in sharing the experience of the film. Thus *It's A Wonderful Life* is not about Frank Capra; rather it is Frank Capra sharing his thoughts about all of us in an intimate fashion, and George Bailey is more of an Everyman than a stand-in for Capra himself.

Like *The Odyssey*, the film begins, *in medias res*, with invocations to the Gods. George Bailey's family and friends pray to heaven to help George, and

Young George (Bobby Anderson) tells Mr. Gower (H. B. Warner) of the poison prescription.

the Lord and St. Joseph settle on one Clarence Odd-body (Henry Travers) as their messenger of mercy and George's guardian angel. But before they send Clarence down to earn his wings, Joseph provides a latter-day version of the epic genealogy, telling Clarence (and us) the history of the key incidents in George's life, pointing out both his inherent courage and honesty (his rescue of his brother Harry, his discovery of the poison prescription) and his romantic desire to quit his small-town home and travel the world.

One early incident in particular sets forth the opposition of comic honesty and resiliency to romantic great expectations. Young George has just recovered from the ear infection he developed after fishing his brother out of the ice. On his first day back at work jerking sodas in Gower's drug store, he finds two little girls waiting for him at the counter. One will grow up to be Vi, the town floozy, and the other will grow up to be Mary, George's wife. Vi (Jeanine Anne Roose) buys two-cents-worth of shoelaces, and asks George (Bobby Anderson) to help her down off her counter stool. George says nothing doing. Vi leaves, and George turns to Mary (Jean Gale), asking her what she wants. Mary replies "a chocolate," and George asks "with coconuts?" When Mary says that she does not like coconuts, George rips a *National Geographic* magazine out of his pocket and says: "Say, brainless, don't you know where coconuts come from? Look at here, from Tahiti, Fiji Islands, the Coral Sea."[2] After this outburst, George returns to the task of constructing Mary's chocolate soda, and as he bends down to scoop ice cream out of the freezer, Mary leans over the counter (closeup on her) and says: "Is this the ear you can't hear on? George Bailey, I'll love you till the day I die." George does not seem to hear this passionate confession, but his reply seems appropriate nevertheless. "I'm going out exploring someday," he asserts. "I'm going to have a couple of harems, and maybe three or four wives." We get a closeup of Mary when George says "wives," and the look on her face indicates that being a wife is just what she has in mind. Mary does, in fact, become George's wife, and she always retains the sense of reserved honesty that she displays here. Her resiliency is demonstrated by the fact that she marries George despite his determination not to be tied down in Bedford Falls. Thus the comic virtues to

Young Mary Hatch (Jean Gale) at the soda counter.

be found in unassuming domesticity are set against the romantic desires of George's dissatisfied provincial imagination.

The movement of the film, therefore, is to educate George, to show him that his dreams, and the despair that seizes him when it becomes absolutely clear that his dreams will never be fulfilled, are based on the false assumption that there is nothing valuable to do in Bedford Falls. George's dreams do, in part, bespeak his sense of vision, and there is nothing necessarily wrong with wanting to see the world or wanting to build great buildings, but, in George's case, there is something amiss. He does not understand his own self-worth. Deeds that he performs as a matter of course, and which therefore seem mundane to him, are in fact courageous and life-preserving. George's disappointment thus stems most directly from his desires for world travel and heroic deeds on a grand scale. What he must learn is that Bedford Falls is grand enough, that deeds done there are as heroic as deeds done elsewhere, and that true value resides not in faraway places but in people: friends are friends, no matter where you find them, and to be a friend is to be the greatest thing a man need ever be.

The moral dilemma in *It's A Wonderful Life* is thus similar to the moral issue in earlier Capra films: faith versus cynicism. At one end of the moral continuum is Peter Bailey (Samuel S. Hinds), George's selfless father, who is the kind of faithful friend to his community that George will eventually become.

George Bailey gets his traveling bag.

At the other extreme is the crippled banker, Henry F. Potter (Lionel Barrymore), a man "sick in his mind, sick in his soul" who "hates everybody who has anything that he can't have." Potter runs the town for the most part, everything but the Bailey Building and Loan, and he is frustrated when he cannot run that as well. Potter's frustration thus results from the same kind of romantic extremism that plagues George. Potter cannot be happy short of having everything he desires. Likewise, George cannot be happy short of seeing everything he wishes to see. The difference between the two is that George is moral, in the same way his father is moral, and he never lets his desires get in the way of his morality. If anything, George lets his morality, being a good neighbor to the people of Bedford Falls, get directly in the way of his own desires.

Potter on the other hand obviously has no sense of morality or community, and represents what George could become were he to devote his life solely to self-gratification in the way that Potter does. The moral continuum is thus worked out in a circle of characters. Peter Bailey is the norm, a moral capitalist devoted to the betterment of the community. Potter is to one side of him on the circle, an amoral capitalist bent on possessing the community and oppressing its people. George is to the other side of his father on the circle, moral like Peter Bailey, but bent on deserting the community for his own ends. The farther George moves away from his father on the circle, the more he lets his own desires determine his actions and attitudes, the closer he becomes to being another Potter. Indeed, George and Potter finally do come together in the "Potters-

Henry F. Potter (Lionel Barrymore): the demon in his den.

ville" sequence, which demonstrates the interrelationship of George's romanticism and Potter's acquisitiveness: George's deserting the community will result in Potter's oppressing the community.

George's past is a long series of frustrations. Just as he is about to leave for Europe, his father dies. Just as he is about to leave for college, he is forced to take over as chief executive of the Building and Loan, lest Potter succeed in taking it over. Four years later, when brother Harry (Todd Karns) returns from college (he went on the money George had saved for his own education), George discovers that Harry has married into a factory in upstate New York and will not be able to take over the Building and Loan so George can finally attend the university. On George's wedding day there is a run on

The run on the Savings and Loan.

the Building and Loan (precipitated by Potter?) and the honeymoon money goes to save the business. When the war breaks out, Harry goes overseas and earns the Congressional Medal of Honor for saving a troop transport from enemy air attack. George stays home, exempt because of his ear, organizing scrap drives, and serving as an air-raid warden. The final back-breaking, frustrating straw, however, is the result of yet another of Potter's attempts to take over the Building and Loan.

Uncle Billy (Thomas Mitchell) is preparing to deposit $8,000 of the Building and Loan's funds in the bank, when Potter is wheeled in. Billy goes over and shows him the headlines that declare Harry Bailey a national hero. In his elation, Billy absent-mindedly slips the money in between the pages of the newspaper, and he gives the paper, money and all, to Potter. Potter's first reaction moments later when he sees the money is to take it back into the bank, but as his office door opens, he sees Billy searching frantically, and Potter realizes that he finally has the Bailey Building and Loan right where he has always wanted it, in his own grubby hands. While George and Billy continue to search for the money, Potter makes sure that the press gets the story about the missing funds and that the District Attorney is notified. When it becomes clear that Billy cannot recall what he did with the money, George finally goes home and expresses his frustration by terrorizing his family. Then, in a last frantic attempt to save the business and avoid scandal, George leaves the house with his life insurance policy and goes to Potter for help.

Potter, of course, has been waiting for years to put the screws to the Bailey family in general, and to George Bailey in particular. His denial of George's appeal is predictable, but the viciousness of the reply is something new. It is no longer George's business that he wants, but George's reputation and life as well:

> You used to be so cocky. You were going to go out and conquer the world. You once called me a 'warped, frustrated old man.' What are you but a warped, frustrated young man, a miserable little clerk crawling in here on your hands and knees and begging for help, no securities, no stocks, no bonds, nothing but a miserable little $500 equity in a life insurance policy. (Potter laughs.) You're worth more dead than alive. Why don't you go to the riff-raff you love

so much and ask them to let you have your $8,000? You know why, because they'd run you out of town on a rail. But I tell you what I'm going to do for you, George. Since the state examiner is still here, as a stockholder of the Building and Loan, I am going to swear out a warrant for your arrest, missappropriation of funds, manipulation, malfeasance (George gets up to leave). Go ahead George, you can't hide in a little town like this.

There is a sadistic side to Potter that we have never seen before in any of Capra's evil capitalists. He is a medieval Despair figure, tempting the discouraged to give up altogether and commit suicide. Misery loves company (as Marlowe's Mephistophilis tells Dr. Faustus), and miserable Potter ("miserable" is his favorite word) loves nothing better than spreading the misery around.

But Despair can only tempt those who are already despairing. George does not consider going to his friends in the community because he believes Potter is right—they will run him out on a rail; and while George may want to leave town, that is not the way he wants to go. George is as wrong as Potter in his judgment of the people, for his friends do band together to save George Bailey and the Bailey Building and Loan. George has let this final frustration become the ultimate proof that morality gets you nothing but heartache and trouble. As in *Mr. Deeds*, the issue is one of faith in the universe and in the moral utility of right action. George has sacrificed all of his desires for the sake of his morals (this provided frustration enough in itself), but the final blow of the missing funds calls into question even the small satisfaction of knowing that sacrifice and frustration are justified. Why be moral when the universe sends Potters out to strangle you? George's decision to commit suicide, then, is not another final noble gesture intended to save the business (even if George might like to think so), but a gesture of ultimate cynicism: life is not worth living and George wishes he had never been born.

George gets that wish (he was never born, never existed), and Clarence gives him the guided tour of Pottersville, a nightmare version of what Bedford Falls would have been without George Bailey. But George does not believe what Clarence shows him. He knows Bedford Falls when he sees it (or so he thinks) and his frantic race through town is in search of someone who will confirm the fact that

George attempts to drown his despair—and then decides to drown himself.

nothing has changed. But things have changed. George's bewildered sprint down Main Street is a subjective montage, constructed so that we are George Bailey, running and stumbling down the street, glancing from one side to the other in search of a familiar face or landmark. What he sees instead are sleazy bars (The Bamboo Room, The Midnight Club, The Indian Club), strip joints ("Girls-Girls-Girls"), and "Dime-a-Dance" halls. The rhythm of the editing is quick, suggesting a high pitch of emotional urgency, and cuts from objective to subjective reveal a strong sense of disorientation.

The main street of Pottersville is cynicism concretized. Big-city decadence has moved into the bloodstream of small-town America, infecting with despair the small-town folk. They are strangers to one another rather than friends, and the sins of the flesh have taken over from the pleasures of the friendly spirit. Pottersville is Capra's version of hell on earth, and just as Odysseus must descend into the underworld before he can return to Ithaca, so must George Bailey visit Potter's den of darkness before he can return to Bedford Falls.

But unlike Odysseus, George at first refuses to acknowledge that hell exists. As Barbara Demming points out in *Running Away From Myself*, George seems singularly uninterested in Clarence's proof that George Bailey's life has made a difference to the people of Bedford Falls.[3] What he is worried about, says Demming, is recognition, going from

the bar to Ma Bailey's Boarding House to the library where the spinster Mary works, and asking in each place "I'm George, don't you know me?" In each case he is denied, and with each denial he becomes increasingly frantic. But this lack of interest does not mean that George is not learning the lesson that Clarence teaches him. He learns it, rather, piece by piece, and the first part of the lesson that he learns is not so much how much the people of Bedford Falls need George, as it is how much George needs the people of Bedford Falls.

The awareness that George finally comes to, then, is concerned with the nature and moral value of friendship. To be without faith in people is to be without friends, and to be without friends is to live in a place like Pottersville where the only community is a community of misery. The second part of the lesson comes after George is finally restored to life. He now knows how much he needs his family and his neighbors, not only in a financial sense, but in a moral sense. He had no idea they would step in, *en masse*, to foil Potter's scheme. But when they

"I'm George, don't you know me?"

do come to his rescue, George has overwhelming proof of their feelings toward him. They need him as much as he needs them, and they are willing to put their money on the line to save him from failure and scandal.

It's A Wonderful Life, then, is a film about friendships. A man's history and self-worth are a function of his deeds and relationships, each serving to enrich the other, all uniting in a vision of community value. Even trust in the universe is set in the context of friendship. Guardian angels are not fuzzy apparitions but likable fellows who carry copies of *Tom Sawyer* around. People can even return favors heavenward, and Clarence can thank George for giving him his wings. But note that Capra does not put forward this vision of friendship as any sort of universal panacea. It may be enough to save George Bailey from arrest and trial, but Potter, like his cynical brethren elsewhere in Capra, has in no way been vanquished. If anything, he has managed to extort another $8,000 from the poor people of the community.

The dream that has been discredited is one of self-sufficiency and self-gratification. George's mistaken sense of frustration has been replaced by a real feeling of satisfaction. Critics like William Pechter, who believe that George's suicide attempt is somehow existentially justifiable, miss the point that most of George's frustration is due not to Potter's schemes, but to his own dreams of faraway places and grandiose deeds.[4] The point is not that George should not feel threatened by Potter, but that George had capitulated to Potter's extremism long before he ever walked into Potter's office to ask for help (he should have gone to the people in the first place). This Potter-like aspect of George's personality is one of the film's greatest strengths. James Agee may complain that the film's "chief mistake or sin—an enormous one—is its refusal to face the fact that evil is intrinsic in each individual."[5] But the film clearly takes account of original sin by showing the best of men subject to the worst of vices.

The bulwark against romantic extremism of any sort is the typical Capra comic family. The subsidiary comic movement of the film, the marriage of George and Mary (Donna Reed), is completed early, but it provides the ethical cornerstone of Capra's personalist morality. "It's deep in the race," says George's father, "for a man to want his own

Mary and George on their wedding night in the old Granville place.

roof, walls, and fireplace" for his family; and it is of no little significance that the Bailey Building and Loan is in the home building business. It is an enterprise dedicated to the notion of family unity. The fertility ritual enacted on the doorstep of the new Martini family home in Bailey Park celebrates the sanctity of this family ethic. Mary hands Mrs. Martini (Argentina Brunetti) a loaf, saying "bread, that this house may never know hunger," and some salt, "that life may always have flavor." George then grabs the wine and hands it to Mr. Martini (Bill Edmunds), completing the litany by wishing "that joy and prosperity may reign forever."

The major image of the film is therefore that of homes and houses. We see the Bailey home, Mary's house, and most importantly the house at 320 Sycamore that George and Mary rebuild as their own home. There is also Bailey Park, which contrasts to the never-seen but often-mentioned tenement shacks owned by Potter. Of the major characters, Potter is the one we most seldom see at home. He is usually in his office, at board meetings, or in his iron-studded carriage. On the one occasion when we do

Dedicating the new Martini home: the ceremony of
wine, bread, and salt.

see Potter at home, he is in his officelike study,
which displays the kind of cold, Napoleonic decor
typical of Capra capitalists. The one picture hanging on Potter's wall is a portrait of himself, the perfect image for Potter's egomania. By contrast, the
Building and Loan office has as its central feature
a model of a Bailey Park home (with a Potter-black
pet raven always hovering near: see still). The individual offices of Uncle Billy and George share the
same kind of homey warmth as the outer office.
George has a picture of his father on the wall and
pictures of the rest of the family on his desk. Uncle
Billy's office is similarly cluttered with memorabilia,
and its generally lived-in appearance contrasts with
the tomblike order of Potter's office and study.

Clearly the most important house of them all is
the old, broken-down, windowless house at 320
Sycamore that serves as the scene for George and
Mary's courtship, their honeymoon, and their entire
life together. The house, the old Granville place, is,
in fact, a symbol for the possibilities for life and
renewal in Bedford Falls. When George and Mary
come drippingly home from the dance in the high
school swimming pool, George insists that they
stop, throw a rock, and make a wish (a privilege
gained by successfully smashing one of the few remaining windowpanes). George throws his rock and
makes his wish, or rather his "whole hatful" of
wishes. Mary asks him what he wished for and he
tells her:

Uncle Billy (Thomas Mitchell), his raven, and George
in the Building and Loan Office.

Mary, I know what I'm gonna do tomorrow, and the next day, and next year, and the year after that. I'm shaking the dust of this crummy little town off my feet and I'm gonna see the world, Italy, Greece, the Parthenon, the Coliseum, and then I'm coming back here and go to college and see what they know, and then I'm gonna build things. I'm gonna build airfields, skyscrapers a hundred stories high. I'm gonna build bridges a mile long . . .

Before George can finish running through the catalogue of his romantic desires, a look both of sadness and determination crosses Mary's face, sadness because George's plans do not include her, and determination that she will be included anyway. She then throws her own rock, breaks her own window,

and, as we find out later, wishes her own wish that she will marry George Bailey, bear his children, and raise her brood of little Baileys in that old rundown yet magically beautiful Granville place. Her wish comes true, implying that the right kind of fertile comic wishes will be rewarded, while George's romantic desires will only meet with frustration and disappointment in an unromantic world.

The depths of George's frustration can be measured by his changing attitude towards the house. Mary has slowly brought it back to life, rebuilding it bit by bit and filling it with a noisy, lively family (and healthy noise, we should note, evidences a healthy family). But the rejuvenation of the old house does not seem to register with George as a

Sadness and determination: Mary makes her own wish.

significant fact. On his final rampage, before he leaves the house to see Potter, he complains that the "drafty old barn" is unfit for human habitation. Of course by this time it is perfectly fit to shelter his family (we see this fitness as the camera follows George in quick succession from the parlor to the living room to the kitchen and upstairs to Susan's bedroom). Mary has successfully built her comic nest, and George's romantic frustration prevents him from recognizing the comic fact of the matter. The dilapidation that he assigns to the house is, in fact, the romantic dilapidation of his own spirit, and this spiritual dilapidation characterizes the house as we see it in the Pottersville sequence, ruined beyond repair, a symbol of hopelessness rather than possibilities.

A prince, rich with love: the *Wonderful Life* of George Bailey.

After George's "rebirth," his attitude towards his home changes completely: it is indeed a wonderful life, and the old barn is a "wonderful, old, drafty house." He finally recognizes that his house is the castle of a prince, rich with love. He finally realizes that living in Bedford Falls is not being out of place, but rather being precisely in place, fulfilling one's role in the grand comic design of the universe. Like *Dirigible* (1931), *It's A Wonderful Life* is an anti-romance that comes to a comic conclusion. The unification of the community behind George Bailey provides us with a *kômos* of solidarity among friends. The film is a celebration of community life and the bonds of faith and trust that tie the community together. It takes into account the ironic possibilities symbolized by Potter, and the tendency for even the best of men to become similarly cynical, but by so doing, it only strengthens the assertion that life can be wonderful. If we can look Potter (and all he implies) in the eye, and still believe in the possibilities for fruitful human relationships, then we are entitled to our comic optimism. *It's A Wonderful Life* is a wonderful film, as richly vital as Ford's *How Green Was My Valley* (1941) or Chaplin's *City Lights* (1931), and if Capra's up-beat sentiment seems slightly out of step with the down-beat pathos of his sentimental contemporaries, then so be it: they need not all march to the same cinematic drummer.

NOTES

[1] Stephen Handzo "Under Capracorn," *Film Comment* 8, no. 4 (1972): 12-4.

[2] All references are directly to the dialogue in the film.

[3] Barbara Demming, *Running Away From Myself* (New York: Grossman, 1969), pp. 112-6.

[4] William Pechter, *Twenty-Four/Times/A/Second* (New York: Harper & Row, 1971), pp. 128-9.

[5] James Agee, *The Nation*, 15 Feb. 1947: 193-4. Manny Farber, writing in *New Republic* (6 Jan. 1947), generally agreed with Agee that *Wonderful Life* was oversimple in its appoach to human problems. The film is, says Farber, Capra's attempt "to convince movie audiences that American life is exactly like the *Saturday Evening Post* covers of Norman Rockwell" (p. 44).

14

Pocketful of Miracles

Pocketful of Miracles was something of a critical and commercial failure when it opened in December 1961. The commercial misfortune probably resulted from poor promotion. The critical failure, however, is harder to fathom. Arthur Knight described *Pocketful* as "overlong, overelaborate, and pretentious."[1] Isabel Quigly remarked that "the odd thing about it isn't its badness but the fact that, bad as it is, it is made by Frank Capra."[2] Even William Pechter, a generally sympathetic critic, could describe the film as "trivial," plagued occasionally by "those big, dull, vacant spaces which money seems infallibly to buy; it suffers from the Hollywood disease—elephantiasis."[3] I find the film one of Capra's most satisfying efforts, every bit as engaging as *Mr. Deeds* (1936) or *Broadway Bill* (1934). It is not, perhaps, one of Capra's great films, not quite up to the standard of *It Happened One Night* (1934) or *Mr. Smith* (1939), but it is a film of considerable merit nevertheless, and one worth attending to if only by virtue of previous critical neglect: reviewers generally gave it the quick once-over blandly, and Capra scholars tend to ignore it altogether, as if Capra had "stopped the world and got off" after *State of the Union* (1948).[4] But *Pocketful of Miracles* is a very moving and enjoyable film, very deeply concerned with the comic drive towards fertile human relationships, and worth much more than just a passing glance.

A common symbol for personal and social fertility is the family, which is often seen in comedy as the ideal context for fruitful human interaction. Such is frequently the case in Capra: from *That Certain Thing* (1928) onward, the family has been at the center of Capra's comic vision, serving as the humanistic foundation of Capra's personalist morality. Many of his films begin with family quarrels and conclude with family reconciliations, as barriers to family and interpersonal harmony are overcome (*e.g., That Certain Thing, The Younger Generation*—1929, *It Happened One Night, Broadway Bill, A Hole in the Head*—1959). *Pocketful of Miracles* fits this pattern of torn-and-mended family relationships very nicely. The film has a double-plot movement, and each plot is concerned either with the maintenance or creation of family ties.

The first plot involves a bootlegger, Dave the Dude, his girlfriend, Queenie Martin, and Dave's business associate, public enemy number one, Steve Darcey. Queenie (Hope Lange) is all that remains of the Martin family after her father, the owner of a lavish speakeasy, is rubbed out for non-payment of large gambling debts. She and Dave fall in love, but their marriage is called off when Dave (Glenn Ford) refuses Queenie's request that he stop dealing with Darcey (Sheldon Leonard) and quit the rackets altogether.

The second plot involves Apple Annie (alias Mrs. E. Worthington Manville: Bette Davis), her illegitimate daughter Louise (Ann-Margaret), the daugh-

The original Apple Annie: May Robson in *Lady For a Day*.

ter's fiancé, Carlos Romero (Peter Mann), his father, the Count Romero (Arthur O'Connell), and Louise's many godfathers, Annie's crew of street beggars. Louise was raised in Spain, and she, her intended, and her future father-in-law are coming to New York to meet the bride's distinguished mother.

The two plots are tied together by Dave's reliance on Annie's good-luck apples. He always gets one before embarking on business ventures, and now that Darcey, the "man from Chicago," is in town, Dave needs more luck than ever if he is to maintain control of his own turf. But Annie is herself in dire need of luck. The prospect of her daughter's visit drives her to drink as she attempts to drown the thought of her impending humiliation and with it her fear that Louise will no longer love her when she finds out that Annie is only an apple woman, not a society matron.

Dave is clearly the only person in the film with the money, the influence, and even half the inclination necessary to carry out the elaborate masquerade that Annie so desperately needs: she has to be Mrs. E. Worthington Manville for the duration of her daughter's visit. But Dave is unwilling to take the time or the trouble: once he gets his apple he wants nothing more to do with the old hag. He has a visitor of his own, Darcey, to worry about.

The moral issue of the film thus centers on Dave the Dude. If he continues his racketeering and the self-centered mercenary attitude required by that profession, he will not only lose Queenie, thereby destroying any possibility of raising a family with her, but he will likewise destroy Annie's family, Annie herself, and with her the very luck that made him a top racketeer in the first place.

But the very fact of Dave's dependence on Annie's apples is evidence enough that he is redeemable. Where Deeds has his tuba and John Doe has his harmonica, Dave the Dude has his lucky apples to symbolize his essential naivete, the vulnerable humanity beneath the self-sufficient gangster facade. He never does anything important without getting a lucky apple from Annie, and her importance is magnified in the film because Dave is in the midst of the most important deal of his career: sewing up complete control of the New York City mobs by forcing Darcey to accept a peace agreement on Dave's terms. Dave is thus vitally involved in a Sternbergian underworld. His future as a big shot depends on his success in negotiating with Darcey. Dave is also vitally involved in the parody underworld of Annie and her beggars. The negotiations with Darcey depend upon Dave's success at keeping Annie and her apples out of trouble. As Dave moves back and forth between one involvement and the other, he slowly begins to understand what true "vitality" is, and Queenie is the one who shows him the way.

The thematic opposition between capitalist self-centeredness and familial responsibility is first specified in the scene where Dave the Dude initially encounters Queenie. The Dude has called for Annie (he has some unknown deal on the fire). She meets him in Rudy Martin's speakeasy, where the Dude is busy blasting open Rudy's safe to learn why the mob bumped him off. Dave finds the reason, $50,000 worth of gambling debts, and he finds a note addressed to himself: "Thanks for everything. Take care of my baby, Queenie." Nobody knows who or what "Queenie" is, and Dave turns to Annie, asking her for an apple worth a triple shot of luck. Annie hands him a big red one, saying "something good's gonna happen to you, now, something real good," and we find out who Queenie is. Just as Annie says "something good" we get a quick cut to a wet and bedraggled young girl poking her head in the speakeasy door. The girl, we find out a moment later when Dave finally gets around to talking with her, is Queenie Martin, Rudy's daugh-

ter. She is all that remains of the Martin family after her father is murdered (and Rudy's gangland death is an example of where racketeering can get you: the bottom of the East River). Queenie is now alone in the world, and the remainder of the film will be, for her, an attempt to create a new family.

Queenie's sense of family is strong, and when she learns that Dave paid for her father's funeral, she thanks him for "being Papa's friend." Of course, Queenie has a thing or two to learn about the Dude and about herself, but she also has an important lesson to teach Dave. She has seen one family destroyed by the lust for money and power, and she is determined, once she falls in love with Dave, that she will not see her second family so destroyed. Accordingly, Queenie has to show Dave that power and money, particularly power and money as Dave conceives of them, will not insure happiness. Queenie has to teach Dave that he does not really need to be another Steve Darcey, constantly hounded by the police on one side and rival mobsters on the other, carted around like a piece of antique furniture in an armored moving van, trapped by the very power that he thought would gain his freedom.

All of which may seem a tall order for a latent homebody like Queenie, but Queenie is more than just a homebody, and Capra makes that clear by use of another significant cut. During the first scene in the speakeasy, Dave asks Annie why he believes that her apples bring him luck. She offers this explanation:

ANNIE: Because the little people like you.
DAVE: What little people?
ANNIE: Oh, you can't see 'em. They live in dreams.
DAVE: Little people like me, huh? Why?
ANNIE: Because they like children, beggars, and poets.
DAVE: You mean that makes me a poet?
ANNIE: You want to believe in something. Right now it's my apple, so the little people jump in it, see? That's why this apple will bring you luck.

Just as Annie begins to explain "the little people," we get another quick cut to Queenie, and the implication, that Queenie is one of the fairy band, is made explicit throughout the course of the film. She literally makes a poet out of Dave the Dude, forcing him to write and direct a fairy-tale comedy with a

Apple Annie (Bette Davis) tells Dave (Glenn Ford) about the "little people" who inhabit her apples, while Joy Boy (Peter Falk) looks on incredulously, from *Pocketful of Miracles. (Copyright © 1961 Franton Productions. All Rights Reserved—Released through United Artists.)*

cast of children (Louise and Carlos, most of the childlike thugs, even the elder Romero and the Spanish consul) and beggars (Annie, the Judge, and the rest of Louise's "godfathers"). And she makes him do it at the very moment when he finally thinks his own dream of money and power is about to come true.

But Queenie is not going to make a romantic poet of the Dude. She is much more concerned to make a domestic poet out of him, and this is made clear in the scene when Queenie, now the star performer at her father's old speakeasy, ceremoniously burns her father's now paid-off debts. She has sold the club, and purchased her freedom. She asks Dave if he is still serious about getting married, and tells him the date and time:

QUEENIE: 10 a.m. Sunday morning we get married, it's all set.

DAVE: You're kidding, you mean really married? us?
QUEENIE: The real us, no more Dude and no more Queenie. To David and Elizabeth, Mr. and Mrs. Conway of Silver Springs, Maryland and their flock of children (she raises her glass).

Dude at first thinks Queenie is kidding, but he quickly discovers that she is serious, and he agrees to the wedding (he has been waiting for years to marry her, and is not going to let sentimental formalities get in his way). The bootlegging racket has dried up with the repeal of Prohibition, and Dave is now respectable enough to show his face in Silver Springs. His attitude towards Queenie's request is one of bemused condescension. He does not fully comprehend the strength of her comic-fertility instinct, and he does not see marriage to Elizabeth as demanding any real change in his own lifestyle.

Dave's unwillingness to attend to Queenie's needs is evidenced moments later in the same scene. No sooner has Dave agreed to the wedding than Joy Boy (Peter Falk) pokes his head in the door to remind Dave that Annie has come with her apples. Dave has something going, and the something is the Darcey deal. When Queenie learns that Steve Darcey, public enemy number one, has come from Chicago to talk with the Dude, she pleads with Dave to grab their bags and flee out the back door (recall Helen Pierce asking the same thing of Frisky in *Dirigible*—1931). But Dude does not want domestic happiness "in the sticks": he wants to be top dog in the city: "I started at the bottom in this town, and I'm going right up to the top. . . . Newsboy, hustler, all the way up, and why? Because I'm good and because I'm lucky. I'm gonna be somebody, Queenie, and you're gonna be somebody with me." Queenie does not want to be this kind of Morris Goldfish somebody, and she gives Dave the choice: either Darcey and the New York City mobs, or herself and Maryland. Dave refuses to choose, and he seems determined as he walks out for his rendezvous with Darcey to have the best of both worlds. He does not give Queenie credit enough to think she will make her ultimatum stick.

The conflict in the film is thus between big-city self-centeredness and comic domesticity: a familiar Capra concern. And as elsewhere in Capra, this conflict is expressed through a variety of characters, ranging from the vice-mongering Darcey at one extreme to the pure-virginal princess, Annie's daughter, at the other. Within this continuum, characters are free to choose the kind of person they wish to be. We have already discussed Dave's dilemma. He must choose between Darcey and Queenie, whether he likes it or not. Queenie, similarly, given Dude's insistence on completing the Darcey deal, has to choose between marriage to Dave and marriage to Howard Potter, the restauranteur (recalling A. B. Charles in *That Certain Thing*) who owns the cafeteria where Queenie used to work. In her choice, Queenie is like Emmadel Jones in *Here Comes the Groom* (1951), leaving the man she really loves for the sake of domestic and financial security. And like Emmadel Jones, Queenie comes to realize that love as a value overrides security. She understands that she cannot desert the man she loves, no matter how crazy his schemes (recall Helen Pierce in *Dirigible*).

What we see happening with Dave and Queenie is thus the same kind of parallel maturation (necessitated by parallel situations) that we saw at work in *Meet John Doe* (1941). Queenie's initial family

The fairytale almost collapses: Annie hugs her daughter's portrait, while Dave and Queenie (Hope Lange) read letter. (*Copyright © 1961 Franton Productions. All Rights Reserved—Released through United Artists.*)

instincts are more proper than Dave's financial ones, but she too is capable of the same type of self-serving ambition: she will sell herself in marriage if that marriage will provide the sort of family security she seeks (although marriage to Howard Potter would only provide a sterile sort of financial rather than emotional security). It is significant that the first move to help Annie is made by Dave. To be sure, he just wants to keep his luck alive, and he has no idea what he is getting into, but he makes Queenie go along to Annie's despite her determination to have nothing more to do with him. Once at Annie's, however, and once Dave has his apple, Queenie takes over, and she is the one who prods Dave into dealing with each successive threat to the success of Annie's masquerade, despite his own determination to drop the whole affair. Through this process of helping Annie, Dave becomes an increasingly better person, more aware of others and more empathetic toward their needs, so that Queenie is finally right to love him without question, no matter what his dealings with Darcey. He says he needs her, and she knows by then that you do not desert a person in need, whether it be a panhandler or a rumrunner.

But ironically, and appropriately, the better person Dave becomes the more he learns that he does not need Darcey. Our interest throughout most of the film is attached to the progress of Annie's comic deception as managed by Dave and Queenie. But the process of managing Annie's fairytale is a process of growth for Dave, and equal with our interest in Annie's fortune is a corresponding interest in Dave's rejuvenation. Each time a new crisis develops in the deception, Dave refuses to go another step further. And on each occasion Queenie insists, cajoles, or badgers, and Dave ends up taking that step, moving that much further outside of his self-centered gangster persona. The more he thinks about Annie's plight, the less he thinks about himself and his own plans. Each time he moves to help Annie, he is forced to keep Darcey waiting, still a prisoner in Dave's armored moving van. Thus to rightly attend to Annie is to rightly ignore Darcey. But again, ironically, the more Darcey is ignored the more willing he is to settle on Dave's terms, so that helping Annie earns Dude everything he desires. By the time Darcey capitulates, however, Dave has come completely to his senses. Now that he has

Annie transformed: Guy Kibbee admires his *Lady For a Day*.

what he wants, he realizes that he no longer wants it. Clearly his experience as godfather and comic poet has made him see the values of love, selflessness, and domesticity, values that provide emotional rewards more real and more lasting than the status capitalist braggarts can claim through terror and oppression.

The depth of this change in Dave's mobster personality is demonstrated in the final crisis. Count Romero insists on a reception to announce the engagement of Louise and Carlos. It is the last straw for Dave. He has managed to come up with a penthouse, a wardrobe, a husband and in-laws for Annie, but he absolutely refuses to stage a party for "one hundred of the four hundred." Queenie pleads with him: "Just once couldn't we help somebody just to help somebody?" And Dave replies: "We're gonna help somebody, we're gonna help me; me, that's who we're gonna help." He then gets ready once again to meet with Darcey, but just before he gets out the door, Carlos and Louise appear to ask "Uncle David" if he will be godfather to their first child. As Queenie points out, Dave is used to being a godfather (to Louise), and apparently the idea still appeals to him, as he quickly plunges in (against Joy Boy's better advice) to planning the gala reception. Dude's mobsters and Queenie's chorus girls will get the instant course in etiquette from The Judge (Thomas Mitchell: Annie's "husband"), and they will be the social set for the evening.

The best-intended plans go oft awry, however, and while Dave is pleading with his boys to get in the spirit of the upper crust (repeating Queenie's speech about doing good for goodness' sake) the cops are outside Queenie's place, making ready to arrest the lot of them. Given this constraining situation, Dave can either leave Annie to impending humiliation, or he can make the greatest sacrifice, do the unheard-of deed: tell the truth to the cops. Dave does just that, even though it rubs against his gangster grain, and the result is that fairy-tale truth overwhelms mundane precinct-station reality. When the Mayor and the Governor hear the "Mother Goose Story," they too are caught up in the comic spirit. They not only agree to free Dave (rather than hold him for kidnapping some snooping reporters), but they volunteer their services as high-class guests for the reception. The success of Annie's

deception is thus assured. Carlos and Louise sail back to Spain to be married and their fairy-tale love affair comes to a happily-ever-after conclusion.

But what does this one successful attempt at overcoming everyday probability imply? Is Capra saying that a belief in fairytales will save us all from poverty, humiliation, and oppression? Or is he saying just the opposite, that poverty, humiliation, and exploitation will bar all but a providentially lucky few from enjoying the comic pleasures of existence?

Surely the film gives the latter answer, and Capra makes this clear through an almost Buñuelian concentration on the grotesque facts of poverty and degradation. No amount of good feeling (of which there is much) can erase the image of a legless beggar riding on a single roller skate through rain-glutted gutters (recall a similar beggar in *Los Olvidados*—1950). No amount of wish fulfillment can obscure our horror at the thought of getting a blowtorch in the armpits (as did Stiff-Arm Sam). People are generally miserable, and racketeers are always there to prey upon their misery. Capra's primary purpose in remaking his own *Lady for a Day* (1933) was to emphasize these "rock-hard" truths of existence.[5] The realistic Dave/Queenie plot concludes with Dave's decision to marry Queenie and move to Maryland, nothing necessarily fantastic or improbable. Darcey is still free to operate his vice rackets ("catering to all human weaknessess"), Annie and her legless, sightless, voiceless beggars are right back on the street, and the rich still live in their high-class hotels where they look down their elevated noses at the beggars below, without empathy or compassion. It is still a hard and generally pitiless world and Capra's humor does not attempt to hide the fact.

As does *It's A Wonderful Life* (1946), then, *Pocketful of Miracles* earns its comic conclusion by encompassing ironic reality. Even the wide screen is exploited for this purpose, letting Capra include the arch-realist Joy Boy as often as possible within the frame to remind us (as he constantly reminds Dave) that Darcey awaits without. The overall structure of the film shifts from high-life to low-life scenes, from penthouses to back alleys, from tattered rags to elegant gowns, from pool halls to billiard table, so that Capra clearly intended us to be aware of both extremes. As I noted in my

Annie waves goodbye as Louise sails for Spain: *Lady For a Day.*

discussion of Capra's style, the scenes of upper-class existence evoke a Minnelli-like appreciation of the beauty that wealth can provide; rich, bright, vibrant tones that enliven the very atmosphere. Capra plays this vibrancy against the cold, somber greys and dark shadows of the streets and tenements, thus demonstrating poverty's bleakness when compared to the colors wealth can lend to life. Of course, one can be too colorful, and the way to avoid that danger is to return to the country where nature provides color enough for the comic life.

But the most noteworthy fact is not just that ironic reality is accounted for, but that its impact is far greater than necessary to justify the quite minor miracle that concludes the film. Dynasties are not overthrown and great political ideals are not reaffirmed. Nevertheless, the film does make a signifi-

cant statement about the relationship between proper concern for others and irresponsible self-centeredness. We have the comic marriages to symbolize properly comic family values, but always hovering nearby are the mutilated beggars, the crippled victims of social disregard, to remind us both how precarious life can be and yet how meaningful it can be even in the worst of circumstances given real empathy and compassion. Thus the beggars can express a certain *joie de vivre* (as they do when they sing in the taxicab) without undercutting their symbolic status as reminders of social reality. They *look* grotesque, and they recall the grotesque possibilities in everyone. Even the best of people, Dave and Queenie, can be all too much like Darcey, cynical, self-centered, emotionally crippled. Nevertheless, for all that Capra can and does say about the "rock-hard" ironies of life, he can still honestly assert a realistic belief in human possibilities for integrity, community, and a life rich with emotion. Even Joy Boy, after all, has a selfless love for his pregnant wife. Sometimes a pocketful of miracles is enough to keep you going.

NOTES

1. Arthur Knight, "A Dissertation on Roast Corn," *Saturday Review,* 11 Nov. 1961: 32.
2. Isabel Quigly, *The Spectator,* 5 Jan. 1962: 18.
3. William Pechter, *Twenty-Four/Times/A/Second* (New York: Harper & Row, 1971), pp. 54, 123.
4. Andrew Sarris, *The American Cinema* (New York: E. P. Dutton, 1968), p. 87.
5. Frank Capra, *The Name Above the Title* (New York: Mac-Millian, 1971), p. 496. Capra makes a similar statement in an interview in *Newsweek,* 18 Dec. 1961: 97-8.

15

The Capra Universe

I began this essay with the assertion that Capra's movies could best be understood in the context of literary history. Such a study provides us with many significant insights into individual films, but more importantly it sets the terms for characterizing the cinema of Frank Capra as a complete and complex whole, a visionary-poetic universe run by laws of probability and morality that often seem only obliquely related to the laws of the world we live in.

But this oblique relationship between the aesthetic image and everyday life is typical of all comedy, and the laws of the Capra universe generally correspond to the laws of the larger comic universe, laws deriving their authority from the recurring and rejuvenating myths of literature and civilization.

As a general rule, comedy attends to and reflects upon human desires for love, life, and fertility. Comic plots emphasize sequences of reversal and recovery that in turn reflect mythological sequences of death and rebirth. Such sequences in themselves are clearly unrealistic: people die and are seldom reborn. But these sequences are symbols of a transcendent emotional truth, the feeling, however, illogical, that life is both miraculous and wonderful.

Elements of the miraculous, the wonderful, and the fantastic are found in all comedies. Shakespeare's comedies abound with fantastic characters and situations. The comedies of Jonson, Middleton, and Massinger are rife with grotesque characters and bizarre plot complications. Similar elements of the improbable and the absurd can be found in Greek Comedy, Roman Comedy, Restoration Comedy, Molière, Shaw, and even in the black comedy of modern playrights such as Beckett and Anouilh.

Capra's films present no exception to this general comic characteristic. Aspects of the improbable, the fantastic, and the unexpected always seem at work in Capra's films, throwing characters off balance, upsetting their sense of equilibrium, deceiving and confusing normally perceptive individuals. Few people, after all, ever find themselves seated beside a runaway heiress on a New York-bound bus. Few people inherit twenty-million dollars. Few Boy Scout leaders suddenly find themselves in the U.S. Senate. Few beggars find themselves hosting the Governor of New York at a penthouse reception.

Hence, the first rule of the comic universe in general and the Capra universe in particular is that normal everyday rules of probability do not always apply. In other words, the everyday rules are "off." Such a suspension of probability allows Capra to put his characters in fantastic situations that require that they rethink their own sense of self and morality, working through the morass of their own emotional and perceptual mistakes towards a renewed awareness of emotional and intellectual reality. Longfellow Deeds, for example, goes to town where he discovers that his romantic dreams are unrealistic given the world he inhabits. Once he does so, how-

Reborn: George (James Stewart) tells Bert the cop
(Ward Bond) that *It's a Wonderful Life*.

ever, he realizes that the world offers realistic rewards enough to satisfy his basic longings and
instincts.

What we see in Capra, then, is actually a latter-
day equivalent of the Roman Saturnalia, a period of
madcap license in which "all normal business and
ceremony [were] put aside for the duration of the
holiday, and masters and servants exchanged roles;
the slaves sat at table wearing their master's clothes
and the *pilleus*, or badge of freedom, and enjoyed
the right to abuse their masters, who served them."[1]
The rules of everyday human interaction are suspended, and the world is turned upside-down (as
Ian Donaldson would put it): the low are made
great, and the great are brought low, and the final
effect is one of "leveling," making all characters
undergo the democratic experience of absolute
equality under the benevolent providence of the
comic spirit (Donaldson, p. 7). The Vanderhoff
household in *You Can't Take It With You* (1938)
is a good example of such saturnalian equality at
work.

This sort of leveling is surely what C. L. Barber
had in mind when he described Shakespeare's festive

The Boy Scout leader in the U.S. Senate: *Mr. Smith Goes to Washington*.

Capra and the clan on the *You Can't Take It With You* set.

comedies as working "through release to clarification," acting out the inversions of holiday revel so that everyday society, to which all revels must eventually return, can be rejuvenated with some of the holiday spirit, made that much more humane, that much more attentive to the emotional needs of all people.[2] Structurally speaking, then, the Saturnalia as a comic pattern corresponds to the scenes of sacrifice and feasting that we discussed in chapter 2: identities are confused, heroes are slain and dismembered, fertility is celebrated, and the rejuvenated society reconstitutes itself at a final festivity, a wedding or *kômos* preparatory to returning from holiday to everyday.

And thus the second rule of the Capra universe is that the "off" rules are always poised to reassert themselves. As in *Pocketful of Miracles* (1961), we are always aware that the fairytales of improbable fortune can return at any moment to the logical fate of everyday life. Taylor might very easily have defeated Jeff Smith. John Doe might very well have jumped (he did in one version). Longfellow Deeds might well have remained silent. Peter might easily have continued assuming that Ellie was a spoiled brat.

Such a balance between wish fulfillment and reality principles is a hallmark of mature comedy. Holiday and everyday only have meaning when placed in opposition. We cannot appreciate the freedom of release unless the bondage of everyday life, with its mundane logic and requirements, remains in our minds. And it is this skill at maintaining the delicate balance between wanting and getting, the probable and the improbable, appealing to our anarchic desires without forgetting our very strong sense of reality and probability, that characterizes Capra's use of the comic form. He is fully aware of human hopes, and yet he is, particularly in the Capra romances, fully cognizant of the ease with which human hopes can lead to disappointment and disaster.

But Capra's mastery of form does not completely account for the great success of his films. Capra's primary concern is with human beings and human emotions. Accordingly, the "reality" of Capra's films depends upon the reality of Capra's characters. Do they act as we would act if we were in their admittedly fantastic shoes? I think the answer to that question is generally an unqualified "yes." Capra creates a sense of emotional necessity: given this situation, these characters would experience these emotions and make these moves. Capra obviously constructs his films to achieve this feeling of emotional verisimilitude, but we never sense the construction. There is a natural "lifelike" flow to Capra's movies, and it is this emotional rhythm that strikes us as realistically accurate. Our reaction as spectators is never "this could never happen to me," but rather "if that did happen to me, that is precisely how I would feel about it, precisely how I would handle it." Therein lies the "truth" of the Capra cinema. His world is self-contained and consistent, yet it arouses and reflects upon actual human emotions.

Thus another key factor in Capra's success is audience identification. His movies are festivities and are about festivities. His characters experience a "rules-off" situation where new emotional and intellectual responses are required, and similarly we as spectators experience a "rules-off" situation where we are free to identify with and feel very deeply about the characters and their struggles. We willingly suspend our disbelief, allowing freer rein to normally controlled emotions and desires, and our experience is roughly equivalent to the experience of the characters: we feel disappointment when they feel disappointment, exhilaration when they feel exhilaration.

But our knowledge and hence our experience is often more complete than that of the characters. We are often aware of situational ironies unknown to the characters themselves. For example, in *It Happened One Night* (1934), we know that Ellie and Peter love each other. Accordingly, our sense of anxiety is in fact greater than that of either Ellie or Peter near the film's conclusion when she is about to marry Westley, for we realize how agonizingly narrow yet how unbridgeably wide is the gap between them: if they would only drop their cynical masks for a moment to see each other as we see them, people deeply in love, the properly comic conclusion would be assured and fertility would symbolically triumph. Our sense of frustration is as great as if not greater than that of the characters. Peter and Ellie are, after all, completely comfortable, in a neurotic sort of way, to be playing their

Peter (Clark Gable) and Ellie (Claudette Colbert) in *It Happened One Night*.

Sharing Clarissa's anxiety: Jean Arthur and Thomas Mitchell in *Mr. Smith Goes to Washington.*

cynical roles. Ellie can even tell her father that "it doesn't matter" what happens, and perhaps it does not matter at that moment to her. But it matters tremendously to us, and the fact that it does matter so much to us is the measure of Capra's genius. We become completely engaged, completely involved, and we come to a new awareness of the relationship between desire (wanting to see Peter and Ellie together) and chance (Peter's last-minute decision to see Andrews at the Andrews mansion).

But Capra does not just put us through an emotional ringer. It is not a matter of cheap thrills and Hollywood daydreams. Peter and Ellie count because they represent a properly attentive sort of human concern: were they not so sensitive to each other they would not be so easily hurt. Thus Capra's point, a mature point at that, is that one should remain both sensitive (as we are when we watch the film) and vulnerable (as we are when we watch the film), willing to risk hurt for the sake of legitimate emotional involvement.

Capra's best films, the ones that earn him his place as one of the greatest Hollywood filmmakers, all depend upon this same sort of involvement. In *The Strong Man* (1926) we feel great concern for Harry Langdon. He is our own childish self that we wish to see protected. In *The Bitter Tea of General Yen* (1933) we experience a similar degree of emotional engagement, hoping against hope that Megan will realize her mistake before it is too late. *Mr.*

Smith Goes to Washington (1939) likewise earns our concerned involvement: we are every bit as anxious as Saunders, sharing her terror when Jeff collapses on the Senate floor, and sharing her elation when Jeff finally triumphs.

Arsenic and Old Lace (1944) gives rise to more complex reactions. We share Mortimer's horror at his aunts' actions, his frantic desire to arrange a plausible coverup that will get both his aunts and his cousin Teddy into Happydale where they so obviously belong, and we also share his desire to escape from the Brewster madhouse and his responsibilities for the open air of Niagara Falls. But there is yet another feeling, a quiet realization that Mortimer was absolutely correct to deny his own escapist tendencies in favor of accepting his family duty. Mortimer is not aware, as we are, that the fact of his bastardy is a poetic reward for his proper behavior, and hence we rejoice as he does not when

proper comic action (accepting the sort of familial responsibility that he had rejected in his anti-marriage tracts) earns an appropriately comic reward, Elaine, his new bride.

It's A Wonderful Life (1946) involves an equally complex set of emotional reactions: we at once sympathize with George Bailey and his romantic frustration, but the flashback structure of the film demands a certain ironic distancing—we know how wrong George is to be frustrated. Such a gap between desire and awareness is the subject of the film as well, for it is the same dissociation between wanting and getting that George must overcome before he recognizes his proper place in the comic universe.

To a great extent, then, the Capra cinema is about involvement, the way situations can demand greater degrees of emotional hazard and commitment than we had at first thought possible or nec-

Mortimer Brewster (Cary Grant) and his bride, Elaine
(Priscilla Lane), in *Arsenic and Old Lace*.

Dancing by the light of the moon: *It's a Wonderful Life*, featuring Donna Reed and James Stewart.

cessary. This is true both for Capra's characters and the members of the audience. Capra's moral code is a function of this involvement: life is a swift-running, exhilarating stream, and each person shares the responsibility of insuring that the stream of existence runs ever onward. Capra's cynics and romantics are thus reprehensible because they refuse to immerse themselves in the rhythm of life. They are captured by their dreams or disappointments, and hence they tend to destroy themselves or to destroy others. But life, human life, is too wonderful and precious to be thus destroyed, and the cinema of Frank Capra serves as an aesthetic reminder both of life's mystery and our responsibility as human beings to insure life's continuity. We must maintain an appropriate sense of commitment, sensitive, vulnerable, deeply felt, in our otherwise everyday lives. The Capra universe is a world upside-down, but thus suspended we are given a closer look at the nature of human emotional reality. Such is the poet's task. Such is Frank Capra's accomplishment.

NOTES

1. Ian Donaldson, *The World Upside-Down* (London: Oxford University Press, 1970), p. 15.
2. C. L. Barber, *Shakespeare's Festive Comedy* (Princeton: Princeton University Press, 1959), p. 6.

Responsibility personified: Jeff Smith's (James Stewart) finest hour.

Filmography

Frank Capra

Fultah Fisher's Boarding House (1922)

Production Company	Fireside Productions, Inc.
Producer	Walter Montague
Director	Frank Capra
Script	Walter Montague, from a poem by Rudyard Kipling
Director of Photography	Roy Wiggins

Released 2 April 1922
Distributors: Pathé Pictures

Capra worked as a film editor and gag writer for Bob Eddy and later for Hal Roach (the *Our Gang* films: directed by Bob McGowan) before joining Mack Sennett at the Keystone lot in 1924. What follows is a list of the Langdon films produced by Sennett. Those directed by Harry Edwards were in all probability scripted by Capra and Arthur Ripley.

Picking Peaches (released 3 February 1924)
Director   Erle Kenton

Smile Please (released 2 March 1924)
Director   Hampton Del Ruth

Shanghaied Lovers (released 30 March 1924)
Director   Roy Del Ruth

Flickering Youth (released 27 April 1924)
Director   Erle Kenton

The Cat's Meow (released 25 May 1924)
Director   Roy Del Ruth

His New Mama (released 22 June 1924)
Director   Roy Del Ruth

The First Hundred Years (released 17 August 1924)
Director   F. Richard Jones

The Luck O' The Foolish (released 14 September 1924)
Director   Harry Edwards

The Hanson Cabman (released October 1924)
Director   Harry Edwards

All Night Long (released November 1924)
Director   Harry Edwards

Feet of Mud (released December 1924)
Director   Harry Edwards

The Sea Squawk (released January 1925)
Director   Harry Edwards

Boobs in the Woods (released February 1925)
Director   Harry Edwards

His Marriage Wow (released March 1925)
Director   Harry Edwards

Plain Clothes (released March 1925)
Director   Harry Edwards

Remember When? (released April 1925)
Director   Harry Edwards

Horace Greely, Jr. (released June 1925)
Director   Alf Goulding

The White Wing's Bride (released July 1925)
Director   Alf Goulding

Lucky Stars (released August 1925)
Director   Harry Edwards
Script   Frank Capra, Arthur Ripley

There He Goes (released November 1925)
Director   Harry Edwards

Saturday Afternoon (released January 1926)
Director   Harry Edwards
Script   Frank Capra, Arthur Ripley

Fiddlesticks (released April 1926)
Director .... Harry Edwards

The Soldier Man (released May 1926)
Director .... Harry Edwards
Script .... Frank Capra, Arthur Ripley

After *The Soldier Man*, Langdon left Sennett, taking Capra, Edwards, and Ripley with him. The remaining Capra/Langdon efforts are feature-length films.

Tramp, Tramp, Tramp (1926)
Production Company .... First National Pictures
Director .... Harry Edwards
Script .... Frank Capra and others
with Harry Langdon and Joan Crawford
Released June 1926
Distributors: First National Pictures

The Strong Man (1926)
Production Company .... The Harry Langdon
                               Corporation
Director .... Frank Capra
Script .... Frank Capra, Hal Conklin,
                               Robert Eddy
Directors of Photography .. Elgin Lessley, Glenn
                               Kershner
with Harry Langdon, Gertrude Astor, William V. Mong, Robert McKim, Priscilla Bonner
Released September 1926
Distributors: First National Pictures

Long Pants (1927)
Production Company .... The Harry Langdon
                               Corporation
Director .... Frank Capra
Script .... Arthur Ripley
with Harry Langdon, Alma Bennett, Gladys Rorkwell, Betty Francisco
Released April 1927
Distributors: First National Pictures

For the Love of Mike (1927)
Producer .... Robert Kane
Director .... Frank Capra
Script .... John Morosso
with Ford Sterling, George Sidney, Ben Lyon, Claudette Colbert
Released September 1927
Distributors: First National Pictures

That Certain Thing (1928)
Production Company .... Columbia Pictures
Producer .... Harry Cohn
Director .... Frank Capra
Script .... Elmer Harris (from a story
                               by Capra?)

Director of Photography .. Joseph Walker
Art Director .... Robert E. Lee
Editor .... Arthur Roberts
Titles .... Al Boasberg
with Viola Dana (Molly), Ralph Graves (Charles Jr.), Burr McIntosh (A. B. Charles).
Distributors: Columbia Pictures

So This is Love (1928)
Production Company .... Columbia Pictures
Director .... Frank Capra
Script .... Elmer Harris, Rex Taylor
Director of Photography .. Ray June
with Shirley Mason, Buster Collier
Released March 1928
Distributors: Columbia Pictures

The Matinee Idol (1928)
Production Company .... Columbia Pictures
Director .... Frank Capra
Script .... Elmer Harris
Director of Photography .. Philip Tannura
Editor .... Arthur Roberts
with Bessie Love, Johnny Walker
Released April 1928
Distributors: Columbia Pictures

The Way of the Strong (1928)
Production Company .... Columbia Pictures
Director .... Frank Capra
Script .... Peter Milne
Director of Photography .. Ben Reynolds
with Mitchell Lewis, Alice Day, Margaret Livingston
Released July 1928
Distributors: Columbia Pictures

Say It With Sables (1928)
Production Company .... Columbia Pictures
Director .... Frank Capra
Script .... Dorothy Howell
Director of Photography .. Joseph Walker
Editor .... Arthur Roberts
with Helene Chadwick, Francis X. Bushman
Released August 1928
Distributors: Columbia Pictures

Submarine (1928)
Production Company .... Columbia Pictures
Director .... Frank Capra
Script .... Dorothy Howell, from a
                               story by Norman Springer
Director of Photography .. Joseph Walker
Editor .... Arthur Roberts
with Jack Holt, Dorothy Revier, Ralph Graves, Clarence Burton, Arthur Rankin
Released September 1928

Distributors: Columbia Pictures

The Power of the Press (1928)

Production Company	Columbia Pictures
Director	Frank Capra
Script	Sonya Levien, Ken Thompson
Directors of Photography	Chet Lyons, Ted Tetzlaff
Editor	Frank Atkinson

with Douglas Fairbanks, Jr., Jobyna Ralston
Released November 1928
Distributors: Columbia Pictures

The Younger Generation (1929)

Production Company	Columbia Pictures
Director	Frank Capra
Script	Sonya Levien, from a story by Fannie Hurst
Dialogue	Howard J. Green
Director of Photography	Ted Tetzlaff
Editor	Arthur Roberts

with Jean Hersholt (Papa Goldfish), Lina Basquette (Birdie), Ricardo Cortez (Morris), Rex Lease (Eddie Lesser), Julanne Johnston, Julia Swayne Gordon, Rosa Rosanova (Mama Goldfish).
Released 4 March 1929
Distributors: Columbia Pictures

The Donovan Affair (1929)

Production Company	Columbia Pictures
Director	Frank Capra
Script	Dorothy Howell, Howard J. Green, from the play by Owen Davis
Dialogue	Howard J. Green
Director of Photography	Ted Tetzlaff
Editor	Arthur Roberts

with Jack Holt, Dorothy Revier, Agnes Ayres, William Collier, Jr., Virginia Browne Faire, Wheeler Oakman, John Roche, Ethel Wales, Hank Mann, Fred Kelsey
Released 11 April 1929
Distributors: Columbia Pictures

Flight (1929)

Production Company	Columbia Pictures
Director	Frank Capra
Script	Howard J. Green, from a story by Ralph Graves
Dialogue	Frank Capra
Directors of Photography	Elmer Dyer, Joe Novak, Joseph Walker
Editors	Maurice Wright, Gene Milford

with Jack Holt (Panama Williams), Ralph Graves (Lefty Phelps), Lila Lee, Alan Roscoe, Harold Goodwin

Released September 1929
Distributors: Columbia Pictures

Ladies of Leisure (1930)

Production Company	Columbia Pictures
Director	Frank Capra
Script	Jo Swerling, from a play by Milton Herbert Gropper
Director of Photography	Joseph Walker
Editor	Maurice Wright

with Barbara Stanwyck (Kay Arnold), Ralph Graves (Jerry Strong), Lowell Sherman, Marie Prevost, Nance O'Neill, George Fawcett, Johnny Walker, Juliette Compton
Released 5 April 1930
98 minutes
Distributors: Columbia Pictures

Rain or Shine (1930)

Production Company	Columbia Pictures
Director	Frank Capra
Script	Jo Swerling, Dorothy Howell, from the play by James Gleason
Director of Photography	Joseph Walker
Editor	Maurice Wright

with Joe Cook, Louise Fazenda, Joan Peers, William Collier, Jr., Tom Howard, David Chasen, Alan Roscoe, Clarence Muse, Edward Matindel, Nora Lane
Released 15 August 1930
90 minutes
Distributors: Columbia Pictures

Dirigible (1931)

Production Company	Columbia Pictures
Producer	Harry Cohn
Director	Frank Capra
Script	Jo Swerling, Dorothy Howell, from a story by Lt. Commander F. W. Wead
Directors of Photography	Joe Wilbur, Elmer Dyer
Editor	Maurice Wright

with Jack Holt (Jack Bradon), Ralph Graves (Frisky Pierce), Fay Wray (Helen), Hobart Bosworth, Roscoe Karns, Harold Goodwin, Clarence Muse, Alan Roscoe
Released 4 April 1931
102 minutes
Distributors: Columbia Pictures

The Miracle Woman (1931)

Production Company	Columbia Pictures
Director	Frank Capra
Script	Jo Swerling, Dorothy Howell, from the play

Bless You Sister by John Meehan and Robert Riskin

Director of Photography   Joseph Walker
Editor   Maurice Wright

with Barbara Stanwyck (Florence Fallon), David Manners (John Carson), Sam Hardy (Hornsby), Beryl Mercer (Mrs. Higgins), Russell Hopton (Wexford), Charles Middleton (Simpson), Eddie Boland (Collins)
Released 20 June 1931
90 minutes
Distributors: Columbia Pictures

Platinum Blonde (1931)

Production Company   Columbia Pictures
Director   Frank Capra
Script   Dorothy Howell (continuity)
                                Robert Riskin (dialogue)
                                Jo Swerling (adaptation)
                                  from a story by Harry E.
                                  Chandlee and Douglas
                                  W. Churchill
Director of Photography   Joseph Walker
Editor   Gene Milford
Technical Director   Edward Shulter

with Loretta Young (Gallagher), Robert Williams (Stew Smith), Jean Harlow (Anne Schuyler), Louise Closser Hale (Mrs. Schuyler), Donald Dillaway (Michael Schuyler), Reginald Owen (Dexter Grayson), Walter Catlett (Bingy), Edmund Breese (Conroy), Halliwell Hobbes (Smyth), Claude Alister (Dawson)
Released 9 May 1932
Distributors: Columbia Pictures

Forbidden (1932)

Production Company   Columbia Pictures
Director   Frank Capra
Script   Frank Capra, Jo Swerling
                                  (adaptation, dialogue)
Director of Photography   Joseph Walker
Editor   Maurice Wright

with Barbara Stanwyck (Lulu Smith), Adolphe Menjou (Bob Grover), Ralph Bellamy (Al Holland), Dorothy Peterson (Helen), Charlotte V. Henry (Roberta)
Released 15 January 1932
Distributors: Columbia Pictures

American Madness (1932)

Production Company   Columbia Pictures
Director   Frank Capra
Script   Robert Riskin
Director of Photography   Joseph Walker
Editor   Maurice Wright

with Walter Huston (Dickson), Pat O'Brien (Matt), Kay Johnson (Mrs. Dickson), Constance Cummings (Helen), Gavin Gordon (Cluett), Robert Ellis (Dude Finlay), Burton Churchill (O'Brien), Arthur Hoyt (Ives), Edwin Maxwell (Clark), Robert Emmett O'Conner (the Inspector)
Released July 1932
76 minutes
Distributors: Columbia Pictures

The Bitter Tea of General Yen (1933)

Production Company   Columbia Pictures
Producer   Frank Capra
Director   Frank Capra
Script   Edward Paramore, from the
                                  novel by Grace Zaring
                                  Stone
Director of Photography   Joseph Walker

with Barbara Stanwyck (Megan Davis), Nils Asther (General Yen), Gavin Gordon (Dr. Strike), Walter Connolly (Jones), Toshia Mori (Mah-Li), Lucien Littlefield (Mr. Jackson), Richard Loo (Capt. Li), Clara Blandick (Mrs. Jackson), Helen Jerome Eddy (Miss Reed), Martha Mattox (Mrs. Avery)
Released January 1933
89 minutes
Distributors: Columbia Pictures

Lady for a Day (1933)

Production Company   Columbia Pictures
Director   Frank Capra
Script   Robert Riskin, from the
                                  story "Madame La
                                  Gimp" by
                                  Damon Runyon
Director of Photography   Joseph Walker
Art Director   Stephen Goosson
Costumes   Robert Kallock
Editor   Gene Havlick
Assistant Director   C. C. Coleman

with Warren William (Dave the Dude), May Robson (Apple Annie), Guy Kibbee (Judge Blake), Glenda Farrel (Missouri Martin), Ned Sparks (Happy), Jean Parker (Louise), Walter Connolly (Count Romero), Barry Norton (Carlos), Robert Emmett O'Conner (The Commissioner), Nat Pendleton (Shakespeare), Hobart Bosworth (The Governor)
Released August 1933
95 minutes
Distributor: Columbia Pictures

It Happened One Night (1934)

Production Company   Columbia Pictures
Producer   Harry Cohn
Director   Frank Capra
Script   Robert Riskin, from the
                                  story "Night Bus" by
                                  Samuel Hopkins Adams

Director of Photography	Joseph Walker
Art Director	Stephen Goosson
Editor	Gene Havlick
Costumes	Robert Kallock
Music Director	Louis Silvers
Assistant Director	C. C. Coleman

with Clark Gable (Peter Warne), Claudette Colbert (Ellie Andrews), Roscoe Karns (Shapeley), Walter Connolly (Alexander Andrews), Alan Hale (Danker), Ward Bond (Bus Driver), Eddy Chandler (Bus Driver), Jameson Thomas (King Westley), Wallis Clark (Lovington), Arthur Hoyt (Zeke), Blanche Frederici (Zeke's Wife), Charles C. Wilson (Henderson), Harry Holman (Auto Camp Manager), Maidel Turner (Manager's Wife), Irving Bacon (Station Attendant), Harry Todd (Flag Man), Frank Yaconelli (Tony), Henry Wadsworth (Drunken Boy), Claire McDowell (Mother), Ky Robinson (Detective), Frank Holliday (Detective), James Burke (Detective), Joseph Crehan (Detective), Milton Kibbee (Drunk), Mickey Daniel (Vender), Oliver Eckhardt (Dykes), George Breakston (Boy), Bess Flowers (Secretary), Father Dodds (Minister), Edmund Burns (Best Man), Ethel Sykes (Maid of Honor), Tom Ricketts (Old Man), Eddie Kane (Radio Announcer), Hal Price (Reporter), and Ernie Adams, Kit Guard, Billy Engle, Allen Fox, Marvin Loback, Dave Wengren, Bert Starkey, Rita Ross (Bus Passengers)
Released 23 February 1934
105 minutes
Distributors: Columbia Pictures

Broadway Bill (1934)

Production Company	Columbia Pictures
Director	Frank Capra
Script	Robert Riskin, from a story by Mark Hellinger
Director of Photography	Joseph Walker
Editor	Gene Havlick

with Warner Baxter (Dan Brooks), Myrna Loy (Alice), Walter Connolly (J. L. Higgins), Douglass Dumbrille (Eddie Morgan), Helen Vinson (Margaret), Raymond Walburn (Col. Pettigrew), Lynne Overman (Happy McGuire), Clarence Muse (Whitey), Margaret Hamilton (Edna), Frankie Darrow (Ted Williams), George Meeker (Henry Early), Jason Robards (Arthur Winslow), Helene Millard (Mrs. Winslow), Edmund Breese (Judge), Clara Blandick (Mrs. Peterson), Inez Courtney (Mae), Claude Gillingwater (Chase), James Blakely (Interne), Alan Hale (Orchestra Leader)
Released November 1934
Distributors: Columbia Pictures

Mr. Deeds Goes to Town (1936)

Production Company	Columbia Pictures
Producer	Frank Capra
Director	Frank Capra
Script	Robert Riskin, from the story "Opera Hat" by Clarence Budington Kelland
Director of Photography	Joseph Walker
Special Effects	E. Roy Davidson
Editor	Gene Havlick
Art Director	Stephen Goosson
Costumes	Samuel Lange
Musical Director	Howard Jackson
Assistant Director	C. C. Coleman

with Gary Cooper (Longfellow Deeds), Jean Arthur (Babe Bennett), George Bancroft (MacWade), Lionel Stander (Cornelius Cobb), Douglass Dumbrille (John Cedar), Raymond Walburn (Walter), Margaret Matzenauer (Madame Pomponi), H. B. Warner (Judge Walker), Warren Hymer (Bodyguard), Muriel Evans (Theresa), Ruth Donnelly (Mabel Dawson), Spencer Charters (Mal), Emma Dunn (Mrs. Meredith), Wryley Birch (Psychiatrist), Arthur Hoyt (Budington), Stanley Andrews (James Cedar), Pierre Watkin (Arthur Cedar), John Wray (Farmer), Christian Rub (Swenson), Jameson Thomas (Mr. Semple), May Methot (Mrs. Semple), Russell Hicks (Doctor Malcolm), Gustav Von Seyffertitz (Dr. Frazier), Edward Le Saint (Dr. Fosdick), Charles [Levison] Lane (Hallor), Irving Bacon (Frank), George Cooper (Bob), Gene Morgon (Waiter), Walter Catlett (Morrow), Barnett Parker (Butler), Margaret Seddon (Jane Faulkner), Margaret McWade (Amy Faulkner), Harry C. Bradley (Anderson), Edward Gargan (Second Bodyguard), Edwin Maxwell (Douglas), Paul Hurst (First Deputy), Paul Porcasi (Italian), Franklin Pangborn (Tailor), George F. Hayes (Farmers' Spokesman), Billy Bevan (Cabby), Dennis O'Keefe (Reporter), George Meeker (Brookfield), Dale Van Sickel (Lawyer)
Released 16 April 1936
115 minutes
Distributors: Columbia Pictures

Lost Horizon (1937)

Production Company	Columbia Pictures
Producer	Frank Capra
Director	Frank Capra
Script	Robert Riskin, from the novel by James Hilton
Director of Photography	Joseph Walker
Special Effects	E. Roy Davidson,

Aerial Photography Elmer Dyer
Technical Advisor Harrison Forman
Editors Gene Havlick,
  Gene Milford
Art Director Stephen Goosson
Interior Decorations Bob Johnstone
Musical Score Dimitri Tiomkin
Musical Director Max Steiner
Costumes Ernest Dryden

with Ronald Colman (Robert Conway), Jane Wyatt (Sondra), Edward Everett Horton (Alexander P. Lovett), John Howard (George Conway), Thomas Mitchell (Henry Barnard), Margo (Maria), Isabel Jewell (Gloria Stone), H. B. Warner (Chang), Sam Jaffe (High Lama), Hugh Buckler (Lord Gainsford), John Miltern (Carstairs), Lawrence Grant (First Man), John Burton (Wynant), John T. Murrary (Meeker), Max Rabinowitz (Seiveking), Willie Fung (Bandit Leader), Wryley Birch (Missionary), John Tettener (Montaigne), Boyd Irwin (Assistant Foreign Secretary), Leonard Mudie (Sr. Foreign Secretary), David Clyde (Steward), Neil Fitzgerald (Radio Operator), Val Durand (Talu), Ruth Robinson (Missionary), Margaret McWade (Missionary), Noble Johnson (Leader of Porters), Dennis D'Auburn (Aviator), Milton Owen (Fenner), Victor Wong (Bandit Leader), Carl Stockdale (Missionary), Darby Clark (Radio Operator), George Chan (Chinese Priest), Eric Wilton (Englishman), Chief Big Tree (Porter), Richard Loo (Shanghai Airport Official), The Hall Johnson Choir, and Beatrice Curtis, Mary Lou Dix, Beatrice Blinn, Arthur Rankin (Passengers)
Released March 1937
125 minutes
Distributors: Columbia Pictures

You Can't Take It With You (1938)
Production Company Columbia Pictures
Producer Frank Capra
Director Frank Capra
Script Robert Riskin, from the
  play by George S. Kaufman and Moss Hart
Director of Photography Joseph Walker
Art Direction Stephen Goosson
Musical Score Dimitri Tiomkin
Musical Director Morris Stoloff
Editor Gene Havlick
Jean Arthur's Gowns Bernard Newman and Irene
Assistant Director Arthur Black

with Jean Arthur (Alice Sycamore), Lionel Barrymore (Martin Vanderhoff), James Stewart (Tony Kirby),
Edward Arnold (Anthony P. Kirby), Mischa Auer (Kolenkhov), Ann Miller (Essie Carmichael), Spring Byington (Penny Sycamore), Samuel S. Hinds (Paul Sycamore), Donald Meek (Poppins), H. B. Warner (Ramsey), Halliwell Hobbes (DePinna), Dub Taylor (Ed Carmichael), Mary Forbes (Mrs. Kirby), Lillian Yarbo (Rheba), Eddie Anderson (Donald), Clarence Wilson (John Blakely), Josef Swickard (Professor), Ann Doran (Maggie O'Neill), Christian Rub (Schmidt), Bodil Rosing (Mrs. Schmidt), Charles Lane (Henderson), Harry Davenport (Judge), Pierre Watkin (Attorney), Edwin Maxwell (Attorney), Byron Foulger (Kirby's Assistant), Russel Hicks (Attorney), Ian Wolfe (Kirby's Secretary), Irving Bacon (Henry), Chester Clute (Hammond), James Flavin (Jailer), Edward Keane (Board Member), Pat Kelton (Inmate), Dick Curtis (Strongarm Man), Kit Guard (Inmate), James Burke (Detective), Ward Bond (Detective), Edward Hearn (Court Attendant), and Robert Greig, John Hamilton (Diners)
Released 29 September 1938
126 minutes
Distributors: Columbia Pictures

Mr. Smith Goes to Washington (1939)
Production Company Columbia Pictures
Producer Frank Capra
Director Frank Capra
Script Sidney Bushman, from the
  novel *The Gentleman from Montana* by
  Lewis R. Foster
Director of Photography Joseph Walker
Editors Gene Havlick, Al Clark
Montage Slavko Vorkapich
Art Director Lionel Banks
Musical Score Dimitri Tiomkin
Musical Director Morris Stoloff
Assistant Director Arthur S. Black

with Jean Arthur (Saunders), James Stewart (Jeff Smith), Claude Rains (Senator Paine), Edward Arnold (Jim Taylor), Guy Kibbee (Governor Hopper), Thomas Mitchell (Diz Moore), Eugene Pallette (Chick McGann), Beulah Bondi (Ma Smith), H. B. Warner (Senator Fuller), Harry Carey (President of the Senate), Astrid Allwyn (Susan Paine), Ruth Donnelly (Emma Hopper), Grant Mitchell (Senator MacPherson), Porter Hall (Senator Monroe), Pierre Watkin (Senator Barnes), Charles Lane (Nosey), Frances Gifford, Lorna Gray, Adrian Booth, Linda Winters [Dorothy Comingore], William Demarest (Bill Griffith), Dick Elliott (Carl Cook), H. V. Kaltenborn (Broadcaster), Kenneth Carpenter (Announcer), Jack Carson

(Sweeney), Joe King (Summers), Paul Stanton (Flood), Russell Simpson (Allen), Stanley Andrews (Senator Hodges), Walter Soderling (Senator Pickett), Frank Jaquet (Senator Byron), Ferris Taylor (Senator Carlisle), Carl Stockdale (Senator Burdette), Alan Bridge (Senator Dwight), Edmund Cobb (Senator Gower), Frederick Burton (Senator Dearhorn), Vera Lewis (Mrs. Edwards), Dora Clement (Mrs. McGann), Laura Treadwell (Mrs. Taylor), Ann Doran (Paine's Secretary), Douglas Evans (Francis Scott Key), Allan Cavan (Ragner), Maurice Costello (Diggs), Lloyd Whitlock (Schultz), Myonne Walsh (Jane Hopper), and Billy and Delmar Watson, John Russell, Harry and Garry Watson, Baby Dumpling [Larry Simms] (The Hopper Boys)
Released 19 October 1939
126 minutes
Distributors: Columbia Pictures

Meet John Doe (1941)

Production Company	Frank Capra Productions
Producer	Frank Capra
Director	Frank Capra
Script	Robert Riskin, from a story by Richard Connell and Robert Presnell
Director of Photography	George Barnes
Editor	Daniel Mandell
Special Effects	Jack Cosgrove
Montage	Slavko Vorkapich
Art Direction	Stephen Goosson
Music	Dimitri Tiomkin
Music Director	Leo F. Forbstein
Assistant Director	Arthur S. Black

with Gary Cooper (Long John Willoughby), Barbara Stanwyck (Ann Mitchell), Edward Arnold (D. B. Norton), Walter Brennan (The Colonel), Spring Byington (Mrs. Mitchell), James Gleason (Harry Connell), Gene Lockhart (Mayor Lovett), Rod La Rocque (Ted Sheldon), Irving Bacon (Beany), Regis Toomey (Bert Hansen), Ann Doran (Mrs. Hansen), J. Farrell MacDonald (Sourpuss Smithers), Warren Hymer (Angelface), Harry Holman (Mayor Hawkins), Andrew Tombes (Spencer), Pierre Watkin (Hammett), Stanley Andrews (Weston), Mitchell Lewis (Bennett), Charles C. Wilson (Charlie Dawson), Vaughan Glaser (The Governor), Sterling Holloway (Dan), Mike Frankovich (Radio Announcer), Aldrich Bowker (Pop Dwyer), Mrs. Gardner Crane (Mrs. Brewster), Pat Flaherty (Mike), Carlotta Jelm (Ann's Sister), Tina Thayer (Ann's Sister), Bennie Bartlett (Office Boy), Sarah Edwards (Mrs. Hawkins), Edward Earle (Radio M.C.), James McNamara (Sheriff), Emma Tansey (Mrs. Delaney), Frank Austin (Grubbel), Edward Geane (Relief Administrator), Lafe McKee (Mr. Delaney), Edward McWade (Joe, a Newsman), Guy Usher (Bixler), Walter Soderling (Barrington), Edmund Cobb (Policeman), Billy Curtis (Midget), Johnny Fern (Lady Midget), John Hamilton (Jim, Governor's Associate), William Forrest (Governor's Associate), Charles K. French (Fired Reporter), Edward Hearn (Mayor's Secretary), Bess Flowers (Secretary), Hank Mann (Ed, a Photographer), James Millican (Photographer), The Hall Johnson Choir, and Knox Manning, Selmer Jackson, John B. Hughes (Radio Announcers at Convention)
Released 3 May 1941
135 minutes
Distributors: Warner Brothers

Prelude to War (1942)

Production Company	The War Department
Producer	Frank Capra
Director	Frank Capra
Script	Anthony Veiller, Eric Knight
Editor	William Hornbeck
Narration	Walter Huston
Music	Alfred Newman
Research	Richard Griffith, Leon Levy, Palmer Williams, Elinor Grey (these people researched all of Capra's War Department and Army Pictorial Service films).

Released October 1942
53 minutes
Part I of the *Why We Fight* series

The Nazis Strike (1943)

Production Company	The War Department
Producer	Frank Capra
Directors	Frank Capra, Anatole Litvak
Script	Eric Knight, Anthony Veiller, Robert Heller
Editor	William Hornbeck
Narration	Walter Huston, Anthony Veiller
Music	Dimitri Tiomkin

42 minutes
Part II of the *Why We Fight* series

Divide and Conquer (1943)

Production Company	The War Department
Producer	Frank Capra

Directors	Frank Capra, Anatole Litvak
Script	Anthony Veiller, Robert Heller
Editor	William Hornbeck
Music	Dimitri Tiomkin

58 minutes
Part III of the *Why We Fight* series

The Battle of Britain (1943)

Production Company	The War Department
Producer	Frank Capra
Director	Anthony Veiller
Script	Anthony Veiller
Editor	William Hornbeck
Narration	Walter Huston, Anthony Veiller
Music	Dimitri Tiomkin

54 minutes
Part IV of the *Why We Fight* series

The Negro Soldier (1944)

Production Company	The War Department
Producer	Frank Capra
Director	Stuart Heisler
Script	Carlton Moss

Released January 1944

The Battle of Russia (1944)

Production Company	The War Department
Producer	Frank Capra
Director	Anatole Litvak
Script	Anatole Litvak, Anthony Veiller, Robert Heller
Editor	William Hornbeck
Narration	Walter Huston, Anthony Veiller
Music	Dimitri Tiomkin

80 minutes
Part V of the *Why We Fight* series

The Battle of China (1944)

Production Company	The Army Pictorial Service
Producer	Frank Capra
Directors	Frank Capra, Anatole Litvak
Script	Anthony Veiller, Robert Heller
Editor	William Hornbeck
Narration	Walter Huston, Anthony Veiller
Music	Dimitri Tiomkin

64 minutes
Part VI of the *Why We Fight* series

Tunisian Victory (1944)

Production Company	The War Department
Producer	Frank Capra
Director	Frank Capra
Editor	William Hornbeck
Narration	Walter Huston, Anthony Veiller
Music	Dimitri Tiomkin

Released in March 1944
70 minutes

Know Your Ally: Britain (1944)

Production Company	The War Department
Producer	Frank Capra
Director	Anthony Veiller
Script	Anthony Veiller
Editor	William Hornbeck
Narration	Walter Huston, Anthony Veiller
Music	Dimitri Tiomkin

42 minutes

Arsenic and Old Lace (1944)

Production Company	Frank Capra Productions
Producer	Frank Capra
Director	Frank Capra
Script	Julius J. and Philip G. Epstein, from the play by Joseph Kesserling
Director of Photography	Sol Polito
Special Effects	Byron Haskin, Robert Burks
Editor	Daniel Mandel
Art Director	Max Parker
Music	Max Steiner
Music Director	Leo Forbstein
Orchestral Arrangements	Hugo Friedhofer
Assistant Director	Jesse Hibbs

with Cary Grant (Mortimer Brewster), Priscilla Lane (Elaine Harper), Raymond Massey (Jonathan Brewster), Jack Carson (O'Hara), Edward Everett Horton (Mr. Witherspoon), Peter Lorre (Doctor Einstein), James Gleason (Lieutenant Rooney), Josephine Hull (Abby Brewster), Jean Adair (Martha Brewster), John Alexander (Teddy Brewster), Grant Mitchell (Reverend Harper), Edward McNamara (Brophy), Garry Owen (Taxi Driver), John Ridgely (Saunders), Vaughan Glaser (Judge Cullman), Chester Clute (Doctor Gilchrist), Charles Lane (Reporter), Edward McWade (Gibbs), Leo White (Man in Phone Booth), Spencer Charters (License Clerk), Hank Mann (Photographer), Lee Phelps (Umpire)
Released September 1944 (filmed in late 1941 and early 1942)

118 minutes
Distributors: Warner Brothers

War Comes to America (1945)

Production Company	The Army Pictorial Service
Producer	Frank Capra
Director	Anatole Litvak
Script	Anatole Litvak, Anthony Veiller
Editor	William Hornbeck
Narration	Walter Huston, Anthony Veiller
Music	Dimitri Tiomkin

70 minutes
Part VII of the *Why We Fight* series

Know Your Enemy: Germany (1945)

Production Company	The Army Pictorial Service
Producer	Frank Capra
Director	Gottfried Reinhardt
Script	Gottfried Reinhardt, Anthony Veiller
Editor	William Hornbeck
Narration	Walter Huston, Anthony Veiller
Music	Dimitri Tiomkin

Know Your Enemy: Japan (1945)

Production Company	The Army Pictorial Service
Producer	Frank Capra
Directors	Frank Capra, Joris Ivens
Script	Allen Rivkin, Robert Heller, Anthony Veiller
Editors	William Hornbeck, Helen Van Dongen
Narration	Walter Huston, Anthony Veiller
Music	Dimitri Tiomkin

Two Down, One To Go (1945)

Production Company	The Army Pictorial Service
Producer	Frank Capra
Director	Frank Capra
Script	Anthony Veiller
Editor	William Hornbeck
Narration	Anthony Veiller
Music	Dimitri Tiomkin

Released 10 May 1945

It's A Wonderful Life (1946)

Production Company	Liberty Films
Producer	Frank Capra
Director	Frank Capra
Script	Frances Goodrich, Albert Hackett, Frank Capra, and Jo Swerling, from the story "The Greatest Gift" by Phillip Van Doren Stern
Directors of Photography	Joseph Walker, Joseph Biroc
Editor	William Hornbeck
Art Director	Jack Okey
Music Director	Dimitri Tiomkin

with James Stewart (George Bailey), Donna Reed (Mary Hatch Bailey), Lionel Barrymore (Mr. Potter), Thomas Mitchell (Uncle Billy), Henry Travers (Clarence), Beulah Bondi (Mrs. Bailey), Frank Faylen (Ernie), Ward Bond (Bert), Gloria Grahame (Violet Bick), H. B. Warner (Mr. Gower), Frank Albertson (Sam Wainwright), Todd Karns (Harry Bailey), Samuel S. Hinds (Peter Bailey), Mary Treen (Cousin Tilly), Virginia Patton (Ruth Dakin), Charles Williams (Cousin Eustace), Sara Edwards (Mrs. Hatch), Bill Edmunds (Mr. Martini), Lillian Randolph (Annie), Argentina Brunetti (Mrs. Martini), Bobby Anderson (Little George), Ronnie Ralph (Little Sam), Jean Gale (Little Mary), Jeanine Anne Roose (Little Violet), Danny Mummert (Little Marty Hatch), Georgie Nokes (Little Harry Bailey), Sheldon Leonard (Nick), Frank Hagney (Potter's Bodyguard), Ray Walker (Joe, Luggage Shop), Charlie Lane (Real Estate Salesman), Carol Coomes (Janie), Karolyn Grimes (Zuzu), Larry Sims (Pete), Jimmy Hawkins (Tommy), Harry Holman (High School Principal), Hal Landon (Marty Hatch), Alfalfa Switzer (Freddie), Bobby Scott (Mickey), Harry Cheshire (Dr. Campbell), Ellen Corby

Released December 1946
129 minutes
Distributors: RKO

State of the Union (1948)

Production Company	Liberty Films
Producer	Frank Capra
Associate Producer	Anthony Veiller
Director	Frank Capra
Script	Anthony Veiller, Myles Connolly, from the play by Howard Lindsay and Russell Crouse
Director of Photography	George J. Folsey
Editor	William Hornbeck
Art Directors	Cedric Gibbons, Urie McClearly
Music	Victor Young

with Spencer Tracy (Grant Matthews), Katharine Hepburn (Mary Matthews), Van Johnson (Spike Mc-

Manus), Angela Lansbury (Kay Thorndyke), Adolphe Menjou (Jim Conover), Lewis Stone (Sam Thorndyke), Howard Smith (Sam Parrish), Maidel Turner (Lulubelle Alexander), Raymond Walburn (Judge Alexander), Charles Dingel (Bill Hardy), Florence Auer (Grace Draper), Pierre Watkin (Senator Lauterbach), Margaret Hamilton (Norah), Irving Bacon (Buck), Patti Brady (Joyce), George Nokes (Grant, Jr.), Carl Switzer (Bellboy), Tom Pedi (Barber), Tom Fadden (Waiter), Charles Lane (Blink Moran), Art Baker (Leith, Radio Announcer), Rhea Mitchell (Jenny), Arthur O'Connell (First Reporter), Marion Martin (Blonde Girl), Tor Johnson (Wrestler), Stanley Andrews (Senator), Dave Willock (Pilot), Russell Meeker (Politician), Frank L. Clarke (Joe Crandall), David Clarke (Rusty Miller), Dell Henderson (Broder), Edwin Cooper (Bradbury), Davison Clark (Crump), Francis Pierlot (Josephs), Brandon Beach (Editor)
Released 30 April 1948
Titled *The World and His Wife* in Great Britain
124 minutes
Distributors: Metro-Goldwyn-Mayer

Westward the Women (1950)

Production Company	Metro-Goldwyn-Mayer
Producer	Dore Schary
Director	William Wellman
Script	Charles Schnee
Story	Frank Capra
Director of Photography	William Mellor
Art Directors	Cedric Gibbons, Daniel B. Cathcart
Set Decoraton	Edwin B. Willis, Ralph S. Hurst
Costumes	Walter Plunkett
Editor	James E. Newcome
Sound	Douglas Shearer
Technical Advisor	Jim Lauch
Music	Henry Russell

with Robert Taylor (Buck), Denise Darcel (Danon), Hope Emerson (Patience), John McIntire (Roy Whitman), Julie Bishop (Laurie), Lenore Lonergan, Henry Nakamura (Ito), Marilyn Erskine (Jean)
Released 11 January 1950
116 minutes
Distributors: Metro-Goldwyn-Mayer

Riding High (1950)

Production Company	Paramount Pictures
Producer	Frank Capra
Director	Frank Capra
Script	Robert Riskin, from his script for *Broadway Bill*,

	Melville Shavelson, Jack Rose
Directors of Photography	George Barnes, Ernest Laszlo
Art Directors	Hans Dreier, Walter Tyler
Editor	William Hornbeck
Costumes	Edith Head
Set Decoration	Emile Kuri
Process Photography	Farciot Edouart
Music Associate	Troy Sanders
Makeup	Wally Westmore
Music	James Van Heusen
Lyrics	Johnny Burke
Music Director	Victor Young
Sound Recording	Hugo Grenzbach, John Cope
Vocal Arrangements	Joseph J. Lilley
Assistant Director	Arthur Black

with Bing Crosby (Dan Brooks), Coleen Gray (Alice Higgins), Charles Bickford (J. L. Higgins), William Demarest (Happy McGuire), Frances Gifford (Margaret Higgins), Raymond Walburn (Professor Pettigrew), James Gleason (Racing Secretary), Ward Bond (Lee), Clarence Muse (Whitey), Percy Kilbride (Pop Jones), Harry Davenport (Johnson), Margaret Hamilton (Edna), Douglass Dumbrille (Eddie Morgan), Gene Lockhart (J. P. Chase), Charles Lane (Erickson), Frankie Darro (Jockey Williams), Paul Harvey (Whitehall), Majorie Lord (Mathilda Winslow), Marjorie Poshelle (Mary Early), Rand Brooks (Henry Early), Willard Waterman (Arthur Winslow), Dub Taylor (Joe)
Released 12 April 1950
112 minutes
Distributors: Paramount Pictures

Here Comes the Groom (1951)

Production Company	Paramount Pictures
Producer	Frank Capra
Associate Producer	Irving Asher
Director	Frank Capra
Script	Virginia Van Upp, Liam O'Brien, Myles Connolly, from a story by O'Brien and Robert Riskin
Director of Photography	George Barnes
Process Photography	Farciot Edouart
Art Directors	Hal Pereira, Earl Hedrick
Set Direction	Emile Kuri
Editor	Ellsworth Hoagland
Costumes	Edith Head
Dance Direction	Charles O'Curran
Music Director	Joseph J. Lilley

Special Effects — Gordon Jennings, Paul Lerpae

Special Orchestral Arrangements — Van Cleave

New Songs — Jay Livingston and Ray Evans

"In the Cool, Cool, Cool of the Evening" — Johnny Mercer and Hoagy Charmichael

with Bing Crosby (Pete), Jane Wyman (Emmadel Jones), Alexis Smith (Winifred Stanley), Franchot Tone (Wilbur Stanley), James Barton (Pa Jones), Robert Keith (George Degnan), Jacky Gencel (Bobby), Beverly Washburn (Suzi), Connie Gilchrist (Ma Jones), Walter Catlett (McGonigle), Alan Reed (Mr. Godfrey), Minna Gombell (Mrs. Godfrey), Howard Freeman (Governor), Maidel Turner (Aunt Abby), H. B. Warner (Uncle Elihu), Nicholas Joy (Uncle Prentiss), Ian Wolfe (Uncle Adam), Ellen Corby (Mrs. McGonigle), James Burke (Policeman), Irving Bacon (Baines), Ted Thorpe (Paul Pippitt), Art Baker (Radio Announcer), Anna Maria Alberghetti (Therese), Laura Elliot (Maid), Dorothy Lamour, Frank Fontaine, Louis Armstrong, Phil Harris, Cass Daley, Chris Appel (Marcel), Odette Myrtil (Gray Lady), Charles Halton (Cusick), Rev. Neal Dodd (Priest), Charles Lane (Burchard), Adeline de Walt Reynolds (Aunt Amy), Charles Evans (Mayor), J. Farrell MacDonald, Carl Switzer (Messenger), Walter McGrail (Newsreel Director), Howard Joslin (Newsreel Cameraman)
Released September 1951
113 minutes
Distributors: Paramount Pictures

Our Mr. Sun (1956)

Production Company	Frank Capra Productions
Producer	Frank Capra
Assistant Producer	Donald Jones
Director	Frank Capra
Script	Frank Capra
Scientific Consultants	Dr. Farrington Daniels
	Dr. Armin Deutsch
	Dr. Donald Menzel
	Dr. Walter Orr Roberts
	Dr. Otto Struve
Sources	*Our Sun,* Donald Menzel, Harvard University Press
	Energy Sources, Eugene Ayres and Charles A. Scarlott, McGraw-Hill
Director of Photography	Harold Wellman
Animation	United Productions of America

Editor	Frank P. Keller
Sets	Wiard Ihnen
Research	Jeanne Curtis
Assistant Director	Arthur S. Black

with Frank Baxter, Eddie Albert, Lionel Barrymore, Marvin Miller
Distributors: Bell Telephone
Bell System Science Series, No. 1

Hemo the Magnificent (1957)

Production Company	Frank Capra Productions
Producer	Frank Capra
Associate Producer	Joseph Sistrom
Director	Frank Capra
Script	Frank Capra
Executive Coordinator	Donald Jones
Principle Advisor	Dr. Maurice B. Virscher
Animation	Shamus Culhane Productions
Editor	Frank P. Keller
Director of Photography	Harold Wellman
Research	Nancy Pitt
Music Supervision	Raoul Kraushaar
Sound Effects	Archie Dattelbaum
Assistant Director	Arthur S. Black

with Frank Baxter, Richard Carlson
Distributors: Bell Telephone
Bell System Science Series, No. 2

The Strange Case of the Cosmic Rays (1957)

Production Company	Frank Capra Productions
Producer	Frank Capra
Associate Producer	Joseph Sistrom
Director	Frank Capra
Script	Frank Capra, Jonathan Latimer
Directors of Photography	Harold Wellman, Ellis Carter
Special Photography	Edison Hoge
Editors	Frank P. Keller, Raymond Snyder
Music Supervision	Raoul Kraushaar
Research	Nancy Pitt
Animation	Shamus Culhane Productions
Assistant Director	Arthur S. Black

with Frank Baxter, Richard Carlson, Bill and Cora Baird's marionettes
Distributors: Bell Telephone
Bell System Science Series, No. 3

The Unchained Goddess (1958)

Production Company	Frank Capra Productions
Producer	Frank Capra

Associate Producer	Joseph Sistrom
Director	Richard Carlson
Script	Frank Capra, Jonathan Latimer
Photography	Harold Wellman
Editor	Frank P. Keller
Animation	Shamus Culhane Productions
Music Supervision	Raoul Kraushaar
Music Editor	Albert Shaff
Research	Nancy Pitt
Assistant Director	Stanley Goldsmith

with Richard Carlson, Frank Baxter
Distributors: Bell Telephone
Bell System Science Series, No. 4

A Hole in the Head (1959)

Production Company	SinCap Productions
Producer	Frank Capra
Director	Frank Capra
Script	Aronld Shulman, from his play
Director of Photography	William H. Daniels
Editor	William Hornbeck
Costumes	Edith Head
Art Director	Eddie Imazu
Music	Nelson Riddle
Orchestrations	Arthur Morton
"All My Tomorrows" and "High Hopes"	Sammy Cahn and James Van Heusen
Assistant Directors	Arthur S. Black, Jr., Jack R. Berne

with Frank Sinatra (Tony Manetta), Edward G. Robinson (Mario Manetta), Eleanor Parker (Mrs. Rogers), Eddie Hodges (Ally), Carolyn Jones (Shirl), Thelma Ritter (Sophie Manetta), Keenan Wynn (Jerry Marks), Joi Lansing (Dorine), George DeWitt (Mendy), Jimmy Komack (Julius Manetta), Dub Taylor (Fred), Connie Sawyer (Miss Wexler), Benny Rubin (Abe Diamond), Ruby Dandridge (Sally), B. S. Pully (Hood), Joyce Nizzari (Alice), Pupi Campo (Master of Ceremonies), Robert B. Williams (Cabby), Emory Parnell (Sheriff), Billy Walker (Andy).
Released July 1959 (Panavision, De Luxe Color)
120 minutes
Distributors: United Artists

Pocketful of Miracles (1961)

Production Company	Franton Productions
Producer	Frank Capra
Associate Producers	Glenn Ford, Joseph Sistrom
Director	Frank Capra
Script	Hal Kantor, Harry Tugend, Jimmy Cannon from the story "Madame La Gimp" by Damon Runyon and the screenplay Lady for a Day by Robert Riskin
Director of Photography	Robert Bronner
Music Director	Walter Scharf
Orchestrations	Gil Grau
Art Directors	Hal Pereira, Roland Anderson
Set Decoration	Sam Comer, Ray Moyer
Process Photography	Farciot Edouart
Editor	Frank P. Keller
Costumes	Edith Head, Walter Plunkett
Choreography	Nick Castle
Song "Pocketful of Miracles"	Sammy Cahn and James Van Heusen
Sound	Hugo Grenzbach, Charles Grenzbach
Makeup	Wally Westmore
Hairstyles	Nellie Manley
Assistant Director	Arthur S. Black

with Glenn Ford (Dave the Dude), Bette Davis (Apple Annie), Hope Lange (Queenie Martin), Arthur O'Connell (Count Romero), Peter Falk (Joy Boy), Thomas Mitchell (Judge Henry Blake), Edward Everett Horton (Butler), Mickey Shaughnessy (Junior), David Brian (Governor), Sheldon Leonard (Steve Darcey), Peter Mann (Carlos), Ann-Margret (Louise), Barton MacLane (Police Commissioner), John Litel (Police Inspector), Jerome Cowan (Mayor), Jay Novello (Spanish Consul), Frank Ferguson (Editor), Willis Bouchey (Editor), Fritz Feld (Pierre), Ellen Corby (Soho Sal), Gavin Gordon (Hotel Manager), Benny Rubin (Flyaway), Jack Elam (Cheesecake), Mike Mazurki (Big Mike), Hayden Rorke (Captain Moore), Doodles Weaver (Pool Player), Paul E. Burns (Mallethead), Angelo S. Rossitto (Angie), Edgar Stehli (Gloomy), George E. Stone (Shimley), William F. Sauls (Smiley), Tom Fadden (Herbie), Snub Pollard (Knuckles).
Released December 1961 (Panavision, Technicolor)
136 minutes
Distributors: United Artists

Reaching for the Stars (1964)

A twenty minute short produced by Frank Capra for the Martin-Marietta Corporation to dramatize their conception for a Manned Orbital Laboratory.

Aborted Projects

In 1934 Capra was loaned to MGM. With Irving Thalberg as Producer, Capra began work on Soviet, "a strong melodrama about an American engineer hired to build a superdam in Russia" starring Wallace Beery, Marie Dressler, Joan Crawford, and Clark Gable. When Thalberg left for Europe, Louis B. Mayer cancelled the film (see *The Name Above the Title;* p. 161).

As part owner of Liberty Films Capra acquired the rights to *Friendly Persuasion* (eventually filmed by William Wyler, 1956) *Roman Holiday* (also filmed by Wyler, 1953), *Woman of Distinction,* and *The Flying Yorkshireman.* When Capra moved to Paramount, he failed to get studio approval for any of these projects.

After completing *A Hole in the Head,* Capra formed a partnership with Bing Crosby, Frank Sinatra, and Dean Martin to film *The Jimmy Durante Story.* Columbia Pictures agreed to co-produce and distribute the film, Capra prepared seventy-five pages of script, but the project was dropped by Capra when it became clear that he would not have production control.

After *Pocketful of Miracles,* Capra planned to film Gore Vidal's *The Best Man,* but disagreements with Vidal forced Capra's departure. The movie was eventually made by Franklin Schaffner (1964).

In 1962 Capra began work on *Circus* starring John Wayne for Paramount. Capra and Joseph Sistrom prepared a script (from a story by Nicholas Ray), made additional casting decisions (David Niven, Claudia Cardinale, Lilli Palmer), and then resigned in favor of Henry Hathaway when Wayne rejected Capra's treatment. The film was released in 1964 as *Circus World.*

While working on *Reaching for the Stars,* Capra obtained an option on Martin Caidin's *Marooned.* Capra presented the project to Mike Frankovich at Columbia, and in May 1964, Capra began preproduction work at Columbia studios. Three years later Frankovich replaced Capra with John Sturges (see *The Name Above the Title, p. 493,* for details).

SOURCES

This filmography is based primarily upon the filmography in the Griffith monograph, *Frank Capra,* New Index Series, no. 3 (London: The British Film Institute, 1951), as checked against Andrew Sarris, *The American Cinema* (New York: E. P. Dutton, 1968), Paul Michael, ed., *The American Movies Reference Book: The Sound Era* (Englewood Cliffs: Prentice Hall, 1969), and the actual screen credits. Additional information from the files of the Museum of Modern Art, *The World of Laughter* by Kalton C. Lahue (Norman: University of Oklahoma Press, 1966), and Capra's autobiography, *The Name Above the Title* (New York: MacMillian, 1971) has been included.

Bibliography

Agee, James. Review of *It's A Wonderful Life. The Nation,* 5 Feb. 1947, pp. 193-94.

————. "Comedy's Greatest Era." *Life,* 4 Sept. 1949, pp. 70-88.

Anstey, Edgar. Review of *Meet John Doe. The Spectator,* 10 Oct. 1941, p. 335.

Aristotle. *The Poetics. Classical Literary Criticism.* Edited by T. S. Dorsch. Baltimore, Md.: Penguin, 1965, pp. 31-75.

Auerbach, Erich. *Mimesis: The Representation of Reality in Western Literature.* Princeton, N.J.: Princeton University Press, 1953.

Barber, C. L. *Shakespeare's Festive Comedy: A Study of Dramatic Form and its Relation to Social Custom.* Princeton, N.J.: Princeton University Press, 1959.

Baxter, John. *Hollywood in the Thirties.* New York: Paperback Library, 1970.

Bazin, André. *What Is Cinema?* 2 vols. Translated by Hugh Gray. Berkeley, Calif.: University of California Press, 1967 and 1971.

Bergman, Andrew. *We're In The Money: Depression America and Its Films.* 1971; rpt. New York: Harper & Row, 1972.

Buchman, Sidney. *Mr. Smith Goes to Washington. Twenty Best Film Plays.* Edited by John Gassner and Dudley Nichols. New York: Crown, 1943, pp. 584-651.

Cameron, Evan. *"It Happened One Night* and *Stagecoach." Screen Education,* July-Aug. 1966, pp. 23-45.

"Capra Corn." *Newsweek,* 18 Dec. 1961, pp. 97-98.

Capra, Frank. "Sacred Cows to the Slaughter." *Stage,* 13, July 1936.

————. "Ce Sont Les Films Qui Font Les Stars." *Anthologie du Cinema.* Edited by Marcel Lapierre. Paris: La Nouvelle Edition, 1946, pp. 333-36.

————. "Frank Capra; 'One Man—One Film'." *Discussion,* no. 3, The American Film Institute, 1971.

————. *The Name Above the Title.* New York: MacMillan, 1971.

———— with Childs, James. "Capra Today." *Film Comment* 8, no. 4 (1972): 22-23.

————. with Bressan, Arthur, and Moran, Michael. "Mr. Capra Goes to College." Andy Warhol's *Interview,* no. 22 (June 1972), pp. 25-31.

Cassirer, Ernst. *The Myth of the State.* New Haven, Conn.: Yale University Press, 1946.

Chaplin, Charles. *My Autobiography.* 1964; rpt. New York: Pocket Books, 1966.

"Columbia's Gem." *Time,* 8 Aug. 1938, pp. 35-38.

Corliss, Richard. "Capra & Riskin." *Film Comment* 8, no. 4 (1972): 18-21.

Cornford, Francis MacDonald. *The Origins of Attic Comedy.* 2nd ed. Cambridge: Cambridge University Press, 1934.

Crowther, Bosley. *The Great Films.* New York: G. P. Putnam's Sons, 1967.

Deming, Barbara. *Running Away from Myself: A Dream Portrait of America Drawn from the Films of the Forties.* New York: Grossman, 1969.

Donaldson, Ian. *The World Upside-Down: Comedy from Jonson to Fielding.* London: Oxford University Press, 1970.

Durgnat, Raymond. *The Crazy Mirror: Hollywood Comedy and the American Image.* New York: Horizon Press, 1969.

————. *Films and Feeling.* Cambridge, Mass.: The M.I.T. Press, 1971.

Eckert, Charles W. "The English Cine-Structuralists." *Film Comment* 9, no. 3 (1973): 45-51.

Farber, Manny. Review of *It's A Wonderful Life. The New Republic,* 6 Jan. 1947, p. 44.

————. *Negative Space.* New York: Praeger, 1971.

Ferguson, Otis. Review of *You Can't Take It With You. The New Republic,* 21 Sept. 1938, p. 188.

————. "Mr. Capra Goes Someplace." *The New Republic,* 1 Nov. 1939, pp. 369-70.

————. "Democracy at the Box Office." *The New Republic,* 24 March 1941, pp. 405-6.

Frye, Northrop. "The Great Charlie." *Canadian Forum,* Aug. 1941, pp. 148-50.

————. *Anatomy of Criticism.* 1957; rpt. New York: Atheneum, 1969.

————. *A Natural Perspective: The Development of Shakespearean Comedy and Romance.* New York: Harcourt, Brace & World, 1965.

Gassner, John, and Nichols, Dudley, eds. *Twenty Best Film Plays.* New York: Crown, 1943.

Gibbons, Brian. *Jacobean City Comedy: A Study of Satiric Plays by Jonson, Marston, and Middleton.* Cambridge, Mass.: Harvard University Press, 1968.

Greene, Graham. Review of *Mr. Deeds Goes to Town. The Spectator,* 28 Aug. 1936, p. 43.

————. Review of *You Can't Take It With You. The Spectator,* 11 Nov. 1938, p. 807.

————. Review of *Mr. Smith Goes to Washington. The Spectator,* 5 Jan. 1940, p. 16.

Griffith, Richard, and Rotha, Paul. *The Film Till Now.* 1930; revised and enlarged 1949 and 1960, Middlesex: The Hamlyn Publishing Group, 1967.

Griffith, Richard. *Frank Capra.* New Index Series no. 3, London: The British Film Institute, 1951.

Handzo, Stephen. "A Decade of Good Deeds and Wonderful Lives: Under Capracorn." *Film Comment* 8, no. 4 (1972): 8-14.

Hartung, Philip T. "Capra and Doe's Little Punks." *The Commonweal,* 28 March 1941, pp. 575-76.

Hellman, Geoffrey T. "Thinker in Hollywood." *The New Yorker,* 5 Feb. 1940, pp. 23-28.

Higham, Charles, and Greenberg, Joel. *Hollywood in the Forties.* New York: Paperback Library, 1970.

Hilton, James. *Lost Horizon.* New York: William Morrow & Company, 1933.

————. "Hollywood." *Cosmopolitan* 101, no. 5 (1936): 22-23, 165-68.

Houston, Penelope. "Mr. Deeds and Willie Stark." *Sight and Sound* 19, no. 7 (1950): 276-85.

Huff, Theodore. *Charles Chaplin.* 1951; rpt. New York: Pyramid, 1964.

Jacobs, Lewis. *The Rise of the American Cinema.* 1939; rpt. New York: Teachers' College Press, 1968.

Kael, Pauline. *Going Steady.* 1970; rpt. New York: Bantam Books, 1971.

Kaul, A. N. *The Action of English Comedy: Studies in the Encounter of Abstraction and Experience from Shakespeare to Shaw.* New Haven, Conn.: Yale University Press, 1970.

Kerr, Walter. *Tragedy and Comedy.* New York: Simon and Schuster, 1967.

Kitses, Jim. *Horizons West.* Bloomington, Ind.: Indiana University Press, 1970.

Knight, Arthur. *The Liveliest Art.* New York: New American Library, 1957.

————. "A Dissertation on Roast Corn." *Saturday Review,* 11 Nov. 1961, p. 32.

Kracauer, Siegfried. *Theory of Film: The Redemption of Physical Reality.* London: Oxford University Press, 1960.

Lahue, Kalton C. *World of Laughter: The Motion Picture Comedy Short 1910-1930.* Norman, Okla.: University of Oklahoma Press, 1966.

————. and Gill, Samuel. *Clown Princes and Court Jesters.* South Brunswick and New York: A. S. Barnes and Company, Inc., 1970.

Langer, Suzanne K. *Philosophy In A New Key: A Study in the Symbolism of Reason, Rite, and Art.* 1942; rpt. New York: New American Library, 1951.

————. *Feeling and Form: A Theory of Art.* New York: Scribner's, 1953.

Leary, Richard. "Capra & Langdon." *Film Comment* 8, no. 4 (1972): 15-17.

Lebel, J.-P. *Buster Keaton.* Translated by P. D. Stovin. South Brunswick and New York: A. S. Barnes and Company, Inc., 1967.

McCaffrey, Donald W. *Four Great Comedians.* South Brunswick and New York: A. S. Barnes and Company, Inc., 1968.

McCarten, John. "Angel of Whimsey." *The New Yorker,* 21 Dec. 1946, pp. 87-88.

Michael, Paul, ed. *The American Movies Reference Book: The Sound Era.* Englewood Cliffs, N.J.: Prentice-Hall, 1969.

Montgomery, John. *Comedy Films: 1891-1954.* 2nd ed. London: George Allen & Unwin, 1968.

Mosher, John. "Meet the Messiah." *The New Yorker,* 22 March 1941, pp. 80-81.

Murphy, William T. "The Method of *Why We Fight.*" *The Journal of Popular Film* 1, no. 3 (1972): 185-96.

Neihardt, John G. *Black Elk Speaks.* 1931; rpt. New York: Pocket Books, 1972.

Pechter, William S. *Twenty-Four/Times/A/Second.* New York: Harper & Row, 1971.

Peckham, Morse. *Man's Rage for Chaos: Biology, Behavior and the Arts.* New York: Schocken Books, 1967.

Perkins, V. F. *Film as Film: Understanding and Judging*

Movies. Middlesex, England: Penguin Books, 1972.

Poague, Leland A. "Mirror, Mirror, on the Wall." Review of *We're In The Money* by Andrew Bergman. *The Potomac Review* 6, no. 1 (1973): 145-47.

Price, James. "Capra and the American Dream" *The London Magazine* 3, no. 10 (1964): 85-93.

Quigly, Isabel. Review of *Pocketful of Miracles. The Spectator,* 5 Jan. 1962, p. 18.

Quigley, Martin Jr. and Gertner, Richard. *Films in America: 1929-1969.* New York: Golden Press, 1970.

Radin, Paul. *The Trickster: A Study in American Indian Mythology.* New York: Philosophical Library, 1956.

Reid, Laurence. "Ballad of Fisher's Boarding House." *Motion Picture News,* 15 April 1922.

Richards, Jeffrey. "Frank Capra and the Cinema of Populism." *Film Society Review* 7, no. 6 (1972): 38-46; no. 7-9 (1972): 61-71.

Riskin, Robert. *It Happened One Night. Twenty Best Film Plays.* Edited by John Gassner and Dudley Nichols. New York: Crown, 1943, pp. 1-59.

————. *You Can't Take It With You* (screenplay, adapted from the play by George S. Kaufman and Moss Hart). *Foremost Films of 1938: A Yearbook of the American Screen.* Edited by Frank Vreeland. New York: Pitman, 1939, pp. 129-46.

Robinson, David. *Buster Keaton.* Bloomington, Ind.: Indiana University Press, 1969.

Salemson, Harold J. "Mr. Capra's Short Cuts to Utopia." *The Penguin Film Review.* no. 7; London: Penguin Books, 1948, pp. 25-34.

Sarris, Andrew. *The American Cinema: Directors and Directions 1929-1968.* New York: E. P. Dutton, 1968.

Sebeok, Thomas A., ed. "Myth: A Symposium." *Journal of American Folklore* 68, no. 270 (1955).

Segal, Erich W. *Roman Laughter: The Comedy of Plautus.* Cambridge, Mass.: Harvard University Press, 1968.

Stebbins, Robert [Sidney Meyers]. "Mr. Capra Goes to Town." *New Theatre,* May 1936; rpt. *American Film Criticism.* Edited by Stanley Kauffmann. New York: Liveright, 1972, pp. 334-35.

Stein, Elliott. "Capra Counts His Oscars." *Sight and Sound* 41, no. 3 (1972): 162-64.

Thomas, Bob. *King Cohn: The Life and Times of Harry Cohn.* New York: G. P. Putnam's Sons, 1967.

Troy, William. "Picaresque." *The Nation,* 14 March 1934, p. 314.

Tyler, Parker. *Magic and Myth of the Movies.* New York: Henry Holt and Company, 1947.

Van Doren, Mark. "Second Comings." *The Nation,* 13 May 1936, pp. 623-24.

Vickery, John B., ed. *Myth and Literature: Contemporary Theory and Practice.* Lincoln, Neb.: University of Nebraska Press, 1966.

Warshaw, Robert. *The Immediate Experience: Movies, Comics, Theatre & Other Aspects of Popular Culture.* Garden City, N.Y.: Doubleday & Company, 1962.

Wiseman, Thomas. *Cinema.* London: Cassell, 1964.

White, David Manning and Averson, Richard. *The Celluloid Weapon: Social Comment in the American Film.* Boston: Beacon Press, 1972.

Wollen, Peter. *Signs and Meaning in the Cinema.* Bloomington, Ind.: Indiana University Press, 1969.

Wood, Robin. *Howard Hawks.* Garden City, N.Y.: Doubleday & Company, 1968.

Zinman, David. *50 Classic Motion Pictures.* New York: Crown, 1970.

Index

The following entries refer (1) to *names,* of actors, of authors, of Capra's collaborators and contemporaries; and (2) to *titles,* of films, and of literary works. Where footnote information is included in the bibliography, I have not (with few exceptions) made an index entry. Similarly, there are no index references to the filmography. (My thanks to Dante Thomas for his advice on matters of indexing.)

DATE DUE

GAYLORD   PRINTED IN U.S.A.

PRINTED IN U.S.A.   23-520-002